D1360476

Understanding
the CHURCH

Understanding the CHURCH

The Biblical Ideal for the Twenty-first Century

COMPILED AND EDITED BY
JOSEPH M. VOGL
AND
JOHN H. FISH III

LOIZEAUX
NEPTUNE, NEW JERSEY

UNDERSTANDING THE CHURCH
First Edition, 1999

A Publication of Loizeaux Brothers, Inc.,
*A Nonprofit Organization Devoted to the Lord's Work
and to the Spread of His Truth*

All rights reserved.
No part of this book may be reproduced or transmitted
in any form or by any means, electronic or mechanical,
including photocopying and recording,
or by any information storage and retrieval system,
without the prior written permission of the publisher,
except in the case of brief quotations
embodied in critical articles or reviews.

———

Individual articles originally appeared in *The Emmaus Journal*

"I Will Build My Church" © 1997 by Karen Frankel
"The Primacy of Scripture and the Church" © 1997 by David J. MacLeod
"The Nature of the Universal Church" © 1997 by Charles T. Grant
"The Character Of the Local Church" © 1997 by James A Stahr
"The Life of the Local Church" © 1997 by John H. Fish III
"The Autonomy of Local Churches" © 1997 by John A. Spender
"The Interdependence of Local Churches" © 1997 by Alexander Strauch

———

ISBN: 0-87213-901-8

Printed in the United States of America
10 9 8 7 6 5 4 3 2 1

CONTENTS

FOREWORD

T he Church. What a myriad of images arise in response to this phrase; images shaped by culture and personal experience; images that reflect the various and divergent historical developments of an observable social institution. But what connection do these images have with the original conception of the Church? To be sure, for some, this very question could not be more irrelevant. But for genuine disciples of the Lord Jesus Christ it assumes enormous importance.

What did the divine Architect have in mind when He announced to a small group of followers, "I will build My Church"? What, in fact, is "the Church"? What were His purposes in forming it? With what resources has it been endowed? Did He provide guidelines for its structure and operation? Did He intend that its function be connected essentially with its nature and purpose? A thoughtful consideration of these and related questions forms the focus of the essays contained in this volume.

Our first essay comprehensively establishes the primacy of Scripture in connection with the Church. The remaining essays go on to: (1) explore the nature of the Church; (2) identify the complementary character and life of local churches; and (3) highlight the twin ideas of autonomy and interdependence that govern interaction between them. When taken together, these six essays lay out in a fresh way the original understanding of the Church: an understanding which has captured the hearts and minds of Christians throughout the past two millennia and still excites us today.

Originally delivered at a colloquium sponsored by Grace Bible Chapel in St. Louis, Missouri on May 15-17,1997, these essays were subsequently published in several issues of *The Emmaus Journal*. They are here for the first time published together.

I know I speak for each of the authors when I express the hope that reading this volume will enhance your understanding of the Church and strengthen your commitment to the Head of the Church—our Lord Jesus Christ.

JOE VOGL
MARCH 1, 1999
ST. LOUIS, MISSOURI

I Will Build My Church

(Chorus)
I will build my Church
And the gates of hell will never tear it down
I will build my Church upon this rock
And the gates of hell will never tear it down

A bride was chosen long before she knew that she was loved
Even though she was my enemy I bought her with my blood
Composed of many peoples yet the many are made one
Hear the mystery now

Her truth divine, her message mine as she stands upon my word
Recognize her by the mark of love, a love that lives to serve
In dying now for others, she will live again
Hear the mystery now

In beauty now behold my Church, all are mine by faith
She's protected through eternity yet still her Lord awaits
When I draw her to my own side then all will be fulfilled
Still the mystery now

KAREN FRANKEL

THE PRIMACY OF SCRIPTURE AND THE CHURCH

BY DAVID J. MACLEOD[1]

INTRODUCTION

During the time of my studies at Dallas Seminary in the 1960s I had the pleasure of meeting Mrs. Winifred G. T. Gillespie, the daughter of W. H. Griffith Thomas, the noted Anglican theologian and Bible teacher and one of the founders of the seminary. She asked me my church denomination, and I told her that I fellowshipped with the group she might know as the Christian Brethren or Plymouth Brethren. "Oh, the Brethren," she said, and with that she had a tale to tell. After Griffith Thomas had been living in North America for some time he took his family on a trip to see family and friends in England. At one of the Anglican Churches where he ministered a tea was held in his honor. His daughter, "Winnie," helped one of the ladies serve the tea. The woman asked Winnie if her father ministered among the Anglicans in America. "No," said Winnie, "he says they're all either 'high' or 'dry.' In America he ministers among the non-conformists" (a term that in Great Britain refers to all non-Anglicans: the Presbyterians, the Baptists, the Congregationalists, the Brethren, etc.). "Oh," the lady said, "I've always thought of the non-conformists as socially inferior and excessively biblical!"[2]

I was reminded of Winnie's story when I read Harold Rowdon's 1986

---

[1]Dave MacLeod is a faculty member at Emmaus Bible College and the Associate Editor of *The Emmaus Journal*.

[2] For many years Mrs. Gillespie, still alive (as I write) at ninety-four years of age, has been in happy fellowship at Christ Congregation, an assembly of Brethren in Dallas. She repeated the above story to me over the phone on May 9, 1989. She also related another story, told to her by her father. A young convert in India was given a copy of Thomas' commentary on Genesis. He enjoyed it greatly and told a friend how much he had profited from reading it. The friend told him that Griffith Thomas was a clergyman in the Church of England. "I'm surprised," said the young man. "He knows his Bible so well I thought he must be a member of the Brethren." Griffith Thomas was later told of this incident, and he said that this was one of the greatest compliments he had ever received.

assessment of the Brethren assemblies in Great Britain.[3] Professor Rowdon raised the question, "What was the essence of the [early Brethren movement]?" He argued that it was not a rejection of clericalism and apostasy; nor was it the quest for unity or a concern for evangelism. The thing that above all distinguished them was the absolute priority which they accorded the Word of God. In fact, he asserted that the most characteristic meeting of those churches was not the "breaking of bread" meeting (although the form that meeting took was distinctive). Rather, it was the weekly Bible reading when they gathered, many with their Greek and Hebrew texts, to study the Scriptures.

A central place was given to the preaching and teaching of the Word. There was much evangelism, to be sure. In his early days as a minister J. N. Darby had seen six hundred to eight hundred persons converted per week in Ireland.[4] Yet they were more well-known for their expository Bible teaching. The regular expositions of B. W. Newton built a congregation of seven hundred in Plymouth,[5] George Müller and Henry Craik had a congregation of several hundred in Bristol,[6] and Bible teachers in Dublin would regularly preach to a congregation of over two thousand at Merrion Hall. Many of their number were prolific writers, and their works consisted of little more than Bible exposition.

The primacy of Scripture is seen in a letter of Darby, one of the two greatest teachers of the first generation of Brethren, the other being Newton. In his fifties he wrote a letter to Professor Friedrich A. G. Tholuck of Halle University, answering the latter's questions about the Brethren. In his letter Darby reminisced about his days as an Anglican clergyman in Ireland. He remembered that as a result of a riding accident—his frightened horse had thrown him against a doorpost—he was laid up for several weeks, during which time he gave himself to the study of the Scriptures and their teaching about the church. He became troubled about the Established Church's doctrinal infidelity, quality of care for Christian people and churches, and lack of spiritual discipline. Doubts entered

---

[3] Harold H. Rowdon, *Who Are the Brethren and Does It Matter?* (Exeter: Paternoster, 1986), 31-33.

[4] J. N. Darby, "Disendowment—Disestablishment: A Word to the Protestants of Ireland, in a Letter to the Ven. Archdeacon Stopford" (dated Feb. 20, 1869), in *The Collected Writings of J. N. Darby*, 34 vols., ed. William Kelly (reprint ed., Oak Park, IL: Bible Truth Publishers, 1972), 20:288. Cf. William Blair Neatby, *A History of the Plymouth Brethren* (London: Hodder and Stoughton, 1902), 16. Neatby says, "600-800 a week," while Darby says "many hundreds."

[5] F. Roy Coad, *History of the Brethren Movement* (Grand Rapids: Eerdmans, 1968), 67.

[6] Harold H. Rowdon, *The Origins of the Brethren, 1825-1850* (London: Pickering & Inglis, 1967), 123, 128.

his mind about his own relationship to the Anglican Church, and those doubts came from the Bible. "I felt...that the style of work was not in agreement with what I read in the Bible concerning the Church and Christianity....These considerations pressed upon me from a Scriptural and practical point of view.... Much exercise of soul had the effect of causing the Scriptures to gain complete ascendancy over me."[7] Darby's remark about the "ascendancy of Scripture" identifies him as a believer in the doctrine of Scriptural authority, a doctrine which says "that the Bible, as the expression of God's will to us, possesses the right supremely to define what we are to believe and how we are to conduct ourselves."[8]

THE PRIMACY OF SCRIPTURE OVER THE CHURCH

OPEN BRETHREN, BIBLICAL AUTHORITY, AND "NEW TESTAMENT CHURCH PRINCIPLES"

The early Brethren found themselves in an era that has some affinities with our own. It was a time of international upheaval, the Napoleonic wars having recently ended. It was also a time of religious upheaval with a smorgasbord of ideas being bandied about in Great Britain. There was the sensational charismatic ministry of proto-Pentecostal minister, Edward Irving (1792-1834). John Henry Newman (1801-90) was beginning to write the tracts on the church Fathers that would lead many, himself included, into the arms of Rome. And there were the Brethren (and other dissenting groups) with their radical commitment to biblical authority and Christian devotion. As Darby noted in his review of Newman's famous work, *Apologia Pro Vita Sua*, he, like Newman and others, was looking for the church, i.e., for the true doctrine of the church.[9]

This question ("What is the church?") is again on the minds of many in this era of sensational charismatic ministries, of celebrated conversions to Anglicanism, Catholicism and Orthodoxy by well-known evangelicals, and of widespread apostasy from the doctrines (and morals) of Scripture by men who claim to be leaders in the church. ,

---

[7] John Nelson Darby, "Letter to Prof. Tholuck, dated c. 1855," in *Letters of J. N. D.*, 3 vols., ed. William Kelly (reprint ed., Oak Park, IL: Bible Truth Publishers, 1971), 3:297-98.

[8] Millard J. Erickson, *Christian Theology*, 3 vols. (Grand Rapids: Baker, 1983), 1:241.

[9] J. N. Darby, "Analysis of Dr. Newman's *Apologia Pro Vita Sua*," in *Collected Writings of J. N. Darby*, 18:146.

The question about the nature of the church was, in part, the impetus behind the conference for which this paper was prepared. It is a question about identity, specifically the identity of the Open Brethren assemblies. Our questions are: (1) "What is the church according to Scripture?" (2) "What do we mean by the autonomy of the local church?" (3) "What is the glue that holds local churches together?" i.e., "in what way are local churches interdependent?"

My assignment at the conference was not so much to answer these questions as it was to set forth the basis upon which they may be answered, viz., the sure foundation of Scripture. My conviction is that the only identity Open Brethren have that is worth keeping is that they are subject to the Bible alone. Their ecclesiology (doctrine of the church) is valuable because it is rooted in and arises from Scripture.

If Open Brethren were to be asked to relate the essentials of the New Testament's teaching about the church, they would include the following items:[10]

The Church Is Apostolic:[11] The New Testament Is Its Sufficient and Authoritative Constitution

The church is founded upon the teaching of the apostles of our Lord Jesus Christ (Eph. 2:20), and it is in the succession of the apostles' teaching (2 Tim. 2:2) that the church is truly apostolic. The teaching of the apostles is the sole and sufficient guide for defining, organizing, and guiding the church.

The church has departed from this essential and has undermined the authority of Scripture in a number of ways: (1) by the Catholic doctrine of apostolic succession in which apostolic authority is passed on from the apostles to each succeeding generation of bishops by an unbroken line of ordinations, (2) by the transformation of the ordinances into sacraments giving them a dominant position ("The Word entirely cedes priority to the Sacrament"),[12] (3) by the

---

[10] Cf. the helpful summaries in William MacDonald, *"Christ Loved the Church"* (Oak Park: Emmaus Bible School, 1956), 9-13 and *passim*.

[11] The first four items in my list of essentials are the traditional attributes of the church found in the Nicene Creed (as enlarged in A.D. 381), "I believe in one, holy, catholic, and apostolic church." Evangelicals generally accept the four attributes as being biblical. They interpret them differently, of course, from Roman Catholics and the Eastern Orthodox. Cf. Philip Schaff, *The Creeds of Christendom*, 3 vols. (New York: Harper, 1877), 1:28.

[12] Emil Brunner, *Dogmatics*, 3 vols., vol. 3: *The Christian Doctrine of the Church, Faith, and the Consummation*, trans. David Cairns (Philadelphia: Westminster, 1962), 67.

assertion that the New Testament is too vague and self-contradictory to be a safe guide in organizing the church, and (4) by the argument that in the New Testament there is an evolution in the development of ecclesiology so that no uniform pattern of church order can be found.

The Church Is Regenerate: It Is the Universal[13] Community of Believers

Every Believer Is a Member of the Church

According to Yale University professor, Paul Minear, the New Testament uses over ninety figures and symbols to depict the church.[14] For the purpose of this paper we need only focus on two: the church is the people of God (1 Pet. 2:9-10) and the body of Christ (Eph. 1:22-23; 1 Cor. 12:27). Those who receive Christ become God's children (John 1:12-13) and are added to the church (Acts 2:41, 47). By a supernatural work of the Holy Spirit they are united to the body of Christ, which is the church (1 Cor. 12:13).

Only Believers Are Members of the Church

The primacy of Scripture concerning the membership of the church has been rejected by the intentional intermixing of believers and unbelievers in Christian communities. French Bible teacher, Alfred Kuen, calls such groups "multitudinous churches," as opposed to "free churches" or, more accurately, "believers' churches."[15]

Kuen argues that a number of factors early in the church's history led to the rise of multitudinous churches: (1) *Moralism*, i.e., the teaching that a Christian is a follower of the moral principles of Christ, rather than a despairing sinner who placed his faith in Christ for salvation,[16] (2) *Intellectualism*, i.e., the shift in the

---

[13] In the traditional list of the attributes of the church the word *catholic* appears. That word is perfectly valid if one means the universality of the church. Unfortunately, it is a term that has been abused in the Anglican, Orthodox, and Roman communions. There it is used in a sectarian sense to exclude all who are not members of those communions.

[14] Paul S. Minear, *Images of the Church in the New Testament* (Philadelphia: Westminster, 1960), 268-69 and *passim*.

[15] Alfred Kuen, *I Will Build My Church*, trans. Ruby Lindblad (Chicago: Moody, 1971), 195-98.

[16] Moralism and a radical shift from the New Testament doctrine of saving grace are already evident in the apostolic Fathers of the second century. Cf. Thomas F. Torrance, *The Doctrine of Grace in the Apostolic Fathers* (Grand Rapids: Eerdmans, 1959), 133-41, and *passim*; Oscar

meaning of faith from trust in the finished work of Christ to the intellectual adherence to a creed.[17] (3) *Sacramentalism*, i.e., the change in meaning of the ordinances of the church from symbolic acts to actual vehicles of divine grace. Infant baptism came to be seen as a rite that actually conferred regeneration.[18] (4) *Ecclesiasticism* or *Institutionalism*, i.e., the change in the understanding of the church from a community of equal brothers to a church of priests[19] who mediate salvation to the laymen and have a legal authority over them.[20]

The Church Is One: It Is a Spiritual Brotherhood United in Christ

In His high-priestly prayer (John 17:20-21) our Lord asks, "that they all may be one." That He means more than just a unity of love is evident from the analogy He draws to the oneness of the Father and the Son.[21] This spiritual union was accomplished at Pentecost when the Holy Spirit united the people of God to Christ and to one another (1 Cor. 12:13). Paul says that there is "one body" (Eph. 4:4). It is striking that the New Testament uses descriptive names (e.g., "believers" [Acts 5:14], "disciples" [Acts 6:1], "saints" [Acts 9:13], "brethren" [Acts 9:30], "Christians" [Acts 26:28], etc.)[22] for the church that include every believer and

---

Cullmann, "The Tradition," in *The Early Church*, ed. A. J. B. Higgins (Philadelphia: Westminster, 1956), 96.

[17] This is not to deny that creeds and confessions had valid origins, viz., in the church's need to counter heresies.

[18] Cf. Brunner, *Dogmatics*, 3: 52, 54, 60, 67, 125. At infant baptism salvation is imparted without making any demands on a person. Henceforth such a person, first a child and then an adult, is asked to live a life he/she can never live, never having been truly born again (Kuen, *I Will Build My Church*, 310).

[19] As Anglican scholar, Melvin Tinker, notes, there is a failure in this ecclesiasticism to distinguish A.D. from B.C., i.e., the new covenant from the old. Failing to see that the Old Testament law was abrogated, the institutional church has lifted practices and models straight from the old covenant and applied them to the church. Thus we have the localization of God in hallowed buildings and the ministry of priestcraft with robes to match. Cf. "Towards an Evangelical View of the Church," in *The Anglican Evangelical Crisis*," ed. M. Tinker (Fearn, Scotland: Christian Focus Publications, 1995), 101.

[20] The church now becomes defined as the visible organization, viz., the Roman Catholic Church. Cf. Brunner, *Dogmatics*, 3:28-29, 30, 58-60. "The Ekklesia of the New Testament is not an institution, but...rather...a world-embracing brotherhood" (p. 35).

[21] The purpose clause (ἵνα) at the end of v. 21 indicates that while the unity envisaged is not institutional, it is meant to be observable. Cf. D. A. Carson, *The Gospel According to John* (Grand Rapids: Eerdmans, 1991), 568.

[22] Cf. W. H. Griffith Thomas, *Outline Studies in Acts* (Grand Rapids: Eerdmans, 1956), 218-25.

exclude none. This is "a strong but silent witness" to the oneness of the body of Christ.[23]

The primacy of Scripture on this important doctrine is undermined by the open divisions in the church.[24] The so-called "Catholic" churches were ripped asunder in 1054, and the various Protestant bodies number in the hundreds. Instead of emphasizing the oneness of the body, some churches name themselves after a great person (Luther, Wesley).[25] Others have taken to themselves the name of an ordinance (e.g., the Baptists), or of the form of church government they favor (e.g., the Presbyterians, Episcopalians, and the Congregationalists). Such denominationalism[26] has led to weakened church discipline, an imbalance of

---

[23] William J. McRae, *The Principles of the New Testament Church* (Dallas: Believers Chapel, 1974), 5.

[24] The modern ecumenical movement sponsored by the World Council of Churches is based on the false premise that denominations are churches. The ecumenism that it promotes is therefore external and institutional. There is a true internal ecumenism, i.e., the unity "in Christ" shared by all true believers. It is a unity of life and a unity in truth. Three important points should be borne in mind: (1) The New Testament never sees "unity" as an end in itself, i.e., as a goal to be achieved in spite of doctrinal error. (2) Not all so-called disunity is wrong. The apostles Paul and John recognize no ground for unity with those who teach doctrinal error [Gal. 1:8; 1 John 2:18-19; 4:1-3] or practice moral evil [1 Cor. 5:5]. (3) Two forms of disunity are recognized in the New Testament, one of which is unacceptable [lack of love, 1 Cor. 1:13], and one of which is necessary [lack of truth]. English reformer, John Jewell (1522-77), reminded his readers that it is possible to be united in error. "There was the greatest consent that might be amongst them that worshipped the golden calf and among them who with one voice jointly cried, 'Crucify Him!'" Another English reformer, Hugh Latimer (1485-1555), remarked, "We ought never to regard unity so much that we would or should forsake God's Word for her sake." Cf. Tinker, "The Anglican Evangelical Crisis," 108-9.

[25] Said Luther, "I pray you, leave my name alone, and do not call yourselves Lutherans, but Christians. Who is Luther? My doctrine is not mine. I have not been crucified for any one. St. Paul would not that any one should call themselves of Paul, nor of Peter, but of Christ. How, then, does it befit me, a miserable bag of dust and ashes, to give my name to the children of Christ? Cease, my dear friends, to cling to those party names and distinctions,—away with them all! and let us call ourselves only Christians, after Him from whom our doctrine comes." Quoted by Philip Schaff, *History of the Christian Church*, 8 vols. (2d ed., New York: Scribner's, 1910; reprint ed., Grand Rapids: Eerdmans, 1970), 7:473.

[26] In the Gospel Halls of Nova Scotia I never heard any name for Christians except those found in the Bible. When I was converted I attended a conference in New England, only to be asked by one of the young people if I was a "Plym." When another friend saw my confusion he said, "You know, he's asking whether you're a P. B." Several years later a seminary classmate approached Dr. Lewis Johnson and Prof. Zane Hodges to ask them the Plymouth Brethren view of something or another—rumor had it that Johnson and Hodges were Brethren. Mr. Hodges responded, "We're not Plymouth Brethren." The student wanted to know why he was so touchy about the name "Plymouth Brethren." After all, "I know a number of students who do not mind being called 'Plymouth Brethren.'" "Well," said Hodges, "if they call themselves 'Plymouth Brethren,' they can't be Plymouth Brethren!"

spiritual gifts,[27] a hardening of existing divisions, a lack of a common forum to resolve disputes, difficulty in effecting reconciliation, a compromising of the church's witness to the world, creedal stagnation, distorted priorities, superficiality,[28] parochialism, and unhealthy competition among churches.[29]

The Church Is Holy: It Is Set Apart to God and to Moral and Doctrinal Purity

The Apostle Paul writes, "The temple of God is holy (ἅγιος, *hagios*), and that is what you are" (1 Cor. 3:17; cf. Eph. 2:21). He uses the imagery of the temple

---

As soon as we develop a "them-us" attitude toward other believers we have denied the oneness of the body. Mr. William Armerding of Vancouver told me of a Christian camp ground on the West coast that rented its facilities to various groups. The Brethren had held a conference there for years, but due to declining numbers the camp notified them that next year they would have to share the facility with a group of evangelical Methodists. One of the Brethren representatives voiced his concern to some friends. "I don't mind the other group being there, but I'm wondering if there'll be enough room for 'the Lord's people.'"

This highlights a problem for anyone who wants to avoid the sin of sectarianism. What does a definable group of churches call itself without compromising its opposition to denominationalism and sectarianism? Have I compromised myself by using the label, "Open Brethren?" The Open Brethren have tried (negatively) to avoid sectarianism and (positively) to affirm the oneness of the body of Christ by accepting all believers to the Lord's Table, supporting worthwhile evangelical efforts outside their assemblies (Inter Varsity, Billy Graham campaigns, etc.), and by inviting gifted men from other groups to their platforms.

But are we a "denomination?" We do not want to be, but the very existence of a definable group of churches ("the assemblies") with shared publications (*Uplook, Counsel, Believer's Magazine, Missions, The Emmaus Journal*, etc.), agencies (CMML, Emmaus Bible College, Stewards Foundation, Stewards Ministries), and spokesmen, suggests something like a denomination. I would make three observations: (1) The only way to avoid being part of a denomination in this sinful age is to adopt absolute independency, which assembly people would not want to do. (2) We must, nevertheless, vigorously and ruthlessly oppose every vestige of sectarianism in our persons and churches. (3) We must recognize that the division in the church is a deep-rooted sin that will exist (even in the assemblies) until our blessed Lord delivers us from this sin cursed earth.

[27] The imbalance of gifts is due to the fact that denominations tend to attract people of similar interests and backgrounds. Some attract intellectuals who often favor teaching; others entrepreneurial types who are often evangelistic; others large-hearted generous types who want to minister to the needy; and others artistic types who are often helpful in music.

[28] Every denomination has Christians who leave at one time or another hungering for something more meaningful. Most denominations have an ethos or style that leaves something out, and people leave looking for that "something."

[29] For a summary of the dangers of denominationalism, cf. John M. Frame, *Evangelical Reunion: Denominations and the Body of Christ* (Grand Rapids: Baker, 1991), 45-56.

which was "sacred," i.e., set apart for God and not to be desecrated in any way. The holiness is objective or positional as the indicative (ἐστε, *este*) in verses 16 and 17 indicates, yet the clear implication is that a functional holiness is expected of Christians.[30] The holiness required is the teaching of pure doctrine in the church, specifically, the foundational doctrine of the gospel itself with its basic content of salvation through Christ.[31] In a number of other passages the early church also testified to its holiness by exercising discipline in the church. Both moral evil (1 Cor. 5) and doctrinal evil (Titus 3:10) were subject to discipline.[32]

The primacy of Scripture in the matter of the church's holiness has been compromised in a number of ways since apostolic times.[33] It was compromised subtly by an institutional interpretation of the phrase "communion of saints" in the Apostles' Creed (7th-8th cent., A.D.). Originally the expression was interpreted personally of the fellowship of all true believers.[34] It came to be interpreted impersonally as "participation in the sacred things," i.e., the sacramental participation in grace through baptism and the Eucharist.[35] The New Testament knows nothing of such a sacramental view of the infusion of grace. The church is holy because it is founded on the sanctifying act and word of God in the work of Christ (Heb. 2:11; 10:10).

The church's holiness is compromised in far more obvious ways in the modern world. Newsmagazines carry stories of bishops who deny the virgin birth and deity of Christ, reject the inspiration of Scripture, and condone the ordination of practicing homosexuals to the ministry. Immoral behavior is tolerated even in evangelical churches. Most churches will not discipline a member even if his/

---

[30] Gordon D. Fee, *The First Epistle to the Corinthians*, NICNT (Grand Rapids: Eerdmans, 1987), 149. Cf. *TDNT*, s.v. "ἅγιος," by O. Procksch, 1:115.

[31] In context the "gold, silver, precious stones," extensively used for adorning ancient temples, were appropriate symbols for pure doctrine. "Wood, hay, stubble" symbolize the false doctrine ("wisdom," 1 Cor. 2:6). The passage, contrary to popular opinion, does not have to do with the individual's personal Christian life. Cf. Fee, *The First Epistle to the Corinthians*, 136, n. 12.

[32] The procedure for discipline involved four steps: (1) private rebuke [Matt. 18:15], (2) plural rebuke [Matt. 18:16], (3) public rebuke [Matt. 18:17a], and (4) official exclusion from the fellowship of the Lord's Table [Matt. 18:17b; 1 Cor. 5:17; 1 Tim. 1:19-20; Tit. 3:10]. Cf. McRae, *The Principles of the New Testament Church*, 26.

[33] Examples of moral (1 Cor. 5) and doctrinal (Tit. 3:10) evil can be found in the apostolic period itself.

[34] Schaff, *The Creeds of Christendom*, 1:22, n. 2.

[35] Brunner, *Dogmatics*, 3:125-26.

her adultery, fornication, drunkenness or homosexuality is commonly known.[36] Theological schools tolerate, then condone, then celebrate false doctrine.

The Church Is Christocentric: Jesus Christ Is Its Head

"Ecclesiology," says University of Basel professor, Karl Ludwig Schmidt, "is simply Christology."[37] He argues that all sociological attempts to explain the church are futile because the church can only be explained by its link to the person and work of Christ. The church is the body of Christ (σῶμα Χριστοῦ, *sōma Christou*), and Christ is the head (κεφαλή, *kephalē*) of the body (Eph. 5:23; Col. 1:18; cf. 1 Cor. 12:12-13, 27). These metaphors stress the unity of Christ and His people, and the term *head* specifically stresses that He is leader or ruler over the church. He exercises a position of power and authority over His people.[38] The early church witnessed to the headship of Christ by recognizing no individual man as the head of the church. Leadership was always invested in a plurality of leaders (first apostles and soon elders). This was true of the universal church and of the local church, which is a replica or a miniature of the universal church.[39]

The primacy of Scripture in its teaching that Christ is the sole head ("Chief Shepherd," 1 Pet. 5:4) of the church was denied in practice soon after the death of the apostles. A plurality of elders gave way[40] to a monarchical bishop,[41] and

---

[36] I am personally aware of a large evangelical church that openly proclaimed its strict adherence to "Lordship salvation." When its elders were advised of a long-term adulterous affair involving two of their members and were asked if they planned discipline, they responded, "That would be too unloving!"

[37] *TDNT*, s.v. "ἐκκλησία," by K. L. Schmidt, 3:512; cf. Brunner, *Dogmatics*, 3:40, 84.

[38] Andrew T. Lincoln, *Ephesians*, WBC (Dallas: Word, 1990), 368. In the interests of feminist ideology the word κεφαλή has been softened by many expositors to mean "source" or "origin" (cf. F. F. Bruce, *The Epistles to the Colossians, to Philemon, and to the Ephesians*, NICNT [rev. ed., Grand Rapids: Eerdmans, 1984], 68). Cf. the definitive article by Wayne Grudem, "Does κεφαλή mean 'Source' or 'Authority Over' in Greek Literature? A Survey of 2,336 Examples," *TrinJ* 6 (Spring 1985): 38-59; Idem., "The Meaning of Kephalē ('Head'): A Response to Recent Studies," in *Recovering Biblical Manhood & Womanhood*, eds. John Piper and Wayne Grudem (Wheaton: Crossway, 1991), 425-68.

[39] Significantly both the universal church (Eph. 1:23) and the local church (1 Cor. 12:27) are described as the body of Christ.

[40] Oxford scholar, George B. Caird, writes, "The twofold ministry of elder and deacon continued unchanged throughout the first century." Cf. G. B. Caird, *The Apostolic Age* (London: Duckworth, 1955), 151.

the institutional Church was ultimately ruled by the Supreme Pontiff, i.e., the Pope, in Rome. Even in the Protestant churches the pastor as an officer over the flock is a firmly entrenched tradition—a tradition that denies to Christ His place as head of the church.[42]

The Church Is Spiritual: The Holy Spirit Is Christ's Vicar in His People

The Apostle Paul spoke of the church as "God's household...being built together into a dwelling of God in the Spirit" (Eph. 2:19-22). What was true of the universal church was also true of the local assembly: "Do you not know that you are a temple of God, and that the Spirit of God dwells in you" (1 Cor. 3:16)? It was the conviction of the early Christians that the risen Christ had poured out the Holy Spirit on the day of Pentecost (Acts 2:33). The Holy Spirit guided the apostles into all truth by taking it from Christ and declaring it to His inspired men (John 14:26; 16:14). He was active in singling out men for service (Acts 6:5) and in appointing elders for the church (Acts 20:28). He equipped each Christian with abilities for service (1 Cor. 12:4-11), gave direction

---

[41] The appearance of the monarchical bishop can be traced back as early as Ignatius (c. A.D. 35-107). "See that you all follow the bishop, as Jesus Christ follows the Father....Let that be considered a valid eucharist which is celebrated by the bishop, or by one whom he appoints" (To the Smyrnaeans 8.1 in The Apostolic Fathers, 2 vols. trans. Kirsopp Lake, LCL [Cambridge: Harvard University Press, 1929], 1:260-61). Also: "Give heed to the bishop, that God may also give heed to you" (To Polycarp 6.1 [1:272-73]). Caird notes that in the latter half of the first century three events occurred that altered the character of the church: (1) the final break between Christianity and Judaism, (2) the beginning of persecution by Rome, and (3) the death of many who had been principal leaders in the early church. The death of the apostles, the crumbling of the old covenant, outbreaks of persecution, and the prevalence of heresy and false prophecy led to the rise of the monarchical bishop. Caird suggests that the vigor with which Ignatius states his case for the bishop's role implies that this new development had been "vigorously opposed" by many in the churches. In any case, the rise of the monarchical bishop is best understood as the expedient by which the early church asserted its right to condemn divergent views in the absence of the apostles. Cf. Caird, The Apostolic Age, 141-55 (esp. pp. 141, 151-52).

[42] This is not to deny that the evangelical church has been blessed by many godly pastors. It is only to assert that Scripture teaches that these men should have been (and should be) part of a team of elders, rather than in a position of solitary authority.

An incident in a Brethren assembly might illustrate a problem in our own thinking. Years ago I was scheduled to preach at a local assembly in Chicago. I arrived in time for the early adult Bible class. The subject was "New Testament Church Principles," a perennial favorite among the Brethren. The moderator started by asking the class, "How do we in the assemblies differ from other Christian groups?" The first person to respond said, "We don't have a pastor." How sad, I thought, to be in a church without even one pastor. How much happier that assembly that can say, "We have several pastor-elders who watch over this flock."

in the sending out of workers (Acts 13:2), and empowered people to preach the Word (Acts 4:8; 1 Thess. 1:5).[43]

This sense of fellowship with the Holy Spirit (Phil. 2:1) was coupled with an understanding of the church as a brotherhood, God's family. Their self understanding was of a fellowship of believing men, not an impersonal institution. They showed hospitality (Acts 16:15; Rom. 12:13; Heb. 13:2) and cared for their needy (Acts 6:1-6). They had meetings in which they ate together in remembrance of Christ (Acts 2:46; 1 Cor. 11:20-34).While there were certain set elements to each meeting (teaching [Acts 11:26], prophesying [Acts 11:28], singing [1 Cor. 14:15], prayer [1 Tim. 2:8], the Lord's Supper [1 Cor. 11:17-26]), there was also an element of spontaneity.[44] There was a looking to the Spirit of God to guide in the meetings of the church (Eph. 5:18-21). There was liberty for various brothers to teach, offer a word of wisdom, give a word of knowledge, etc. 1 Corinthians 14:26 indicates a lack of fixed order[45] in the meetings. Cambridge professor, C. F. D. Moule, wrote:

> The most characteristic Christian way of guidance was in the kind of setting indicated in [1 Cor. 14], where the Christians assemble, each with a psalm or a teaching or a revelation or a burst of ecstasy: and the congregation exercises discernment. That is how Christian ethical decisions were reached: informed discussion, prophetic insight, ecstatic fire—all in the context of the worshipping, and also discriminating,

---

[43] Cf. Klaus Runia, "The God-Given Ministry Between Spirit and Situation," in *God Who is Rich in Mercy*, eds. Peter T. O'Brien and David G. Peterson (Homebush West, NSW, Australia: Lancer Books, 1986), 267.

[44] Cf. the discussion in Robert Banks, "From Fellowship to Organisation: A Study in the Early History of the Concept of the Church," *RTR* 30 (September 1971): 79-89.

[45] Well-known is George Müller's comment that the church can function "without any rules" (Harold H. Rowdon, *The Origins of the Brethren, 1825-1850* [London: Pickering & Inglis, 1967], 122). One needs to be careful, however, not to miss the fact that in the context of freedom the Apostle does impose some order (1 Cor. 14:26-33). He sees no value in chaos. All Christian groups have some form to their meetings—if they didn't they wouldn't know where and when to meet! Most would agree that there has to be some uniformity in order for there to be worship. Novelty turns the attention of the worshiper away from God to the novel activity. C. S. Lewis, an Anglican, had these wise words, "As long as you notice, and have to count the steps, you are not yet dancing but only learning to dance. A good shoe is a shoe you don't notice. Good reading becomes possible when you need not consciously think about eyes, or light, or print, or spelling. The perfect church service would be one we were almost unaware of; our attention would have been on God." Cf. *Letters to Malcolm: Chiefly on Prayer* (New York: Harcourt, Brace, Jovanovich, 1963), 4.

assembly, with the good news in Jesus Christ behind them, the Spirit among them, and before them the expectation of being led forward into the will of God.[46]

The primacy of Scripture with regard to the Spirit's role in the life of the church was undermined by the formalization of the church's life.[47] Paul confronts this tendency in Thessalonica: "Do not quench the Spirit; do not despise prophetic utterances. But examine everything carefully; hold fast to that which is good" (1 Thess. 5:19-21). In the years following the passing of the apostles there occurred a series of decisive shifts of emphasis. First, there was the formalization of ministries. Biblical eldership was replaced by episcopacy in which rank was divorced from function. The bishop now stood in the place accorded by Paul to the Spirit. He was owed submission due to his official position, not by virtue of his works. Ignatius wrote, "Let no one do any of the things appertaining to the Church without the bishop."[48] There was the formalization of worship with simple familial "meetings" being replaced by formal gatherings with liturgical forms of service. In place of mutual ministry of the Word, prayer, and common involvement in the Supper, extemporaneous elements began to disappear, ritual was introduced, and official control of the Supper was placed in the hands of the bishop.

The Church Is a Priesthood: Every Believer Is a Minister of God

During O. T. times the nation of Israel had a priesthood, a class of mediatorial men, distinct from their fellow Israelites, who carried out the ministerial work of sacrifice, representation, and access to God. They wore distinctive clothing and had special privileges; they alone could approach the altar and enter the sanctuary. Under the new covenant all this changed. Every believer is a priest of God (1 Pet. 2:5, 9; Rev. 1:5-6). The mediatorial ministry of Christ is undelegated and untransmissible. The eldership of the church is essentially pastoral, never mediatorial, and the words *priest, sacrifice,* and *altar* as terms of clerical status and privilege are not characteristic of apostolic teaching. When the term *priest* is used of the church it is always in the plural, "priests," (Rev. 1:6), or else it is

---

[46] C. F. D. Moule, *The Birth of the New Testament* (3d ed., San Francisco: Harper & Row, 1982), 272-73. I quote Moule although I am a cessationist, i.e., someone who believes that some gifts of the early church have passed off the scene, their foundational function having ended.

[47] Cf. Banks, "From Fellowship to Organisation," 85-88.

[48] Ignatius, *To the Smyrnaeans* 8.1, in *The Apostolic Fathers*, 1:260-61.

used collectively, i.e., "priesthood" (1 Pet. 2:5). "The truth, therefore, is that Christianity *is*, not *has*, a priesthood."[49] In the New Testament all Christians are "laity," i.e., "the people of God" ("people" = λαός, *laos*, cf. Tit. 2:14), and all Christians are "ministers" (Eph. 4:12).[50] All have access to the presence of God through Christ (Heb. 10:19-25), all may offer sacrifices (Rom. 12:1-2; Heb. 13:15-16), all are gifted to serve (1 Cor. 12:4-11), and all were free to participate in the meetings of the church (1 Cor. 14:26).

The primacy of Scripture was jettisoned within a century with the formalization of responsibilities and the establishment of a clerical class. Elaborate titles, special garments, impressive rituals, religious calendars, and ecclesiastical ornaments set these "professional Christians" apart from the laity. Eduard Schweizer says the church as a body consisting of members living in their mutual addressing, asking, challenging, comforting, and helping one another has been exchanged for a church of services in which a theater audience looks on while paid actors act out their parts on the stage.[51]

The Church Has Ritual: It Practices Symbolic Acts That Were Instituted by Christ

The Head of the church instituted two practices or ordinances that were to be permanently practiced by His people. An ordinance[52] may be defined as a symbolic rite that sets forth the central truths of the Christian faith and was (1) instituted by our Lord in the Gospels, (2) practiced by the early church in the Book of Acts, (3) expounded by the apostles in the epistles, and (4) obligatory upon every believer.[53] There are two practices in the New Testament that fit this definition: baptism (Matt. 28:19-20; Acts 8:38; Rom. 6:4-6), and the Lord's Supper

---

[49] W. H. Griffith Thomas, *The Principles of Theology: An Introduction to the Thirty Nine Articles* (rev. ed., London: Church Book Room Press, 1956), 316. Idem., "Is the New Testament Minister a Priest?" *BS* 136 (January 1979): 65-73.

[50] Robert Banks, "Fulfilling the Promise of the Priesthood of All Believers," *CBRF Journal* 129 (December 1992): 25.

[51] Eduard Schweizer, "The Service of Worship," in *Neotestamentica: German and English Essays 1951-1963* (Stuttgart: Zwingli Verlag, 1963): 334-36. Cf. Banks, "From Fellowship to Organisation," 82, n. 9.

[52] The word *ordinance* is derived from the Latin *ordo*, meaning "a row," then "an order, arrangement."

[53] A. H. Strong, *Systematic Theology* (Old Tappan, NJ: Revell, 1907), 930. This definition excludes five of the seven sacraments (viz., ordination, confirmation, matrimony, extreme

(Luke 22:19-20; Acts 20:7; 1 Cor. 11:23-26). Baptism, i.e., the immersion of believers in water (Acts 2:41; 8:12, 36-38; 9:18; 10:44-48; 16:30-34; 18:8; 19:1-5), is an act which symbolizes one's entrance into the church, the body of Christ (1 Cor. 12:12-13).[54] The Lord's Supper, the regular partaking of the elements of bread and wine with other believers, symbolizes one's continuance in the body, or life in it (cf. 1 Cor. 11:25).[55]

The primacy of Scripture has been seriously compromised by the corrupt practices that appeared in the second and third centuries. With the ascendancy of Emperor Constantine (A.D. 312) came the baptism of unbelievers and the multitudinous church. Sprinkling and pouring gradually replaced biblical baptism (immersion), and sacramental notions gradually replaced the symbolic meaning of the act. The Catholic doctrine of baptism is sacramental,[56] imparting salvation (the new birth) in an event which makes no personal claim on the person. It works automatically and mechanically (*ex opere operato*), even if the baptized is an infant who is incapable of saving faith.[57] The doctrine of baptismal regeneration has produced generations of people who have never been genuinely born again.

The diminishing of Scripture is seen even more dramatically in the evolution of the Lord's Supper into the sacrament of the mass. In New Testament times the Supper was an act of fellowship, which believers regularly repeated in obedience to the command of the Lord in order to build themselves up and strengthen their hope in His return. It came to be viewed as a miracle in which the elements were

---

unction, penance, baptism, and the eucharist) of the Roman Catholic Church. It also excludes, in spite of the adamant assertions of a brother on the East coast, the view that the woman's head covering in meetings of the church is a sacrament! One should not try to protect what one believes is a biblical practice by unbiblical claims for that practice.

[54] The visible act of submersion spoke of the believer's dying and rising with Christ. The visible act was regarded as one with the inner event, i.e., Spirit baptism, that joined the believer to the body of Christ. Cf. Brunner, *Dogmatics*, 3:53.

[55] S. Lewis Johnson, Jr., "The First Passover," *BBB* (Sept. 27, 1981): 1.

[56] The word *sacrament* is derived from the Latin *sacramentum*, which was applied to anything sacred or consecrated. In ecclesiastical usage it meant an oath or solemn pledge. The connection of the term with the rites of baptism and the Lord's Supper lies in the use of *sacramentum* in the Vulgate to translate the Greek μυστήριον (*mystērion*), or "mystery (cf. Eph. 5:32; 1 Tim. 3:16; Rev. 1:20). Because of the mysterious element of the term and the almost magical power (imparting of regeneration and turning the elements into the body and blood of Christ) associated with the sacraments in Catholic theology, many evangelicals prefer the term *ordinance*. Cf. Robert Saucy, *The Church in God's Program* (Chicago: Moody, 1972), 191.

[57] Brunner, *Dogmatics*, 3:54.

changed into the body and blood of Christ and by which saving grace was infused into the faithful. Due to this miracle the Sacrament becomes more important than the Word. "The Supper, understood as Sacrament, is now placed without competitor in the center." Instead of a lowly supper, it became a sacrifice offered in a holy place upon an altar. Once again there was a barrier between the administrator of the holy things and the "profane" people. The new covenant concepts of the people of God as "brothers" and "saints" and the whole of everyday life as sanctified to service for God (Rom. 12:1-2) was annulled by a return to the division between the sacred and the profane sphere.[58]

The Church Is Self-Supported: Only Christians Contribute to Its Work

In the early church there was a conviction that the Christian life was a stewardship in which the Lord has "richly supplied us with all things" (1 Tim. 6:17). Financial giving to the work of the Lord was an expression of the grace of God (2 Cor. 8:1-2) and the believers' dedication to Christ (2 Cor. 8:5). In Acts 11:29 it is the "disciples," i.e., believers, who contribute to help the poor in Judea. In 3 John 7 the Apostle commends servants of the Lord who accepted no financial support from the Gentiles, i.e., from unbelievers. That only Christians should support the Lord's work is evident because: (1) only Christians are stewards of God's grace, (2) this is apostolic practice [Acts 11:29], and (3) it protects the free offer of grace from confusion [Matt. 10:8; 2 Cor. 11:7; Acts 20:35]. Not only did the apostolic church believe that only Christians should give, but that every Christian, rich (1 Tim. 6:17-19) and poor (2 Cor. 8:1-2), should give.

Money was given to repay God's servants (1 Cor. 9:13-14; Gal. 6:6), care for the needy among God's people (Rom. 15:26-27; 2 Cor. 8:13-15), and extend Christ's message (Phil. 4:10-19). Giving was to be voluntary, not forced (2 Cor. 8:3; 9:5,7), generous, not parsimonious (2 Cor. 8:2; 9:6,13; 1 Tim. 6:18), enthusiastic, not grudging (2 Cor. 8:4, 11-12; 9:7), deliberate, not haphazard (2 Cor. 9:7; Acts 11:29), regular, not spasmodic (1 Cor. 16:2), proportionate, not arbitrary (1 Cor. 16:2), sensible, not reckless (2 Cor. 8:11-12; 1 Cor. 16:2; Acts 4:34-35), and unobtrusive, not ostentatious (Matt. 6:1-4).[59]

The Apostle Paul's approach to money is instructive. He preached without

---

[58] Brunner, *Dogmatics*, 3:60-66. Caird (*The Apostolic Age*, 154) writes, "The records of the apostolic age are silent on three other points of church order also. There is no evidence from our period that the administration of the sacraments was the monopoly of any ministerial office, that ordination involved the laying on of apostolic hands, or that the ministry was ever regarded as a priesthood."

charge so as not to harm his message (Acts 18:3; 20:34-35), yet he could candidly rebuke an assembly for financially taking advantage of him (2 Cor. 11:7-8).[60] He did not solicit funds for himself, yet he mentioned the needs of other workers and elders (Tit. 3:13; 1 Tim. 5:17-18). He solicited funds only from believers and did not use pressure tactics.

The giving of money for the promotion of the work of Christ is another area where the primacy of Scripture over our lives has been seriously compromised. In multitudinous churches baptized unbelievers are regularly solicited for money. Christian organizations repeatedly appeal to secular foundations for grants to support their causes. The unbelieving world looks on with bemused disgust as TV preachers raise large sums to promote their lavish lifestyles.[61] Religious organizations take funds from professing Christians and contribute them to political and military causes.

BIBLICAL AUTHORITY AND THE STRUCTURE OF THE CHURCH

Robert Saucy, professor of systematic theology at Talbot Theological Seminary, has said that it is "the move toward leadership in the church by a plurality of elders" that "has given rise to the [recent] question of authority" in the church.[62] It is to this issue, therefore, that we must turn our attention.

The Pre-Critical Opinions[63]

Prior to modern critical scholarship it was generally accepted that there was a single pattern for governing the church. This view is still accepted, in different

---

59 Murray J. Harris, "Christian Stewardship," *Interest* (February 1979): 4-5.

60 "Ministers are underpaid because we are not doing our duty to finance the work of God....We need to understand that it is not our job to enforce other people's voluntary sacrifice. I am not called to enforce your charity. I am responsible to God for the stewardship of my own money." Cf. R. C. Sproul, "Pastors and Paychecks: Ticket for Low Morale," *Eternity* (May, 1988): 56.

61 There is an oft-repeated anecdote about a visit Thomas Aquinas (the "angelic doctor," A.D. 1225-74) paid to the pope, Innocent IV (d. 1254). He found the pontiff watching as money was being counted. The pope smiled and said, "Well, Thomas, the church can no longer say, "Silver and gold have I none." "No, your holiness, she can't," said the great theologian, "and neither can she say, 'In the name of Jesus Christ of Nazareth, rise up and walk'" (Acts 3:6).

62 Robert L. Saucy, "Authority in the Church," in *Walvoord: A Tribute*, ed. Donald K. Campbell (Chicago: Moody, 1982), 219.

63 Cf. W. D. Davies, "A Normative Pattern of Church Life in the New Testament?" in *Christian Origins and Judaism* (Philadelphia: Westminster, 1962), 199-229.

ways by Roman Catholicism, Eastern Orthodoxy, High Anglicanism, and by many Reformed and Evangelical Protestants. Catholicism,[64] Orthodoxy,[65] and Anglo-Catholicism[66] are hierarchical churches with their bishops claiming apostolic succession in direct continuity with the early church. Reformed and Evangelical groups holding to presbyterian or congregational church structure claim apostolic succession in their professed obedience to the teaching of the apostles found in the New Testament.

Of particular interest to readers of this essay are the opinions of the early Brethren on this question.[67] Early leader, Anthony N. Groves, argued that eldership was taught in Scripture.[68] At the well-known assembly in Plymouth leadership was provided by a plurality of elders. After a two-week retreat (February 1839) to consider church order, George Müller and Henry Craik, of Bethesda Chapel in Bristol, concluded that the church should be governed by a plurality of elders.[69] Similar conclusions were arrived at by Müller's friend, the saintly Robert Chapman, who carried on a work in Barnstable.

The views of John Nelson Darby were quite different, and his views had

---

[64] Cf. Pierre Batiffol, *Primitive Catholicism*, trans. H. L. Brianceau (New York: Longmans, Green, 1911), vi-vii and *passim*.

[65] Cf. Timothy Ware, *The Orthodox Church* (rev. ed., New York: Penguin, 1983), 21-22, 35-36, 252-57 and *passim*.

[66] Cf. the various essays in Kenneth E. Kirk, ed., *The Apostolic Ministry* (reprint ed., London: Hodder & Stoughton, 1957). Kirk (p. 8) defends the theory of doctrinal development in which later practices were present in apostolic times in seed form. Christ endowed His people with two gifts, viz., the means of grace (the word and sacraments) and the ministry of grace (the apostles and their fellow-laborers). Both (means and ministry) were in a state of fluidity for many years. It took some time before the Word was crystallized into the canon, and it took some time before the term "bishop" was reserved for the distinct office of "Essential Ministry," i.e., those men in apostolic succession. Evangelical Anglicans reject a Catholic view of apostolic succession, and they are less inclined to insist that episcopacy is found in any form in the New Testament, but they do see it as a legitimate development. Cf. Edward Arthur Litton, *Introduction to Dogmatic Theology*, ed., P. E. Hughes (1892; new ed., London: James Clarke, 1960), 400-402.

[67] The Open Brethren tended to be restorationists, but the Exclusives felt this was an impossible ideal because of the ruin of the church. They opted for a primitive piety, rather than a primitive church order. Cf. James Patrick Callahan, "Primitivist Piety: The Ecclesiology of the Early Plymouth Brethren," Ph. D. dissertation: Marquette University, 1994.

[68] Cf. G. H. Lang, *Departure: A Warning and an Appeal* (2d ed., London: C. J. Thynne and Jarvis, 1926), 48.

[69] Cf. Coad, *History of the Brethren Movement*, 75, 154-55 and *passim*; Rowdon, *The Origins of the Brethren*, 125-26 and *passim*. Less than twenty years after Müller's death his own assembly had abandoned biblical eldership for Darby's views (Coad, p. 212).

tremendous influence on the Exclusive wing of the Brethren as well as on the third stream of Brethren, called by McLaren, "the revival Brethren."[70] This third group is particularly relevant to us in that they carried on much of the evangelistic and assembly-planting efforts in North America.

Darby taught that churches or missionaries today cannot lawfully appoint elders because there is no one with God-given authority to officially appoint them. He defended his position with two arguments: (1) In the New Testament only apostles or their delegates appointed elders [Acts 14:23; 1 Tim. 5:22; Tit. 1:5]. Because there are no longer apostles and apostolic delegates in the church elders can no longer be appointed.[71] (2) The church fell into spiritual ruin with the departure of the apostles, and God did not allow the office or any external structure of the church to continue after their time.[72]

---

[70] Ross Howlett McLaren, "The Triple Tradition: The Origins and Development of the Open Brethren in North America," *EMJ* 4 (Winter 1995): 193-208.

[71] Cf. J. N. Darby, "Reply to Two Fresh Letters from Count De Gasparin," in *The Collected Writings of J. N. Darby*, ed. William Kelly (reprint ed., Sunbury: Believers Bookshelf, n.d.), 4:368. It is true that the Apostles and their delegates have departed. What is not true is Darby's assumption that only apostles can appoint elders. It is very important, especially for loyal followers of a revered figure like J. N. Darby, to carefully distinguish what the Bible says from what Mr. Darby infers that it means. The Bible just does not say that only apostles and their delegates may appoint elders. Furthermore, the timing of Paul's instructions concerning the qualifications and appointment of elders suggests that another, quite different, interpretation of the facts is the correct one. That fact that the apostle's written instructions appear in Timothy and Titus, written toward the end of his career, suggests that he was arranging for the perpetuation of the office (not its demise) after his departure. A local assembly can still give heed to the "apostles' teaching" on these matters, even though the apostles themselves have left the scene (cf. Acts 2:42).

Paul's comments in Acts 20:28 suggest that, in the final analysis, eldership is not an office or authority which can be conferred by man. It is the Holy Spirit who appoints elders. By means of the qualifications spelled out by Paul in 1 Timothy and Titus godly men are enabled to recognize those whom the Spirit has separated to the work. In short, it is not the function of the church to confer authority on men but to recognize the authority of those whom the Holy Spirit has appointed. Additionally, it might be inferred, although Scripture does not explicitly say so, that the elders of an established assembly, as the official overseers of the church, would have the authority (implied in their office) to develop and appoint others as elders. However, the emphasis of the New Testament is not upon the authority of those who appoint elders, but upon the recognition of the authority the Spirit has given to some as elders.

[72] Cf. R. A. Huebner, *The Ruin of the Church, Eldership, and Ministry of the Word by Gift* (Morganville: Present Truth Publishers, n.d.), 33-35. The New Testament certainly cites examples of failure in the apostolic churches, and it warns of the dangers of apostasy both in the present and in the end-time. The history of Christendom furnishes numerous examples of the scarlet sins of the visible church. Nevertheless, it is erroneous to argue, as does Darby, that the

The Modern Critical Consensus

Modern biblical scholarship brought about a new understanding of church government in the nineteenth century. New tools and disciplines brought about an examination of the Scriptures that was in many cases more exact, but in others more unbelieving.[73] New Testament commentator and Anglican bishop, J. B. Lightfoot, is an example of the kind of devout scholarship that represents the finest work of the time. In a now celebrated essay he demonstrated that the churches of the New Testament era were governed by elders. The term *bishop* was a designation of the same office, i.e., the elders were the bishops. Episcopacy developed out of the office of elder, and was not a direct development out of the office of apostle.[74]

A more negative conclusion was offered by Lightfoot's friend, Cambridge scholar F. J. A. Hort, who asserted that there is no evidence in the New Testament that either our Lord or His apostles established any church offices that were permanently binding.[75] Following a sociological approach, Oxford scholar Edwin Hatch argued that organization in the early church developed gradually and that the various elements of that organization were patterned on contemporary

---

church is completely in ruins. In fact, the many revivals and renewal movements of church history (including the Protestant reformation and the Brethren movement itself) show that the Holy Spirit has sovereignly pulled many in the church "back to the Bible" and apostolic practice on numerous occasions.

Darby points to the loss of the doctrine of justification by faith in the Fathers ("Miracles and Infidelity," in *Collected Writings*, 32:187) as but one illustration of the church's ruin. In the providence of God, however, that great doctrine was recovered by Martin Luther. We might also cite the doctrine of biblical eldership as a truth lost in the clerisy of the Middle Ages. Yet this doctrine was recovered by George Müller and others in the nineteenth century. In spite of the pervasive apostasy and unbelief in our day, faithful Christians can still gather together and organize themselves on the basis of apostolic instruction and example as provided by the New Testament Scriptures.

[73] W. D. Davies cites lexicographical, theological, sociological, and historical studies. He also mentions the baneful influence of the Enlightenment in substituting political and environmental factors for exegetical and theological explanations for the church's organization. Cf. "A Normative Pattern of Church Life in the New Testament?" 200, 206-7.

[74] J. B. Lightfoot, "The Christian Ministry," in *St. Paul's Epistle to the Philippians* (12th ed., London: Macmillan, 1913), 193, 196. The first edition of this important work was published in 1868. He writes, "The episcopate was formed not out of the apostolic order by localization but out of the presbyterial by elevation."

[75] Fenton John Anthony Hort, *The Christian Ecclesia* (1897; reprint ed., London: Macmillan, 1914), 230.

societies of various kinds.[76] In short, New Testament ecclesiology was a culturally relative thing.

Similar discussions were being carried on in nineteenth century German scholarship. In an oft-cited book Leipzig scholar, Rudolf Sohm, argued that the early church had no formal organization. Where the risen Christ is present ("Where two or three are gathered together in My Name," Matt. 18:20) there is the church. There was no need for human officers and organization. Such developments are the essence of Catholicism and are due to sociological influences, especially the example of the state. Such outward forms represent a new law that has become binding on every Christian. [77] Sohm did not deny the existence of apostles and elders in the New Testament church, but he argued that their leadership was of a "purely spiritual" variety. All Christians were ministers, and there was no official leadership class. The visible church with an ordained hierarchy is due to "the impulses of the natural man."[78]

Sohm's views were strongly opposed by the great church historian, Adolf Harnack,[79] who wrote with the critical assumptions of liberal biblical scholarship. The early church was organized from the beginning, he argued. It had two distinct kinds of ministry—a universal and a local. The first, a charismatic ministry comprising Apostles, Prophets, and Teachers, was universal and derived its authority from divine appointment. The second consisted of elder-bishops and deacons, appointed by popular election in particular local churches with functions limited to the church that had elected them.[80] By the time the *Didache*[81] was written the former charismatic ministry was passing away and was bequeathing its honors to the administrative class of bishops and deacons.

---

[76] Edwin Hatch, *The Organization of the Early Christian Churches*, The Bampton Lectures for 1880 (2d ed., London: Rivingtons, 1882), 56-58, 83-87 and *passim*. Elders are based on the system of government by heads of families, or the seniors of a tribe; bishops follow the model of contemporary associations that were governed by a president, etc.

[77] Rudolf Sohm, *Outlines of Church History*, trans. May Sinclair (trans. of 8th German ed. of 1893, London: Macmillan, 1913), 32-39.

[78] Sohm, *Outlines of Church History*, 35. He wrote, "The natural man is a born Catholic." Cf. similar comments in Brunner, *Dogmatics*, 3:19-84.

[79] Cf. Adolf Harnack, *The Constitution and Law of the Church*, trans. F. L. Pogson (New York: Putnam's, 1910), 175-258.

[80] Harnack, *The Constitution and Law of the Church*, 190.

[81] Harnack's views were first aired in his edition of the *Didache* (1884). The *Didache* or "Teaching of the Twelve Apostles" (early 2d cent.?) purports to be the instruction given to the nations in obedience to Jesus' commission in Matt. 28:18-20. It was first discovered in the

Harnack saw church organization as due to the desire of man to externalize his religion. When he spoke of the divine appointment of the charismatic ministry he really meant that it was a human necessity, i.e., man by nature demands such organization.[82]

The next major voice to address the topic was Oxford scholar, B. H. Streeter. He is the chief protagonist of a view that has had great influence in the twentieth century. He argued that in the New Testament there can be traced an evolution in church order. He maintained that at the end of the New Testament era there existed, in different provinces of the Roman empire, different systems of church government. "Among these the Episcopalian, the Presbyterian, and the Independent can each discover the prototype of the system to which he himself adheres."[83] Streeter's view that the churches of the New Testament era are like a "coat of many colors," varying both in foundation and in organization has received the benediction of many later scholars.[84] His book was welcomed with relief, the Archbishop of Canterbury humorously observed, as the solution to the whole debate over New Testament ecclesiology. The question had at last been

---

nineteenth century and is a manual of church instruction. Cf. Kirsopp Lake, *The Apostolic Fathers*, 2 vols., LCL (Cambridge: Harvard University Press, 1912), 1:305-7.

[82] Cf. Davies, "A Normative Pattern of Church Life in the New Testament?" 203-4; Batiffol, *Primitive Catholicism*, xx–xxi; J. A. Robinson, "The Christian Ministry in the Apostolic and Sub-Apostolic Periods," in *Essays on the Early History of the Church and the Ministry*, ed. H. B. Swete (London: Macmillan, 1918), 60-68.

[83] Burnett Hillman Streeter, *The Primitive Church Studied with Special Reference to the Origins of the Christian Ministry*, The Hewett Lectures for 1928 (London: Macmillan, 1930), ix. The church in Jerusalem was governed by elders, with James as a kind of bishop (pp. 72-74). In Corinth preeminence in the church depended on the personal possession of some spiritual gift and government was something like modern Congregationalism (pp. 77-80). In response to the Corinthian situation Paul began to lay greater stress upon the offices of the church (cf. Phil. 1:1), and in 2 and 3 John there has clearly emerged a mono-episcopacy in the person of John ("elder" in the singular, cf. pp. 83-89).

[84] Davies, "A Normative Pattern of Church Life in the New Testament?" 212, 217. Cf. C. H. Dodd, "The Church in the New Testament," in *Essays Congregational and Catholic*, ed. Albert Peel (London: Congregational Union of England and Wales, 1931), 3; T. W. Manson, *The Church's Ministry* (London: Hodder and Stoughton, 1948), 60, 65; George Johnston, *The Doctrine of the Church in the New Testament* (Cambridge: Cambridge University Press, 1943), 65-66, 95-96; Myles M. Bourke, "Reflections on Church Order in the New Testament," *CBQ* 30 (1968): 493; Millard J. Erickson, *Christian Theology*, 3 vols. (Grand Rapids: Baker, 1985), 3: 1084. Dodd asserted that Streeter's conclusions could not be shaken, and Manson said the New Testament era was marked by "a good deal of fluidity" in church organization and that "it is idle to look for any hard and fast system."

settled and, in the words of *Alice in Wonderland*, "Everybody has won, and all shall have prizes."[85]

The present state of affairs in liberal, academic scholarship is illustrated by three German scholars who are frequently cited in contemporary works. Edward Schweizer, New Testament professor at the University of Zurich, flatly states, "There is no such thing as *the* New Testament Church Order." In New Testament times circumstances were quite varied in different churches, he asserts, and it is vital for the ecumenical dialogue that we admit this.[86] Ernst Käsemann, formerly Professor of New Testament at the University of Tübingen, likewise asserts that there were different church governments in the New Testament era, with elder rule in place in Jerusalem but no formal structure in the Pauline churches.[87] Hans Küng, one of Catholicism's most influential theologians, sees significant change within the New Testament era, but in the Pastoral Epistles he sees the stage being set for a monarchic episcopate.[88]

What is particularly significant for the present study is the attitude of such scholars to the veracious authority of Scripture. They do not believe that the Bible tells the truth, and therefore they do not believe that the Bible can determine the true path for the people of God in practicing church government. The question at hand is the New Testament's teaching on elders. In the Book of Acts (cf. 14:23) and in the Pastoral Epistles it says that Paul appointed elders and gave detailed instructions about their qualifications.[89] These scholars make the following three observations: (1) Paul does not use the term *elder* in his nine letters to churches [Romans, 1 and 2 Corinthians, Galatians, Ephesians, Philippians, Colossians, and 1 and 2 Thessalonians], so it is clear that he did not have a consistent doctrine

---

[85] Michael Ramsey, *The Gospel and the Catholic Church* (2d ed., London: Longmans Green, 1956; reprint ed., Cambridge, MA: Cowley, 1990), 68.

[86] Edward Schweizer, *Church Order in the new Testament*, trans. Frank Clarke (London: SCM, 1961), 13. Cf. Walter Brueggemann, "Rethinking Church Models Through Scripture," *Theology Today* 48 (July 1991), 128-38. Brueggemann writes, "There is no one single or normative model of church life. It is dangerous and distorting for the church to opt for an absolutist model that it insists upon in every circumstance" (p. 129).

[87] Ernst Käsemann, "Ministry and Community in the New Testament," in *Essays on New Testament Themes* (London: SCM, 1964), 86. He wrote, "The Pauline community had had no presbytery during the Apostle's lifetime."

[88] Hans Küng, *The Church*, trans. Ray and Rosaleen Ockenden (New York: Sheed and Ward, 1967), 408-10 and *passim*.

[89] The case for biblical eldership is far more extensive than this. See below, my discussion, "The Biblical View Defended," pp. 37-48.

of eldership.[90] (2) Luke is historically unreliable when he says that Paul appointed elders in the churches.[91] (3) The Pastoral Epistles are not authentic, i.e., they were written by someone other than Paul.[92]

An evangelical response to these dogmas of "critical orthodoxy" is beyond the scope of this paper. It will suffice to say that evangelical scholars with impeccable academic credentials and believing hearts have vigorously responded to them all.[93]

The Contemporary Evangelical Impasse

Happily all discussion about church order in the nineteenth and twentieth centuries has not been marred by rejection of biblical authority and a denial of the Bible's sufficiency in the realm of church government. Mention has already been made of Lightfoot's famous essay which, while disastrous to episcopacy, was a fine example of devout biblical scholarship in search of truth. During this time period there were many examples of Christian scholars who, while differing among themselves over which form of church government was correct, agreed that the Bible contained authoritative guidelines for believers to follow. Proponents of episcopacy,[94] presbyterianism,[95] congregationalism,[96] and elder

---

[90] Küng, The Church, 402; Käsemann, "Ministry and Community in the New Testament," 86; Schweizer, Church Order in the New Testament, 99.

[91] Küng, The Church, 405; Käsemann, "Ministry and Community in the New Testament," 89; Schweizer, Church Order in the New Testament, 70-71.

[92] Küng, The Church, 400; Käsemann, "Ministry and Community in the New Testament," 89; Schweizer, Church Order in the New Testament, 77-78.

[93] On the historicity of Acts, cf. I. Howard Marshall, The Acts of the Apostles, TNTC (Grand Rapids: Eerdmans, 1980), 34-44; Colin J. Hemer, The Book of Acts in the Setting of Hellenistic History (Tübingen: J. C. B. Mohr, 1989); F. F. Bruce, The Acts of the Apostles: Greek Text with Introduction and Commentary (rev. ed., Grand Rapids: Eerdmans, 1990), 27-34. For a defense of the Pauline authorship of the Pastorals, cf. Donald Guthrie, New Testament Introduction (4th ed., Downers Grove: InterVarsity Press, 1990), 607-49, and Theodor Zahn, Introduction to the New Testament, 3 vols., trans., M. W. Jacobus et al (Edinburgh: T. & T. Clark, 1909), 2:85-133 (§37).

[94] For the Anglo-Catholic position, cf. Ramsey, The Gospel and the Catholic Church, 68-85. An evangelical Anglican approach is offered by Leon Morris, Ministers of God (Chicago: InterVarsity Press, 1964), 98 and passim; Kevin Giles, What On Earth is the Church? (Downers Grove: InterVarsity Press, 1995), 149-50 and passim; and Tinker, "Towards an Evangelical View of the Church," in The Anglican Evangelical Crisis, 94-110.

[95] Presbyterianism, i.e., that form of church government in which local elders are also members of a presbytery which has authority over several churches, is defended by: Louis Berkhof,

rule of independent churches[97] all wrote defenses of their systems, and all used the Bible to support their conclusions.

At the same time, however, there is a growing chorus of evangelical voices denying that Scripture gives authoritative guidance for the organization of the church. That denial usually comes in one of three ways: First it is asserted by some that there is no single form of church organization taught in the New Testament.[98] Second, other scholars make an exaggerated distinction between the interpretation and application of narrative texts, in this case, the texts that describe the apostolic practice of appointing elders. The second objection is often coupled with the assertion that the Pastoral Epistles, for example, are a form

---

Systematic Theology (4th ed., Grand Rapids: Eerdmans, 1949), 581-92. A recent Presbyterian ecclesiology is that of Edmund P. Clowney, *The Church* (Downers Grove: InterVarsity Press, 1995), 211-12.

[96] Congregational church government with a single strong pastor is defended by A. H. Strong, *Systematic Theology* (Old Tappan: Revell, 1907), 914-17; C. Peter Wagner, *Leading Your Church to Growth* (Ventura: Regal, 1984), 73 and *passim*; David L. Smith, *All God's People: A Theology of the Church* (Wheaton: Bridgepoint, 1996), 375. Congregational government which allows for a plurality of elders but insists that authority is ultimately vested in the congregation is defended by Saucy, "Authority in the Church," 219-38.

[97] Cf. Wayne Grudem, *Systematic Theology* (Grand Rapids: Zondervan, 1994), 932-35; John F. MacArthur, Jr., *The Master's Plan for the Church* (Chicago: Moody, 1991), 87-94, 179-99. Bible teachers from the Open Brethren assemblies have made the most significant contribution here. Cf. Donald L. Norbie, *New Testament Church Organization* (Chicago: *Interest Magazine*, 1955), 35-50; Kenneth A. Daughters, *New Testament Church Government* (Kansas City: Walterick, 1989), 37-59 and *passim*; Neil Summerton, *A Noble Task* (2d ed., rev., Carlisle, UK: Paternoster, 1993); Alexander Strauch, *Biblical Eldership* (3d ed., rev., Littleton, CO: Lewis and Roth, 1995). Strauch has also written, with Richard Swartley, two training manuals for mentoring new elders: *Study Guide to Biblical Eldership* (1995) and *The Mentor's Guide to Biblical Eldership* (1995), both published by Lewis and Roth.

[98] Cf. George Eldon Ladd, *A Theology of the New Testament*, ed. Donald A. Hagner (rev. ed., Grand Rapids: Eerdmans, 1993), 579; Morris, *Ministers of God*, 111; F. F. Bruce, "Practice or Principle (2)," *Harvester* 68 (February 1989): 7; Harold H. Rowdon, "Elders and Deacons," *Aware* 70 (May 1991): 12-13, Idem., "Elders and Deacons: An Alternative," *Aware* 70 (June 1991): 12-13. Bruce offers a quote from Henry Craik, George Müller's fellow elder, that sounds much like the viewpoint of B. H. Streeter, mentioned above. Cf. Henry Craik, *New Testament Church Order* (Bristol: W. Mack, 1863), 3-4: "I may be regarded as advocating very latitudinarian opinions, but I am disposed readily to admit that there are passages in the inspired writings that seem, to some extent, to favor a species of Episcopacy; others that may appear to support Presbyterianism; very many, again, that uphold Congregationalism, and others, as clearly teaching what may be described as less systematic than any of the above organizations." Craik (47-64) later seems to treat elder rule as normative. Cf. Coad, *History of the Brethren Movement*, 154-55; Rowdon, *The Origins of the Brethren*, 124-25.

of *ad hoc* correspondence[99] addressing the specific problems of a single audience and are not to be applied to our modern situation.[100] Third, there are Christian scholars and writers who apply a kind of pragmatic cultural relativism to the question of church government. "The major forms of church structures [Episcopalianism, Presbyterianism, Congregationalism, etc.] are a matter of history and culture rather than of revelation and apostolic tradition....Church structure must be flexible and adaptable, never fixed or restrictive." It must adapt to its "environment and cultural milieu" and be able to work "among a people with a unique psychology." [101] "Church order—certainly in our time—should be loose-leaf."[102]

In summary, the contribution of evangelical scholars to the debate is somewhat troubling. While they are to be lauded for treating the Bible seriously, they present less than a united voice to a local congregation looking for counsel in organizing itself. On the one hand there are vigorous defenses of conflicting church polities, and on the other there is the view that the Bible offers no normative view. In light of this apparent impasse, I would like to ask (and answer) three important questions.

---

[99] *Ad hoc* may be defined as follows: "for a special case only, without general application." Cf. *Webster's New World Dictionary of the American Language*, ed. D. B. Guralnik (New York: Simon and Schuster, 1984), 17.

[100] Cf. Gordon D. Fee, "Reflections on Church Order in the Pastoral Epistles with Further Reflection on the Hermeneutics of *Ad Hoc* Documents," *JETS* 28 (June 1985): 141-51.

[101] George W. Peters, *A Theology of Church Growth* (Grand Rapids: Zondervan, 1981), 169, 172. Most Christians are objective enough to admit—at least about church governments other than their own—that history and culture have shaped church polity. And they can see that such structures can become binding, blinding, and blighting. Tradition can hinder progress, efficiency, and effectiveness. The question at hand, however, is whether or not there is a form of church government that is normative for all churches because it is prescribed by the apostles of Jesus Christ. If there is such a form it is highly unlikely that it will be a hindrance to the growth and development of the body of Christ. In that the church is a society gathered out from "all the world" and includes "men from every tribe and tongue and people and nation" (Mark 16:15; Rev. 5:9,10) it is certain that any apostolic guidelines for church government will be "easily capable of universal application. Methods and forms which have only local or racial or class suitability are contrary to the genius and the need of the church." Cf. G. H. Lang, *The Churches of God* (London: Paternoster, 1959), 32.

[102] Hendrikus Berkhof, *Christian Faith*, trans., Sierd Woudstra (rev. ed., Grand Rapids: Eerdmans, 1986), 388. Well-known pastor and writer, Gordon MacDonald wrote, "Today a church should be willing to change anything except its doctrinal distinctives." Cf. "Ten Conditions for Church Growth," *Leadership* 4 (Winter 1983), 45.

The Biblical View Defended

Does the New Testament Teach a Single Form of Church Government?

Leadership by a Council of Elders. In spite of widespread opinion to the contrary the evidence in the New Testament for a single form of church government, viz., pastoral oversight by a council of elders,[103] is overwhelming.[104] Elders are found in early, middle, and later time periods in the New Testament era; they are found in key cities in three different geographical areas (Palestine, Greece, and Asia Minor); and they are found in both Jewish and Graeco-Roman settings. They are found in Judea and the surrounding area around A.D. 41 (Acts 11:30).[105] They governed the church in Jerusalem at the time of the great council in the autumn of A.D. 49 (Acts. 15). Among the Pauline churches leadership by elders was established in the churches of Derbe, Lystra, Iconium,[106] and Antioch[107] (Acts 14:23 [A.D. 48-49]); in the church at Ephesus (Acts 20:17 [A.D. 57]; 1 Tim. 3:1-7; 5:17-25 [A.D. 60]); in the church at Philippi (Phil. 1:1 [A. D. 62])[108]; and in the island of Crete (Titus 1:5 [A. D. 66]).[109]

---

[103] It is generally agreed that the terms *elder*, (πρεσβύτερος) *overseer* (ἐπίσκοπος), and *pastor* (ποιμήν/ποιμαίνω) are used to describe the same office. This is clear from Acts 20:17, 28 where the elders are called overseers and are said to shepherd (i.e., pastor) the flock (also see Titus 1:5, 7; 1 Pet. 5:2). Cf. Lightfoot, *Philippians*, 95-99.

[104] The best summaries of the evidence are found in: Strauch, *Biblical Eldership*, 101-17, and George W. Knight III, *The Pastoral Epistles: A Commentary on the Greek Text*, NIGTC (Grand Rapids: Eerdmans, 1992), 175-77. My own summary is adapted from these two works.

[105] The dates used here are from Harold W. Hoehner, "A Chronological Table of the Apostolic Age" (unpublished class notes, Dallas Theological Seminary, 1972).

[106] Every church in which leadership is referred to in Asia Minor, either under Paul and his associates or under Peter's ministry, has a plurality of elders. Cf. Knight, *Pastoral Epistles*, 177.

[107] Antioch was the center for the Gentile mission.

[108] Philippi was in Macedonia.

[109] The assertion by critical scholars that elders are not mentioned in any of Paul's letters to churches needs to be challenged. They are mentioned in Philippians, although the term *overseers* (ἐπίσκοποι) is used and not *elders* (πρεσβύτεροι). They are mentioned in 1 Thessalonians 5:12, although προϊστάμενοι ("those who have charge over") is used instead of πρεσβύτεροι (cf. 1 Tim. 3:4, 5; 5:17). They are also probably mentioned in 1 Corinthians. In the list of 12:28 there are those who have some sort of office (apostles, prophets, teachers, helps, and administrators) as well as those who have a gift not associated with an office (miracles, healings, and tongues). Setting aside the foundational offices (apostles and prophets, cf. Eph. 2:20) and the non-office gifts, we are left with the three categories: teachers (διδάσκαλοι), helps (ἀντιλήμψεις), and

Elders are acknowledged or commended by virtually every New Testament writer who writes about church leadership (Luke, Paul, author of Hebrews, James, Peter).[110] According to Peter's first epistle elders existed in churches throughout northwestern Asia Minor: Pontus, Galatia, Cappadocia, Asia, and Bithynia (1 Peter 1:1; 5:1). There are strong indications that elders existed in churches in Thessalonica (1 Thess. 5:12), and James (5:14-15) and the author of Hebrews assume the same pattern (Heb. 13:7, 17).

A variety of arguments have been raised in defense of the singularity of pastors, i.e., the view that the New Testament supports the notion of a single pastor over each congregation. The main arguments are nicely summarized by Baptist scholar, Manfred Kober:[111] (1) Paul's use of the singular *overseer* when listing the qualifications of the elder in 1 Timothy 3:1-2 suggests a single pastor because he uses the plural *deacons* when he sets forth the qualifications of deacons. In short, each church should have one pastor and several deacons. It is clear, however, that the singular ἐπίσκοπος in 1 Timothy 3 is generic because in 1 Timothy 5:17 he moves to the plural πρεσβύτεροι.[112]

(2) The individual "angels" to whom the seven letters of Revelation 2 and 3 are sent are best understood as the "messengers," i.e., the individual pastors[113]

---

administrators (κυβερνήσεις). In 1 Timothy 3 Paul mentions two duties of the overseer, viz., teaching (v. 2) and caring/ruling (vv. 4-5), which parallel the teachers and administrators of 1 Corinthians 12:28. The gift of "helps" is likely a reference to deacons. In short, the Corinthian assembly had elders/overseers who Paul refers to as teachers and administrators and deacons who are called *helpers*. It is likely, furthermore, that elders are also mentioned in Ephesians 4:11 as pastors and teachers. Cf. Knight, *The Pastoral Epistles*, 176; Lightfoot, *Philippians*, 194; *TDNT*, s.v. "κυβέρνησις," by H. W. Beyer, 3:1036.

[110] I am excluding John (2 John 1, 3 John 1) because his use of the term elder refers to an individual and not to a situation of church government.

[111] Manfred E. Kober, "The Case for the Singularity of Pastors," *Baptist Bulletin* (June 1982): 8-10, 19. I am omitting Dr. Kober's third argument, viz., "the argument from the nature of the pastorate," because it does not really deal with the question at hand, viz., the plurality (or singularity) of elders in each congregation. Cf. also: Iain H. Murray, "The Problem of the 'Eldership' and Its Wider Implications," *The Banner of Truth* 395-96 (August 1996), 36-56.

[112] Similarly, in Titus Paul moves from the plural πρεσβύτεροι ("elders") in 1:5 to the generic singular ἐπίσκοπος ("overseer") in 1:7.

[113] Albert Barnes, *Notes on the New Testament: Revelation*, ed. Robert Frew (New York: Harper, 1851; reprint ed., Grand Rapids: Baker, 1972), 57-58.

[114] Richard Chenevix Trench, *Commentary on the Epistles to the Seven Churches in Asia* (6th ed., rev., London: Kegan Paul, Trench, Trubner and Co., 1897), 57-60. On the basis of this interpretation Trench argued that the episcopate had appeared in the church by the latter part of the first century A.D.

or bishops[114] of the seven churches. This does not do justice to the term ἄγγελος, however, which elsewhere in Revelation (1:1; 5:2,11; 7:2,11, etc.) refers to superhuman beings, i.e., angels.[115]

(3) The New Testament gives several examples of local pastoral leadership by one individual: Timothy in Ephesus [1 Timothy 1:2, 3], James in Jerusalem [Acts 15:13], Epaphras in Colossae [Col. 4:12; Philemon 23], Epaphroditus in Philippi [Phil. 2:25], and Titus in Crete [Tit. 1:4, 5].

To call these men pastors is to read post-apostolic practice back into the New Testament. Timothy and Titus were apostolic delegates who served in the spreading of the gospel and strengthening the various churches under Paul's care. They did pastoral work, to be sure, but always under Paul's authority and direction (cf. 1 Thess. 3:2; Phil. 2:19, 20; 1 Cor. 16:10, 11; 1 Tim. 1:3). Epaphroditus was an envoy of the Philippian church who was sent to minister to Paul. Epaphras was probably the original evangelist in Colossae (Col. 1:7-8; 4:12-13). At the time Colossians was written (A.D. 61) he was with the Apostle in Rome and had no immediate plans to return home.[116] Although he did labor among the churches of Colossae, Laodicea, and Hierapolis, there is no evidence that he was the solitary pastor of any of them. James was an apostle who ministered to the Jews and was considered a "pillar" of the Jerusalem church. Significantly, neither Paul nor Luke makes clear his formal relationship to either the Twelve or to the Jerusalem elders.

Two further observations are in order: First, a number of the churches in which these men worked had a plurality of pastor-elders (Jerusalem, Ephesus, Philippi). Kober never makes clear the relationship of these key men (Timothy, Titus, James, etc.) to the pastor-elders of the churches. If they were the individual pastors of their churches, who were the other pastors (elders/overseers) mentioned in those churches? Second, the doctrine of a plural eldership does not deny that God raises up extraordinarily gifted men to teach and lead His people. There are evangelists, missionaries, teachers, and preachers whom God raises

---

[115] R. H. Charles, *The Revelation of St. John*, ICC, 2 vols. (Edinburgh: Clark, 1920), 1:34; *TDNT*, s.v. "ἄγγελος," by G. Kittel, 1:86-87. The angels of Revelation 2 and 3 are variously interpreted. I take them to be the guardian angels of the churches. Charles took them to be the heavenly doubles or counterparts of the churches. Mounce says that each of the seven angels is the personification of the prevailing spirit of that church. Cf. Robert H. Mounce, *The Book of Revelation*, NICNT (Grand Rapids: Eerdmans, 1977), 82.

[116] If Epaphras was the solitary pastor of the Colossian church, it is striking that Paul kept him with him in Rome. This would imply that the Apostle was willing to leave the assembly without pastoral care—a most unlikely thought.

up to plant churches, teach, counsel, write, and correct His people. He may even gift one of the elders to be *primus inter pares* ("first among a council of equals")[117] among his fellow elders in a church. In fact, James may have been just such a man in Jerusalem.

(4) In the New Testament era the Christians of a given city or locality made up the local church of that area. This local church (e.g., the 5,000 member- church of Jerusalem) would then be divided up into various house churches. While the city or locale might have a plurality of elders, it is likely that each house church had only one.[118] In that the local church in our culture is based on the individual house church, it is best that we have a single pastor over each congregation. [119]

Four observations are in order: First, the churches in such places as Lystra, Iconium, and Antioch do not seem to have been large, yet Paul appointed elders (plural) in each church (Acts 14:23).[120] Second, the believers addressed in the Epistle to the Hebrews, it is commonly believed,[121] met as a house church, yet they are exhorted to submit to their leaders (plural, cf. Heb. 13:17). Third, the church in Jerusalem, several thousand persons in size, is consistently spoken of as the *church* in Jerusalem, not *churches* (Acts 5:11; 8:1,3; 11:22; 12:1,5; 15:4, 22; 18:22). Until times of persecution the believers of that city met on the east side of the outer court of the Temple, a place known as Solomon's colonnade (Acts 2:44,46; 5:12,42). They viewed themselves as a united congregation (Acts 2:44, 46; 5:12; 6:2), and were led by the Twelve Apostles, and later by the elders and James (Acts 2:42; 4:35,37; 5:2-6; 6:2-4,6; 8:14-17; 9:27; 15:4-29). Finally, the

---

[117] Cf. Strauch, *Biblical Eldership*, 45-50, for an explanation of this important concept. Kober ("The Case for the Singularity of Pastors," 19) argues that this concedes the whole argument to proponents of a single pastor. To acknowledge one man's unusual gifts is biblically proper. To be "first among equals" on a council of elders is quite different from being the only elder, i.e., the first over subordinates!

[118] This is a common assertion today. Cf. Thomas D. Lea and Hayne P. Griffin, Jr., *1, 2 Timothy, Titus*, NAC (Nashville: Broadman, 1992), 109; R. Alastair Campbell, *The Elders: Seniority Within Earliest Christianity* (Edinburgh: T. & T. Clark, 1994), 172; Rex A. Koivisto, *One Lord, One Faith* (Wheaton: BridgePoint, 1993), 27-28, 244.

[119] Kober ("The Case for the Singularity of Pastors," 10), following Strong, hedges his bets at this point by conceding that some house churches may have had a plurality of elders. Cf. Strong, *Systematic Theology*, 915-16.

[120] John H. Fish III, "Brethren Tradition or New Testament Church Truth," *EmJ* 2 (Winter 1993): 135.

[121] William L. Lane, *Hebrews 1–8*, WBC (Dallas: Word, 1991), liii; Paul Ellingworth, *The Epistle to the Hebrews*, NIGTC (Grand Rapids: Eerdmans, 1993), 26. Cf. Harold W. Attridge, *The Epistle to the Hebrews*, Hermeneia (Philadelphia: Fortress, 1989), 12.

Christians at Ephesus who met in various homes (cf. 1 Cor. 16:19) are spoken of by Luke as the "church" in Ephesus and not "the churches" (Acts 20:17). He also speaks of the "flock," not the "flocks," over which the Holy Spirit has placed elders (Acts 20:28). The most natural reading of the text indicates that there was one church in Ephesus and one body of elders to guide it. How the elders organized themselves among the various house churches the text just does not say, and it is pure speculation to argue that each house church had a single pastor.[122]

(5) Dr. Kober's final argument is based on the symbolism of a shepherd and his flock. Just as there is one Chief Shepherd, viz., Christ, over the universal church (John 10:11, 16), so there should be one shepherd (pastor) over the local church who is solely responsible for it (1 Pet. 5:2, 3). This final point is actually an assertion with no support other than the traditional practice of Kober's own denomination. I would make two points in response: First, Christ is the Chief Shepherd in the church, whether in its universal or local form. He, not a human pastor, is the "head" of the church (Eph. 1:22-23). Jesus did not say, "Where two or three have gathered together, there the pastor is in the midst." What He did say is, "there I am in their midst" (Matt. 18:20). Second, in the very passage Kober cites (viz., 1 Pet. 5:1-4) Peter addresses the "elders" (plural) who shepherd a flock (sing.) under the Chief Shepherd.

A Twofold Pattern for the "Official" Ministry. A twofold pattern for official ministry[123] (ἐπίσκοπος [*episkopos*], i.e., oversight and διάκονος [*diakonos*], i.e., service) is outlined in 1 Timothy 3:1-13 and is uniform throughout the New Testament era. The same twofold pattern is found in the Philippian assembly (Phil. 1:1). It is reflected in the early division of labor at Jerusalem between the oversight, ministry of the Word, and prayer by the Apostles and the aid to the

---

[122] Strauch, *Biblical Eldership*, 143.

[123] It should be noted that 1 Timothy 3:1 does not use the term "office." The term ἐπισκοπή ("office of overseer," NASB) is rare in secular Greek and never has the sense of "office." Knight (*The Pastoral Epistles*, 153) has "position of overseer." The NIV is perhaps best: "If anyone sets his heart on being an overseer...." As Schweizer (*Church Order in the New Testament*, 171-80) notes, nowhere in the New Testament do the apostles refer to elders or deacons as "officers." This is striking in that the Greek language has a wealth of terms for "office" or "officer," e.g. ἀρχή ("one at the head, ruler"), ἄρχων ("ruler"), τιμή ("position of dignity"), τέλος ("power of office"), λειτουργός ("priestly office"), πρᾶξις ("public office"), ἱερατεία ("priest's office"). The caution of the apostles is due to the fact that they viewed the work of elders and deacons as tasks, functions or ministries, not as official platforms that distinguished the leaders from the people in a clergy-laity fashion. If by office, however, one simply means a formally recognized position with appropriate duties, then the elders and deacons were "officers" in the church. Cf. David Mappes, "The New Testament Elder, Overseer, and Pastor," *BS* 154 (April 1997): 169.

widows on the part of the Seven (Acts 6:1-4). As Knight observes, there is not only conceptual parallel but also linguistic parallels.[124] Peter, one of the twelve apostles, later refers to himself as a "fellow elder" (συμπρεσβύτερος, 1 Pet. 5:1). The task for which the Seven were elected is referred to as the daily διακονία (*diakonia*, v. 1, "serving") without further qualification, and their activity is described as διακονεῖν τραπέζαις (*diakonein trapezais*, v. 2, "to serve tables"). The linguistic connection with 1 Timothy 3:8-13 and to those who are described as διάκονοι (*diakonoi*) and by the verb διακονεῖν (*diakonein*)[125] is striking and is in accord with the division of labor in conceptual terms in Acts 6. In summary, these three passages (Acts 6:1-4; Phil. 1:1; 1 Tim. 3:1-13) show a twofold division of labor in early, middle, and later time periods in the New Testament era church, in key cities, in three various geographical areas (Palestine, Greece, and Asia Minor), and in both Jewish and Gentile settings.

Does the New Testament Teach a Normative Form of Church Government?

It is the conviction of the present writer that "the instructions given to elders, as well as the eldership structure itself, are to be regarded as apostolic directives (Titus 1:5) that are normative for churches today."[126] How are we to reply, then, to those who argue that passages describing church government are no more than *ad hoc* advice for the time and not normative instructions for all time? I would respond, first of all, by saying that we should not deny the obvious situational setting of various passages of Scripture. George Knight says we should go further. "Every book within the canonical Scriptures would seem to warrant the designation of being *ad hoc*. That is the very nature of Scripture. It consists of documents given by God through the writers to His people in the particular situations in which they find themselves."[127]

The fallacy that some contemporary scholars draw from this observation is that the contents and teachings of the documents therefore must be *ad hoc*. Knight offers two reasons why it is wrong to conclude that *ad hoc* documents

---

[124] Knight, *The Pastoral Epistles*, 175. Cf. the extended discussion of Acts 6:1-6 in Alexander Strauch, *The New Testament Deacon* (Littleton, CO: Lewis and Roth, 1992), 15-54.

[125] It is clear from the list of qualifications of the men described in 1 Timothy 3:8-13 that the noun (διάκονος) and verb (διακονέω) are used in a technical sense to describe "the deacon as a church official." Cf. *TDNT*, s.v. "διάκονος," by Beyer, 2:89.

[126] Strauch, *Biblical Eldership*, 116.

[127] George W. Knight III, "The Scriptures Were Written for Our Instruction," *JETS* 39 (March 1996): 3-13. The above quote is on p. 3.

contain only *ad hoc* teaching. First, those addressing *ad hoc* situations often intend to give general teachings and lasting principles that apply to all human beings. A classic example is the giving of the Ten Commandments. Although given in an *ad hoc* situation (cf. Exod. 20:2), our Lord, James, and the apostle Paul all appeal to them as God's intended standard for conduct for all human beings, including Gentiles (Matt. 19:17-19; Mark 10:19; Luke 18:20; James 2:8-13; Rom. 13:8-10). Another example is found in the seven letters to the churches in Asia Minor where the *ad hoc* commendations, warnings and promises to individual first century churches are clearly intended for the church at large—"He who has an ear, let him hear what the Spirit says to the churches" (Rev. 2:7, etc.).

Second, the Apostle Paul specifically says that these Scriptures "were given for our instruction" (Rom. 15:4; cf. 1 Cor. 9:8-10; 10:5,11). His insistence on the fact that the Scriptures were written for us, which he reinforces by a denial that they were written only for the original recipients or subjects (Rom. 4:23-24) has "enormous implications for our overarching approach to Scripture and for our general hermeneutical stance or approach to Scripture. To let an *ad hoc* approach become our first or dominant approach is…to go exactly counter not only to the hermeneutical approach Paul himself uses, but also that which in these passages he demonstrates to be the approach faithful to God's purpose in causing the Scriptures to be written for us."[128] What is so instructive about Paul's use of the Scriptures is "his understanding that they directly instruct us and apply to us. He writes almost as if there were no gap at all between the Scriptures written years before and the 'us' for whom they are written as instruction. …Since this principle is true of the OT Scriptures written before the end of the ages has come, how much more is it true of the NT Scriptures written in the period of the end of the ages" (1 Cor. 10:11).[129]

There are indications in the New Testament that the pattern of oversight by a plurality of elders is normative and not just *ad hoc*. Not only is there a consistent pattern of plural elders among the churches, but there is also instruction about elders given to the churches,[130] and there is instruction and exhortation given directly to elders.[131]

---

[128] Knight, "The Scriptures Were Written for Our Instruction," 7.

[129] Knight, "The Scriptures Were Written for Our Instruction," 12.

[130] Strauch (*Biblical Eldership*, 106-7) offers as examples: James' instructions to call for the elders (James 5:14), Paul's instruction to financially support them (1 Tim. 5:17-18), his instructions about their protection, disciplining, and restoration (1 Tim. 5:19-22), his instructions about their qualifications (1 Tim. 3:1-7; Tit. 1:5-9), his encouragement of those who aspire to the work (1 Tim. 3:1), his instructions about their examination (1 Tim. 3:10; 5:24-25), Peter's

Furthermore, eldership best harmonizes with and promotes the true nature of the New Testament church.[132] There are at least four ways in which leadership by a plurality of elders complements the nature of the church:[133] First, it complements the church's nature as a family of brothers and sisters.[134] A plural eldership, unlike a formal clerical structure with its special titles, sacred clothes, chief seats,[135] and lordly terminology, best expresses the church's character as a brotherhood.[136] Second, it complements the church's nature as a nonclerical

---

instructions about submission to them (1 Pet. 5:5), the author of Hebrews' instruction to obey them (Heb. 13:17), Paul's teaching about their responsibilities (Tit. 1:7; 1 Thess. 5:12; Tit. 1:9), and Paul's instruction to the church to be at peace with its elders (1 Thess. 5:12-13).

[131] Strauch (*Biblical Eldership*, 107-8) offers as examples: James' instruction about prayer for and anointing the sick (James 5:14), Peter's charge to shepherd and oversee the flock (1 Pet. 5:1,2), his warning against authoritarianism (1 Pet. 5:3), his promise of reward at the return of Christ (1 Pet. 5:4), his exhortation to humility (1 Pet. 5:5), Paul's reminder that elders are appointed by the Holy Spirit (Acts 20:28), his exhortation to guard against false teachers (Acts 20:28) and false doctrine (Acts 20:31), his reminder of the need for hard work, compassion, and generosity (Acts 20:35), his exhortation to be at peace with the congregation (1 Thess. 5:13).

[132] The critical consensus is that church order is irrelevant to the gospel and theology. Pragmatism (i.e., necessity or expediency) is the determining factor in choosing a form of church government (Streeter, *The Primitive Church*, 261-62). T. W. Manson argued that all forms of church government have been effective. The one test that applies to all forms is pragmatic, not theological. Church order in the New Testament is secondary, "derivative, dependent, and functional," not doctrinal in its significance (*The Church's Ministry* [London: Hodder & Stoughton, 1948], v, 100-103). Cf. Davies, "A Normative Pattern of Church Life in the New Testament?" 218-19. This critical orthodoxy is rejected by more than proponents of plural eldership. Michael Ramsey, for example, argues that episcopacy best expresses the Gospel and the nature of the church. Church order is not a matter of indifference, but is related to the inner meaning of the church and the Gospel itself (*The Gospel and the Catholic Church*, vi, 65 and *passim*).

[133] Strauch, *Biblical Eldership*, 109-15. Earlier in his book (pp. 38-44) Strauch enumerates three practical reasons for a plurality of elders: (1) balancing people's weaknesses, (2) lightening the work load, and (3) providing accountability.

[134] Australian scholar, Robert Banks (*Paul's Idea of Community* [Grand Rapids: Eerdmans, 1980], 53-54), says that of all the metaphors used in the New Testament for the church, those comparing the Christian community to a family are the most significant metaphors of all. Among other observations, he notes that God is our Father (1 Thess. 1:1), we have been adopted as sons (Gal. 4:4-5), we are children and heirs (Rom. 8:14-17), we are members of God's household (Gal. 6:10), and fellow Christians are our brothers (Gal. 1:2; 1 Cor. 16:20, etc.).

[135] In the Fall of 1995 my wife and I were given a tour of St. John's University in St. Cloud, Minnesota. In the beautiful church building we saw dramatically illustrated the hierarchical nature of the Catholic Church. Elevated behind the altar was the bishop's chair, a little lower were pews for the ordained priests, and a little lower pews for the brothers in training. Lowest of all were the pews for the laity.

community. The New Testament knows nothing of a consecrated class of clerics who carry out the ministry for the laymen. Instead, every member of the church is a holy saint (1 Cor. 1:2), a royal priest (1 Pet. 2:5-10), and a Spirit-gifted member of the body of Christ (1 Cor. 12; Eph. 4:12).[137]

Third, the plural eldership complements the church's nature as a humble-servant community. When it functions properly, shared leadership manifests mutual regard for one another, submission to one another, patience with one another, consideration of one another's interests, and deference to one another. Finally, plural eldership complements the church's nature by guarding and promoting the preeminence and position of Christ over the local assembly. The apostles practiced a form of church government that reflected the distinctive, fundamental truth that Christ was the Ruler, Head, Lord, and Pastor of the church. "There is only one flock and one Pastor (John 10:16), one body and one Head (Col. 1:18), one holy priesthood and one great High Priest (Heb. 4:14-16), one brotherhood and one Older Brother (Rom. 8:29), one building and one Cornerstone (1 Pet. 2:5-8), one Mediator, one Lord. Jesus Christ is 'Senior Pastor,' and all others are His undershepherds (1 Pet. 5:4)."[138]

Does the New Testament Teach a Supra-Cultural Form of Church Government?

Well-known British scholar, Alec Motyer, has said that "it is not as much as hinted in the New Testament that the church would ever need—or indeed should ever want or tolerate—any other local leadership than that of the eldership group."[139] What then is to be said in answer to those who argue for a "circumstantial flexibility" in most aspects of church government; who assert that to insist upon

---

[136] The family character of the church is displayed in a number of ways: the early believers met in homes (Rom. 16:5; 1 Cor. 16:19), they shared material possessions (Acts 2:44-45; 1 Cor. 16:1), they ate together (Acts 2:46; 20:11), they greeted one another with affection (Rom. 16:16; 1 Cor. 16:20), they showed hospitality (Acts 16:15; Rom. 12:13), they cared for widows (Acts 6:1-6; 1 Tim. 5:1-16), and they disciplined their members (1 Cor. 5–6; 1 Cor. 2:1-11). Cf. Strauch, *Biblical Eldership*, 110.

[137] It is startling to find in a conservative evangelical journal the comparison of a Protestant pastor to a priest. "Like Old Testament priests, pastors are part of a formally designated and consecrated ministry, the nature of which calls for priestly acts at their deepest level." The pastor, it is asserted, bears the responsibility for the service of worship and preserving the dignity of God's house, while others arrange the flowers and organize the choir. Cf. John E. Johnson, "The Old Testament Offices as Paradigm for Pastoral Identity," *BS* 152 (April 1995), 194-95.

[138] Strauch, *Biblical Eldership*, 115.

[139] Alec Motyer, *The Message of James*, BST (Downers Grove: InterVarsity Press, 1985), 189.

one normative form is rigidly to level all local bodies before an "insensitive monolithic" standard;[140] and who insist that the form of polity adopted by a local community of Christians depends upon the cultural norms or sociological realities of the area in which the church finds itself.[141]

I would make four observations in answer to the argument that church government should vary with the culture in which Christians find themselves.[142] First, it is untrue to the cultural universality of New Testament ecclesiology,[143] i.e., the presence of elder rule in every cultural grouping of the apostolic age. It is often argued that because the first Christians were Jews, the office of elder was taken over from the religious environment with which they were familiar, viz., those of the synagogue.[144] This assertion is weak for two reasons: (1) It fails

---

[140] A. Boyd Luter, New Testament Church Government: Fidelity and Flexibility," *Michigan Theological Journal* 2 (1991): 127,135; Howard Snyder, *The Problem of Wineskins* (Downers Grove: InterVarsity Press, 1975), 124. Modern missiology with its demands for indigenous churches rather than biblically modeled churches offers many illustrations of this perspective. For example, Mahlon M. Hess argues that the form of church polity adopted by a given tribe will depend upon whether the indigenous government is basically local (congregational), regional (presbyterian), or a kingdom (episcopal). Cf. "Political Systems and African Church Polity," in *Readings in Missionary Anthropology*, ed. William A. Smalley (Tarrytown, NY: Practical Anthropology, 1967), 193-94.

[141] Cf. Berkhof, *The Christian Faith*, 388.

[142] In this section I am closely following an unpublished paper by J. Gary Inrig, "Ecclesiology, Cultural Relativism, and Biblical Absolutism," written for a course at Dallas Seminary in May 1969.

[143] The supra-cultural nature of the church may be illustrated in at least two ways: (1) The relation of Jews and Gentiles in the church. The conventional wisdom of the modern "church growth" movement would dictate sub-cultural churches with side-by-side Jewish and Gentile assemblies each following their own cultural preferences. This, in fact, is what a vigorous and outspoken faction of the early church wanted. They did not want an integrated church, but a purely Jewish church, in which Gentiles gave up their cultural identity. The apostles ultimately rejected this idea [Gal. 2:11-14]. In spite of the cultural and evangelistic expediency of such a policy, it was rejected—there would be no church structure along racial and national lines. The reason was doctrinal—it would be a denial of the equal standing of Jews and Gentiles in the body of Christ [Eph. 2:11-22]. (2) Slavery. The attitude of the Apostle Paul toward slavery is a striking illustration of the New Testament's attitude toward culture. On the one hand he exhorts them to respect their masters (1 Tim. 6:1,2), to give service to them as to God (Eph. 6:5-8), and to recognize the hand of God in their position (1 Cor. 7:20-24). On the other hand Paul undermines his culture's authority by arguing that slavery has no validity within the church (1 Cor. 7:22; Gal. 3:28) and that slaves are to be treated as brothers (Philemon 16).

[144] Morris, *Ministers of God*, 70. Cf. C. W. Dugmore, *The Influence of the Synagogue Upon the Divine Office* (2d ed., Westminster: Faith Press, 1964), 7-10 and *passim*.

to take seriously the sovereign control of Israel's history by which the Lord guided the nations so that the office was already familiar to the earliest Christians.[145] (2) It does not take seriously the installation of elders in Gentile churches. A case in point is the Philippian assembly. When Paul came to the city he did not go to the synagogue, because there were not enough Jews in the city to have one.[146] Of Jewish converts we hear nothing, yet Paul addresses his epistle, "To all the saints in Christ Jesus who are in Philippi, including the overseers (i.e., the elders) and deacons" (Phil. 1:1).

Second, it is insubordinate to the apostolic demand for uniform practice in the churches. In 1 Corinthians 11–14 the Apostle Paul deals with problems of church order in the Corinthian assembly. "His expectation and demand is that there will be uniformity in practice throughout the churches." [147] He writes, **"But if one is inclined to be contentious, we have no other practice, nor have the churches of God"** (1 Cor. 11:16). Such ecclesiastical relativism seeks to evade the clear teaching in Scripture about the ordering of the church. At times it merges with the ecclesiastical pragmatism I have addressed above. "If it works, that's enough!" Jim Elliot, the young and forthright missionary to Ecuador, wrote of this attitude,

> Further, J. says "the [Plymouth Brethren] worship service is most satisfying to me as an individual." What in all eternity has that got to do with it? Have her personal likes and dislikes any right to dictate method in the holy church of God….J.'s letter was interesting. Her attitude toward the church of God is like the majority of Fundamentalists—"anything will do." The pivot point hangs on whether or not God has revealed a universal pattern for the church in the New

---

[145] The indebtedness of the early church to the synagogue can be overstated. To cite just two examples: (1) Elders predate the synagogue in Israel's history [Exod. 19:7; Judg. 21:16], and (2) the synagogue had a chief officer ["head of the synagogue," Luke 8:49; 13:14; Acts 18:8,17], yet the New Testament assemblies never adopted this practice. Cf. Emil Schürer, *The History of the Jewish People in the Age of Jesus Christ*, 3 vols., ed. Matthew Black *et al* (rev. ed., Edinburgh: T. & T. Clark, 1979), 2:433-39.

[146] The minimum number for a synagogue was ten men, as this was the quorum for a religious meeting (Schürer, *The History of the Jewish People*, 2:438). Cf. *Aboth* 3.6 in *The Babylonian Talmud: Seder Nezikin*, 4 vols., ed. I. Epstein (London: Soncino, 1935), 4:30, which reads, "Rabbi Ḥalafta [ben Dosa] of Kefar Ḥanania said, 'When there are ten sitting together and occupying themselves with Torah, the Shechinah abides among them, as it is said: God standeth in the congregation of God [Ps. 82:1].'"

[147] Cf. Noel Weeks, *The Sufficiency of Scripture* (Edinburgh: Banner of Truth, 1988), 158-59.

Testament. If He has not, then anything will do so long as it works. But I am convinced that nothing so dear to the heart of Christ as His Bride should be left without explicit instructions as to her corporate conduct.[148]

Third, it is demeaning to the important place of the local church in the plan of God. The church lies at the heart, not the periphery of God's program. It is, says Paul, "The pillar and support of the truth" (1 Tim. 3:15). God has designed the church to show very important truths to the world, and He has so designed it that those truths can only be shown by a certain form of church structure.

Finally, ecclesiastical relativism is inconsistent with the evangelical view of biblical authority. Evangelicals insist that the Word of God is sufficient for every area of faith (theology) and practice; sufficient, that is, in every area except one, viz., church government. In this area cultural variation is important, many evangelicals insist. This is puzzling because evangelicals normally insist that the Bible must be the judge of culture and not be conformed to it. They recognize that culture is often a Satanic means of sheltering people from God. They know that the New Testament means something closely akin to "culture" when it speaks of the κόσμος (kosmos, i.e., the "world"), the Satanic system opposed to God.

They reject cultural relativism when it says that biblical morality and doctrine are not to be applied to a specific people. They rightly reject the relativistic notions of anthropologists who oppose the preaching of the gospel to native peoples on the ground that it "Westernizes" them. They totally reject the moral relativism that would minimize or trivialize the evils of adultery, divorce, homosexuality, lying, idolatry, drunkenness, and other practices prohibited by Scripture. Yet they inconsistently deny the possibility of following the New Testament in its teaching on church order because our culture is different.

Such relativism is unknown to the apostles. Paul advises Timothy that he is writing so that "you may know how one ought (δεῖ, dei) to conduct himself in the household of God, which is the church of the living God, the pillar and support of the truth" (1 Tim. 3:15). "There is a divine necessity about New Testament church order," says Gary Inrig. "It is not optional, no matter what the culture, because of the local assembly's relation to divine truth."[149]

---

[148] Elisabeth Elliot, *Shadow of the Almighty* (New York: Harper and Row, 1958), 138-39.

[149] Inrig, "Ecclesiology, Cultural Relativism, and Biblical Absolutism," 14.

THE PRIMACY OF SCRIPTURE IN THE CHURCH

THE CENTRALITY OF THE WORD AMONG THE ACTIVITIES OF THE CHURCH

Paul's expression "the pillar and support of the truth" (1 Tim. 3:15) says a great deal about his understanding of the function of the local church. The context of the expression is his letter to Timothy in which he instructs him to confront the doctrinal error being perpetrated by some of the Ephesian elders.[150]

The word *pillar* (στῦλος, *stylos*) would have special significance to the Ephesians in that their city was the site of the Temple of Diana which had 127 marble pillars upon which announcements were regularly affixed. The local church was a pillar upon which the truth was to be held up that all might see it. By "truth" (ἀλήθεια, *alētheia*) Paul means the full revelation of God in Christ as verse 16 makes clear. The truth is the orthodox Christian faith, i.e., the fundamental doctrines of the Bible as they center in Christ. The church is a household called to manifest the truth in its message and to conform to it in its conduct.[151] Paul adds that the church is the "support" or buttress (ἑδραίωμα, *hedraiōma*) of the truth. The church, the Apostle implies, exists to maintain the faith and protect it from all danger.

A survey of the New Testament reveals that the elders of the church are men who daily deal with biblical truth. They are warned to guard the flock against "wolves," i.e., false teachers (Acts 20:17,28-31; Titus 1:5-9), and they are instructed to be teachers of the Word of God (John 21:17; 1 Tim. 3:2; 4:13). The man is to be honored who works hard at preaching and teaching (1 Tim. 5:17-18). As James Orr (1844-1913), the well-known Scottish theologian, remarked, "If there is a religion in the world which exalts the office of teaching, it is safe to say that it is the religion of Jesus Christ."[152]

---

[150] In support of the hypothesis that the church in Ephesus was being misled by some of the elders, Fee offers this evidence: (1) The errorists were teachers [1 Tim. 1:3, 7; 6:3], and teaching was a task of elders [3:2; 5:17]. (2) A significant part of the letter is allotted to the character, qualifications, and discipline of church leaders [3:1-13; 5:17-25], and many of the guidelines stand in obvious contrast to what is specifically said of the false teachers. It is noteworthy that two of the ringleaders are named and excommunicated [1:19-20]. Cf. Gordon D. Fee, *1 and 2 Timothy, Titus,* NIBC (Peabody, MA: Hendrickson, 1988), 7–8.

[151] Cf. Knight, *The Pastoral Epistles,* 181.

[152] James Orr, *The Christian View of God and the World* (1893; reprint ed., Grand Rapids: Eerdmans, 1954), 20.

The Centrality of Biblical Preaching/Teaching

In Luke's brief description of the first meetings of the church (Acts 2:42), he says, "they were continually devoting themselves to the apostles' teaching." Commenting on this text, biblical commentator John R. W. Stott writes, "The Holy Spirit opened a school in Jerusalem that day; its teachers were the apostles whom Jesus had appointed; and there were 3,000 pupils in the kindergarten!"[153] He rightly observes that from the outset the church rejected anti-intellectualism. There was never a hint that instruction was unnecessary.

The believers listened attentively because the apostles were a living link with the Savior. The Holy Spirit enabled them to remember infallibly what they had heard Jesus say (John 14:28; 15:26-27), and they were given authority to communicate divine revelation (cf. 1 Cor. 2:10; Gal. 1:11-12). It was their duty to lay the foundation of normative Christian teaching for the Christian church (Eph. 2:20). What they taught was the voice of God to the church (cf. 1 Pet. 1:25; 1 John 4:6; John 14:26; 1 Thess. 2:13).[154] Their teaching, as Acts 28:31 makes clear, concerned the Lord Jesus Christ—the facts of His life and teaching and the significance of His death and resurrection (Acts 2:22-36).

The living apostles no longer expound the truth[155] in the meetings of the church, but apostolic teaching still goes forth in every place where faithful men hand the truth on to those who can teach others (2 Tim. 2:2). Their teaching is found in the canon of the New Testament, and the faithful church is one which seeks to understand, proclaim, and conform to the unique, infallible teaching of the apostles of Jesus Christ.

D. Martyn Lloyd-Jones, in his lectures to the students of Westminster Theological Seminary, said, "The most urgent need in the Christian Church today is true preaching....It is obviously the greatest need of the world also."[156] John Stott added, "Preaching is indispensable to Christianity. Without preaching a

---

[153] John Stott, *The Spirit, the Church, and the World: The Message of Acts*, BST (Downers Grove: InterVarsity Press, 1990), 82. Cf. R. B. Rackham, *The Acts of the Apostles* (London: Methuen, 1901), 33.

[154] Cf. Robert Culver, "Apostles and the Apostolate in the New Testament," *BS* 134 (April 1977): 136-37.

[155] The term teaching in Acts 2:42 (διδαχή) refers to the act of teaching. It later came to refer to established and formulated doctrine. Cf. *TDNT*, s.v. "διδαχή," by K. H. Rengstorf, 2 (1964): 163-65.

[156] D. Martyn Lloyd-Jones, *Preaching and Preachers* (Grand Rapids: Zondervan, 1972), 9.

necessary part of its authenticity has been lost. For Christianity is, in its very essence, a religion of the Word of God."[157]

The Decline of Biblical Preaching/Teaching

Professor John R. de Witt of Reformed Theological Seminary says that today "most congregations are largely indifferent to preaching." They "are satisfied with mediocrity in the pulpit, provided the [preacher] is inoffensive and does not trespass too much on their time."[158] These low expectations are self-fulfilling, says Regent College professor, James Packer. Having become cool and blasé about preaching we expect little from them and "should not wonder that God deals with us according to our unbelief."[159]

John Stott has concluded that preaching is a dying art.[160] Many reasons have been offered for its demise. Some have noted the mood of our age which is decidedly anti-authority. All elements of the old order (family, school, state, Bible, church) are being challenged. We should remember, however, that mankind has always been hostile to God and authority (cf. Rom. 8:7). We should also remember that Christianity is inherently dogmatic due to the doctrine of revelation.[161]

Others have pointed to the cybernetics (= mechanisms of communication) revolution. TV makes people physically lazy, intellectually uncritical, emotionally insensitive, psychologically confused, and morally disordered.[162] Because of TV "the power of speech to communicate significance has become suspect."

---

[157] John R. W. Stott, *Between Two Worlds: The Art of Preaching in the Twentieth Century* (Grand Rapids: Eerdmans, 1982), 15.

[158] John R. de Witt, "Contemporary Failure in the Pulpit," *Banner of Truth* (March 1981), 23. A newspaper columnist recently quipped that when the average church member asks the minister, "What will the sermon be about?" he does not want to know the subject. He really wants to know whether it will be about ten minutes long or about thirty minutes long.

[159] J. I. Packer, "Why Preach?" in *The Preacher and Preaching*, ed. Samuel T. Logan, Jr. (Phillipsburg: Presbyterian and Reformed, 1986), 5.

[160] Stott, *Between Two Worlds*, 50.

[161] I remember reading an interview with Dr. Billy Graham. He was asked how he could preach about hell from the Bible to unchurched people who reject biblical authority. He answered, "I just read to them verses about hell and watch them sweat!" Graham had great confidence in the Bible as a living book (cf. Heb. 4:12-13).

[162] Stott, *Between Two Worlds*, 64, 75. Stott counsels Christians and preachers to: (1) exert greater discipline over our children's use of TV, (2) penetrate the world of media and learn to use it, and (3) reckon with a TV-conditioned congregation in our church meetings.

Calm and chatty intimacy is considered genuine, while strong feelings expressed in dynamic preaching look and sound artificial.[163]

Adding his reasons for the modern demise of preaching, J. I. Packer says that much of it is non-preaching.[164] They are either speeches delivered without opening the Bible, lectures aimed at informing the mind, or addresses expressing the preacher's opinion. In short, they are often less than messages from God. Preaching, he notes, is teaching *plus* application (invitation, direction, summons), and the *plus* is often lacking in many church discourses today.

Second, he notes that topical preaching,[165] as opposed to expository preaching,[166] has become the general rule. Such sermons fall short because their biblical content is made to appear as the speaker's own wisdom. The text is reduced to a peg upon which the speaker hangs his own opinions. "This destroys the very idea of Christian preaching, which excludes the thought of speaking for the Bible and insists that the Bible be allowed to speak for itself in and through the speaker's words." The true preacher must allow himself to become a mouthpiece for messages from the biblical text.[167]

---

[163] Packer, "Why Preach?" 6.

[164] Packer, "Why Preach?" 3-7.

[165] There is, of course, a form of topical preaching that is valid, viz., the exposition of topics and doctrines of Scripture basing one's remarks on the central passages that underlie those topics and doctrines.

[166] Expository preaching is not just a running commentary on a passage, nor is it merely a lesson in ancient history. Rather, it is the communication of the exact and full meaning of a passage of Scripture in terms of our contemporary culture with the specific goal of helping people to understand and obey the truth of God. Cf. Stott, *Between Two Worlds*, 137-44.

[167] Among many evangelicals there is a fundamental misunderstanding of preaching. According to the *Second Helvetic Confession* 18 (1566) the sermon is "the voice of Christ." As John Murray notes in his comments on Romans 10:14-15, Paul views the sermon as the vehicle through which Jesus Christ Himself speaks. It is the means by which God addresses Himself to sinners. Christ speaks in the gospel proclamation; He is heard in the message spoken by His messengers. There is a great want of earnestness seen in much preaching today. Gone is the sober attitude of Richard Baxter,

"I preached as never sure to preach again,
And as a dying man to dying men."

This absence of the authoritative, prophetic note in much preaching is illustrated by an introduction I have heard too many times, "Brother So-and-So is now going to 'share' what the Lord has laid on his heart." The word "share" is one of the most despicable platitudes ever used to describe a sermon. I agree with de Witt, "The minister must come from God, bearing God's message, speaking God's Word, standing in a sense even in God's place, addressing us with that which in no way rests on his own authority." Cf. "Contemporary Failure in the Pulpit," 19-20, 23; John Murray, *The Epistle to the Romans*, 2 vols., NICNT (Grand Rapids: Eerdmans, 1965), 2:58; Philip Schaff, *The Creeds of Christendom*, 3 vols. (New York: Harper, 1877), 1:412.

Third, in some Christian groups today "a cult of spontaneity militates against preaching." A holdover from the 1960s and 70s, this viewpoint prizes crudeness as a sign of sincerity. Folk-style songs, extempore prayer marked by earnest incoherence, Charismatic "prophecy," and under-prepared and intellectually imprecise sermons are some of the manifestations of this attitude.[168]

Fourth, the fascination with liturgical forms by some evangelicals militates against preaching. It is striking that J. I. Packer, an Episcopalian, should make this observation. He is bothered that numerous Christians are flowing into liturgical churches because of the shallowness and mediocrity of the churches of their upbringing. The problem is that they are throwing the baby (preaching of the Bible) out with the bathwater (shallow worship services).

The Substitutes for Biblical Preaching/Teaching

John MacArthur, well-known pastor and seminary president, has argued that a new pragmatism in our time is undermining "the four priorities of the early church," namely, "the apostles' teaching, fellowship, the breaking of the bread, and prayer" (Acts 2:42).[169] MacArthur is particularly concerned about a change in ministry philosophy in which entertainment is being used as a tool for church growth.[170] He cites similar concerns by the late A. W. Tozer who feared that frivolous diversions would eventually destroy people's appetites for real worship and the preaching of the Word.[171] Such things are defended by an Arminian

---

[168] In many groups spontaneity is valued above substance and passion above preparation (Packer, "Why Preach?" 5).

[169] John F. MacArthur, Jr., "Truth vs. Technique," *Reformation & Revival Journal* 3 (Fall 1994): 17-42. According to many Reformed Christians there are three "marks" of the church, viz., the pure preaching of the Word, the pure administration of the sacraments, and the exercise of church discipline (*Belgic Confession* [A.D. 1561], Article 29, in Schaff, ed., *The Creeds of Christendom*, 3:419). Cf. G. C. Berkouwer, *Studies in Dogmatics: The Church*, trans. James E. Davison (Grand Rapids: Eerdmans, 1976), 14-15. Some, citing Acts 2:47, would add a fifth priority to MacArthur's list of four, viz., evangelism.

[170] MacArthur offers as examples: up-tempo music; guest speakers who are comedians, not preachers; drama and entertainment instead of exposition; a church that featured a wrestling match featuring church employees; a pie fight during a Sunday morning service; a church with a special-effects system that can produce smoke, fire, sparks, and laser lights, etc. I am sure that MacArthur would not condemn all contemporary music or all use of film or drama. But his overall warning is salutary. There is a tendency in modern society for technique to replace truth.

[171] Some time ago my good friend, Paul Sapp of Ohio, had a conversation with Dr. James M. Boice, the able pastor and Bible teacher from Philadelphia's Tenth Presbyterian Church. "What you win them with you win them to, and what you win them to you keep them with." cautioned Dr. Boice.

pragmatism ("Does it work?") that denies the growth process found in Scripture: "I planted, Apollos watered, but God was causing the growth. So then neither the one who plants nor the one who waters is anything, but God who causes the growth" (1 Cor. 3:6-7). "The new pragmatism sees preaching as passé.[172] Plainly declared biblical truth is deemed too offensive and utterly ineffective. We're now told we can get better results by first amusing people and thus wooing them into the fold."[173]

Other substitutes for preaching have emerged in our time. D. Martyn Lloyd-Jones, in his famous Westminster Seminary lectures, noted the increased emphasis on "personal work" or "counseling."[174] Others have bemoaned the

---

[172] Instructive here are the observations of a secular work, Neil Postman's *Amusing Ourselves to Death* (New York: Penguin, 1985), 63-4 and *passim*. He argues that the television age tends to turn everything into entertainment and amusement. Significantly, this secular commentator describes the pre-television age as the age of Exposition. "Exposition is a mode of thought, a method of learning, and a means of expression." Exposition, he explains, is "the sophisticated ability to think conceptually, deductively, and sequentially; a high valuation of reason and order; an abhorrence of contradiction; a large capacity for detachment and objectivity; and a tolerance for delayed response." He notes that the age of Exposition has been replaced by the Age of Show Business.

[173] A number of years ago I spoke at a seminar in Chicago on the subject of preaching. A young friend of mine, at that time a full-time worker in a progressive Brethren assembly, told me that he had abandoned the "Dallas style" exposition he had learned under Haddon Robinson. "It's too confrontational. I believe in preaching in a more relational fashion—teaching the Christian life as a world view. Gradually people accept this world view as their own." Lost in his understanding was the biblical view that the gospel is "a stone of stumbling and a rock of offense" (Rom. 9:33; 1 Pet. 2:8).

[174] D. Martyn Lloyd-Jones, *Preaching and Preachers* (Grand Rapids; Zondervan, 1972), 17, 29-30, 37, 39. Dr. Lloyd-Jones, a physician by training, did not dismiss the need for personal work/counseling. Neither do other critics of the modern counseling movement. What he and other biblical men are saying may be summarized as follows: (1) Good biblical preaching should relieve the need for much counseling, and (2) biblical theology must not be replaced by pop-psychology in the pulpit.

John White, the well-known writer and psychiatrist, also decried the present trend to substitute counseling for the exposition of the Word of God. He wrote, "Until about fifteen years ago psychology was seen by most Christians as hostile to the gospel. Let someone who professes the name of Jesus baptize secular psychology and present it as something compatible with Scripture truth, and most Christians are happy to swallow theological hemlock in the form of 'psychological insights.'

Over the past fifteen years there has been a tendency for churches to place increasing reliance on trained pastoral counselors....To me it seems to suggest weaknesses in or indifference to expository preaching within evangelical churches....

Why do we have to turn to the human sciences at all? Why? Because for years we have failed to expound the whole of the Scripture. Because from our weakened exposition and our

psychologizing of the Christian message.[175] Lloyd-Jones, an astute observer of modern evangelicalism, asserts that as biblical preaching—preaching that is expositional, pastoral, doctrinal, and relevant—goes down, the need for counseling goes up. True preaching, applied by the Holy Spirit to individuals who are listening, has been the means in the past of dealing with many of the personal problems of people. As Harold John Ockenga observed long ago, biblical preaching will communicate the same ideas that one gives in counseling. "You might as well handle a thousand people as one or ten."[176]

Other voices have stressed the need for an evangelical social activism to deal with the social conditions and political injustices of society.[177] It is not evangelism and Bible teaching designed to convert and nurture individual souls that is needed so much as programs that will bring about social transformation.[178] Key proponents[179] of this view argue that evangelicals need to return

---

superficial talks we have produced a generation of Christian sheep who have no shepherd. And now we are damning ourselves more deeply than ever by our recourse to the wisdom of the world.

What I do as a psychiatrist and what my psychologist colleagues do in their research or their counseling are of infinitely less value to distressed Christians than what God says in His word. But pastoral shepherds, like the sheep they guide, are following…a new Pied Piper of Hamelin who is leading them into the dark caves of humanistic hedonism" (*Flirting With the World* [Wheaton: Shaw, 1982], 114-17).

Old Testament scholar, Walter C. Kaiser, Jr., added, "There just are no substitutes for declaring the whole counsel of God to the whole body of believers. All additives prove in the end to be more carcinogenic and detrimental to our spiritual health than we had ever imagined" ("The Future Role of the Bible in Seminary Education," *Concordia Theological Quarterly* 60 [October 1996], 250).

[175] Let me add one caveat here. I am not suggesting that all counseling or therapy is wrong— it is often very helpful to talk our problems out with a responsible, mature Christian elder, pastor, or counselor, and there may be occasions when a Christian will need medical help from a physician with psychiatric training. What I am saying is that our modern society has rejected the biblical explanation of evil. It has rejected the biblical terminology of sin for a new moral vocabulary that is largely psychological. Therapy is deadly when it encourages us to think of ourselves as helpless victims instead of the full-scale sinners and responsible moral beings that we really are.

[176] "Harold J. Ockenga: Chairman of the Board," *Christianity Today* (Nov. 6, 1981): 28.

[177] It has been suggested that Walter Rauschenbusch (1861-1918), the father of the social gospel, lost his faith in orthodox Christianity during a trip to the holy land. He saw for himself the deplorable condition of the Palestinian roads for which Jesus had done nothing. He lost sight of the fact that Christ had better things to do than to busy Himself with physical comforts. Paul Verghese, a member of the Orthodox Syrian Church, said that the temptation of the Protestant churches is to replace evangelization with service. Cf. Kuen, *I Will Build My Church*, 291-92.

[178] A major shift in evangelical thinking was first widely heralded at the Congress on World Evangelization held in Lausanne in 1974.

to their roots, i.e., the socially-concerned and active evangelicalism of the nineteenth century.[180] Lloyd-Jones has argued that such activism is at best secondary, [and] very often not even secondary. The primary task of the church is the preaching of the Word of God.[181]

Another substitute for preaching and teaching the Bible is the current concentration on liturgy that I mentioned earlier. The past two decades have seen a steady stream of evangelicals out of Bible teaching churches into the liturgical services of the Roman, Greek Orthodox and Anglican communions. Tired of the "religious individualism and kitsch" of their churches they have sought a more austere God-centered worship in the set liturgies of these older churches. J. I. Packer, himself an evangelical Anglican, is stunned by this movement. "It saddens me to observe that this liturgical interest, which has led them to leave churches that highlighted the ministry of the Word, seems to have elbowed all concern about preaching out of their minds."[182]

---

[179] Proponents include C. Rene Padilla, Samuel Escobar, Jim Wallis, Ron Sider, and (sadly) John Stott. Carl F. H. Henry, who first called modern evangelicals to social action in his *The Uneasy Conscience of Modern Fundamentalism* (Grand Rapids: Eerdmans, 1947), has more recently expressed concern at where his ideas have led them. Cf. Carl Henry, "The Uneasy Conscience Revisited," in *Twilight of a Great Civilization: The Drift Toward Neo-Paganism* (Westchester: Crossway, 1987), 170-72.

[180] The social action of the nineteenth century was different than that advocated by today's evangelicals in several ways: (1) The nineteenth century movement was preceded by the widespread proclamation of the gospel and the mass conversions of the Methodist revival. (2) The nineteenth century leaders were all agreed upon salvation by faith and the inerrancy and centrality of the Scriptures. (3) The nineteenth century evangelicals insisted on the personal nature of sin. (4) Nineteenth century social action was limited to social welfare, i.e., the attempts to alleviate existing problems. The differences are striking: (1) Modern evangelical social action has not been preceded by a widespread proclamation of the gospel and mass conversions. It has, in fact, been accompanied by a massive decline in personal morality and family breakdown. (2) Modern socially active evangelicals are marked by uncertainty about vital matters of faith and morality [witness the defections on inerrancy, the softness on personal sins of adultery, homosexuality, etc.]. (3) Modern social activists speak more of "structural sin," "transforming society," and "extending the kingdom" [understood in terms of political change] than they do of personal sin and discipleship. (4) Modern social activists are far more ambitious than their nineteenth century counterparts. They speak of the transformation of society, often in Marxist tones, often with little consideration of what is socially, economically, or politically possible. Cf. Rachel Tingle, "Evangelical Social Action Today: Road to Recovery or Road to Ruin?" in Melvin Tinker, ed., *The Anglican Evangelical Crisis*, 186-202.

[181] Lloyd-Jones, *Preaching and Preachers*, 19.

[182] Packer, "Why Preach?" 5-6.

The Importance of Biblical Preaching/Teaching

Dr. Donald Coggan says that this modern attitude to preaching is "a specious lie" perpetrated by "Our Father Below," as C. S. Lewis called the devil.[183]

Preaching is important, says Packer, for three reasons:[184] First, it is God's revealed way of making Himself and His work known to us. Many New Testament texts stress the need for preaching (Matt. 10:6-7; Mark 3:14; 13:10; Luke 24:45-49; Acts 5:42; 6:2-4; 10:42; Rom. 10:6-17; 1 Cor. 1:17-24; 9:16; Phil. 1:12-18; 2 Tim. 4:2-5; Tit. 1:3). Second, preaching communicates the force of the Bible as no other way of handling it does. Packer derives this argument from the nature of Scripture itself, which is, in and of itself, preaching. Many sections in the prophets, the Gospels, the Acts, and the epistles are sermons on paper. The rest of the Scriptures as well were written to edify.

Finally, preaching focuses the identity and clarifies the calling of the church as no other activity does. The church has an identity crisis today, says Packer. Is it a social club, like the Rotary? Is it a special interest group, like a political party, or is it, perhaps, an athletic center? No, the church is the people of God, and preaching keeps before the believers their calling to be an obedient, Word oriented, worship oriented, and witness oriented company of people.

The Rehabilitation of Biblical Preaching/Teaching

If we—I am writing primarily to those in Open Brethren assemblies—are to be Spirit-filled churches, the powerful preaching of apostles' doctrine must be rehabilitated.[185] We must recognize that the primary task of the church is the proclamation of God's Word (2 Tim. 4:2; cf. Acts 6:4; 1 Tim. 4:13; 6:2; 1 Cor. 1:17,

---

[183] Quoted in Stott, *Between Two Worlds*, 50.

[184] Packer, "Why Preach?" 15-21. Packer (pp. 8-14) defines preaching as follows: (1) Its *content* is God's message to man. (2) Its *source* is a passage from the Bible, and the sermon will be grounded on that passage. (3) Its *purpose* is to inform, persuade, and call forth an appropriate response to the God whose message is being delivered. (4) Its *perspective* is applicatory. "Preaching is God-centered in its viewpoint, Christ-centered in its substance, and life-changing in its thrust." (5) Its *authority* is divine in so far as the preacher is truly under the authority of Scripture.

[185] As John Stott observed, the account in Acts 2 of the church's baptism and indwelling by the Spirit is the ideal place to find out what a Spirit-filled church looks like. Acts 2:42 and its immediate context point to the following elements: the preaching of the Word, the fellowship of other Christians, the worship of God in the celebration of the Lord's supper, the asking for divine aid in prayer, and the evangelism of the lost. Cf. "Setting the Spirit Free," *Christianity Today* (June 12, 1981), 17-21.

23; 2 Cor. 4:5).[186] In our assemblies we must allow/encourage men to give themselves to preaching.[187] Recognizing the biblical principle of difference in spiritual gifts—not everyone is a preacher/teacher, not even every elder—we must free the gifted men from other responsibilities in order that they might give themselves to this task.[188]

Furthermore, we must commit ourselves to the complete authority of the Word—in our church life, in our business life, and in our family life. Also, we must preach the great doctrines of the Bible, and we must preach them from the texts in which they are found. In addition, as preachers we must be certain of our relationship to Christ and maintain a strong Christian life. Finally, we must be aware that we are role models for younger men, and we must set for them a good example in the earnest discipline we bring to the preaching task.

THE CENTRALITY OF THE WORD IN THE MESSAGE OF THE CHURCH

John Stott wrote, "It is the contention of evangelicals that they are plain Bible Christians, and that in order to be a biblical Christian it is necessary to be an

---

[186] James Montgomery Boice, "Manifesto for Effective Preaching," *Eternity* (October 1975): 73.

[187] For a number of years F. F. Bruce contributed a brief discussion question to *The Harvester* magazine. After the magazine ran an article on Martyn Lloyd-Jones, Bruce wondered if, "in order to realize his full potential as a great preacher, a man requires a pulpit of his own to serve as his base" ("Professor Bruce Asks," *The Harvester* [Dec. 1980], 349). In a subsequent issue (February 1981, p. 16), well-known Bible teacher H. L. Ellison offered this response, "I have frequently asked staunch upholders of 'assembly principles' whether C. H. Spurgeon or Dr. Campbell Morgan, if they had been assembly members, subject to all the limitations placed on such members, could have achieved the results that they did. The answer was always, 'No.' Whereupon I suggested that not our principles, but our understanding of them, was at fault. We have fallen down and worshipped the Moloch of no one-man-ministry and failed to recognize the principle of recognition of gift. God challenges our feeble understanding by raising up the exceptional man…and showing us how little room there is for [him] in our traditions. As the late G. H. Lang used to say, 'If the Apostle Paul were to come to the average assembly, the elders would have to say to him, 'Sorry, Brother Paul, but we are booked solid for the next six months.'"

[188] A man who gives himself to forty hours of administration or counseling will not have time for preaching. This will come as a shock to men who glibly say it takes two hours to prepare a sermon. In a recent volume by experienced preachers, all contributors said that it took from ten to twenty hours to prepare a sermon. The shortest preparation time was six hours, and the longest was forty. In evaluating these figures one should remember that all these preachers preached at least once a week, and all came to the task with a wealth of experience. How much longer should it take a neophyte? Cf. Haddon W. Robinson, ed., *Biblical Sermons* (Grand Rapids: Baker, 1989), 27 and *passim*.

evangelical Christian."[189] This is a bold assertion because Stott is not saying that evangelicals are an interesting and distinctive group within the Christian spectrum; he is saying that evangelicalism is authentic, biblical Christianity.[190]

The word *evangelical* comes from the Greek word εὐαγγέλιον (*euangelion*), meaning "gospel" or "good news." Evangelicals are those people whose beliefs and practice are shaped by what the Apostle calls "the truth of the gospel" of Jesus Christ (Gal. 2:5, 14). They are "cross-centered people, for the heart of the gospel is the declaration of Christ's atoning death and victorious resurrection with its summons to faith and a life of discipleship."[191] Because they are Bible people, evangelicals[192] give the Scriptures the place of primacy in their life, practice, and theology. The fundamental perspectives of the Bible's teaching must be central in what is regularly proclaimed from the pulpit.

The Authority of Scripture: A Distinctive View of Revelation and Theology[193]

At least six biblical truths give evangelical theology its basic shape. The most basic of these is its view of the Bible. Evangelicals follow their Lord who

---

[189] John R. W. Stott, *Christ the Controversialist* (Downers Grove: InterVarsity Press, 1970), 32. As Stott notes (pp. 27-32) the word evangelical has a long history. It was used around A.D. 200 by Tertullian in defense of biblical truth against the heresies of Marcion. Luther used the term to describe his doctrine. It was used in 1532 by Sir Thomas More in his attack on William Tyndale and his followers. He referred to them as "those evangelicalles." Cf. Mark Thompson, "Saving the Heart of Evangelicalism," in *The Anglican Evangelical Crisis*, ed. Melvin Tinker (Fearn, Scotland: Christian Focus Publications, 1995), 29.

[190] As Anglican theologian, Mark Thompson, notes, "This is a dangerous business." It is saying that other religious traditions (Catholic, charismatic, Liberal) involve some kind of error ("Saving the Heart of Evangelicalism," 41). J. Gresham Machen saw this years ago. His famous work is not entitled, *Evangelical Christians and Liberal Christians*; it is entitled *Christianity and Liberalism* (1923; reprint ed., Grand Rapids: Eerdmans, 1972).

[191] Thompson, "Saving the Heart of Evangelicalism," 28-29. Thompson pointedly rejects contemporary works that attempt to define evangelicalism in terms of sociology or spirituality. It must be defined theologically.

[192] Open Brethren are evangelicals. They are "Brethren" because they share a common history with a group of churches and because they believe certain church practices are biblical and normative. They are "Open" because they believe that within the framework of evangelical theology there are differences of opinion, and allowances must be made for these in that the pervasive influence of sin on our hearts and minds keeps all of us from perfection in this life. Open Brethren make room for these differences without resorting to disenfranchising those who differ. Cf. Thompson, "Saving the Heart of Evangelicalism," 40.

[193] In this exposition of evangelical distinctives, I am closely following Thompson's important essay, "Saving the Heart of Evangelicalism," 29-38.

explained Himself and His work in terms of Scriptural teaching (Luke 24:27). They affirm with the apostles (2 Tim. 3:14-17; 2 Pet. 1:21) that the Scriptures come from the mouth of God and are His full and sufficient provision that they might be thoroughly equipped to live the Christian life.

The Seriousness of Sin: A Distinctive View of Human Nature

In defining the predicament of man evangelicals must resist the modern approach of using the language of psychotherapy. They must instead explain the problems of people by the categories which the Bible supplies. The seriousness of the human predicament is seen in the death of Jesus. That death is "a barbaric overreaction on God's part" if human beings are not in very serious danger.

The greatest of dangers facing people is a long-standing one, originating with the decision of Adam and Eve to disobey God (Gen. 3; Rom. 5:12). That self-centered and self-seeking decision has involved the entire human race in their corruption and guilt. Every human being has a bias towards sin (Rom. 3:23), is alienated from God (Isa. 59:1-2; Col. 1:21), and is under the threat of God's terrifying judgment (Heb. 9:27; 10:31). The most basic need of men and women is not justice for the oppressed, international peace, or environmental awareness, as important as these may be. The most basic need, according to Scripture, is for forgiveness of sin and reconciliation with God.

The Penal Substitutionary Atonement of Christ: A Distinctive View of Salvation

Beginning with Genesis 3:15 and gradually unfolding through the Scriptures is the promise of a full, final, and effective solution to the problem of sin. That solution is offered by the Suffering Servant of the Lord who takes upon Himself "the iniquity of us all" (Isa. 53:6). Jesus Christ is the promised "lamb of God" (John 1:29) who gives His life a "ransom for many" (Mark 10:45). The Bible teaches that He died in our place and bore the curse of God for us (2 Cor. 5:21; Gal. 3:13; 1 Pet. 3:18; 1 John 2:2). This is God's answer to the human dilemma. If Scripture is to have a place of primacy in the church the penal substitutionary death of Christ as a satisfaction of God's righteous demands must not be reduced to just one of many "theories" of atonement. It must be proclaimed as the basic biblical understanding without which other perspectives are devoid of any real meaning.[194]

---

[194] Cf. S. Lewis Johnson, Jr., "Behold the Lamb: the Gospel and Substitutionary Atonement," in The Coming Evangelical Crisis, ed. John H. Armstrong (Chicago: Moody, 1996), 119-38.

Justification by Faith Alone: A Distinctive View of Christian Response

The Judaism of Jesus' time was a grotesque mutation of the religion given to Moses.[195] It had changed the religion of promise into a performance-oriented attempt to relate to God on the basis of one's own self-righteousness. While the Pharisees boasted in their own righteousness (Luke 18:14) Paul taught that God "justifies the ungodly" (Rom. 4:5). It is those who put their faith in Jesus who are made right with God (Rom. 4:1-5). They are acquitted in God's courtroom and have a new standing with Him (Rom. 8:1-4). If Scripture has primacy then this important doctrine will be proclaimed. It safeguards the initiative of God in salvation and undermines all human boasting.

The Necessity of the New Birth: A Distinctive View of Grace and the Spirit

Human beings, lost in their sins, are called to respond to God's marvelous provision. Such a response is impossible for those who are spiritually dead (Eph. 2:1), deaf (1 Cor. 2:14), and blind (2 Cor. 4:3-4). They are unable to believe without the miraculous intervention of God. They need to be born again (John 3:3,5). God in His grace provides both the objective and subjective requirements for salvation. He has provided the atonement by Christ, and He brings us to new birth by His Spirit. As Thompson has noted, it is wrong to say that evangelicals have ignored the work of the Spirit. They have always maintained His importance in creation, redemption, and the life of the church and Christian. They have always asserted His vital role in the greatest miracle of all: bringing a person from death to life. What they have refused to do is to trivialize His work and to sever His work from the Scriptures, the "sword of the Spirit" (Eph. 6:17).

---

[195] Beginning with E. P. Sanders (*Paul and Palestinian Judaism* [Philadelphia: Fortress, 1977]) some very sophisticated attempts have been made to modify the biblical doctrine. Sanders argued that Judaism in the first century was not a religion of "works." Rabbinic religion was not characterized by legalistic works-righteousness. Sanders has influenced the thinking of such men as James Dunn, Alister McGrath, and N. T. Wright. They emphasize the relational aspect of justification at the expense of the forensic. Righteousness, they argue, is covenant faithfulness and sin is covenant faithlessness. The word "justify" is to be understood as meaning "declaring to be within the covenant." McGrath translates "justify" by "rectify." Wright opposes what he calls the "invention" of the word "impute" to describe how righteousness can be taken from point A to point B. Cf. Geoffrey Thomas, "The 1994 Westminster Conference," *The Banner of Truth* 382 (July 1995), 11, a report on the address "The Council of Trent and Modern Views of Justification by Faith," by Philip Eveson.

The Imminent Personal Return of Jesus to Judge: A Distinctive View of Universal History

The urgency of the gospel call is anchored in the future reality of judgment, a reality guaranteed by the resurrection of Jesus from the dead (Acts 17:31). The New Testament is full of warnings about the imminency and unexpectedness of the return of Jesus to the earth (John 14:1-3; Rom. 8:19,23,25; 1 Cor. 1:7; Phil. 3:20; 4:5; 1 Thess. 1:9-10; 4:13-18; Tit. 2:12-13; James 5:7-8; Jude 21; Rev. 22:20-21). Christians are described as those who have "turned to God from idols to serve the living and true God, and to wait for His Son from heaven" (1 Thess. 1:9-10).

Although evangelicals differ on certain chronological matters with regard to our Lord's coming, we also agree that the only hope of rescue lies in Jesus Christ Himself. It is no surprise, says Thompson, that evangelism is (or should be!) at the forefront of evangelical practice. This springs from our understanding of Scripture, of the future, of the human predicament, of the work of Christ and the necessity of faith and new birth by the Spirit.

Summary

It is a shift from these basic biblical truths that characterizes a shift from evangelicalism. Such a shift does not usually come at first from a negative attack. Rather it usually comes from a modification by addition. That is why evangelical theology has often been summarized by the Reformation slogans: "Scripture alone," "Christ alone," "Grace alone," and "Faith alone." These slogans guard against modification by addition.

J. I. Packer wrote, "You cannot add to evangelical theology without subtracting from it. By augmenting it, you cannot enrich it; you can only impoverish it. Thus, for example, if you add to it a doctrine of human priestly mediation you take away the truth of the perfect adequacy of our Lord's priestly mediation. If you add to it a doctrine of human merit, in whatever form, you take away the truth of the merits of Christ....The principle applies at point after point. What is more than evangelical is less than evangelical. Evangelical theology, by its very nature, cannot be supplemented; it can only be denied."[196]

As Mark Thompson put it, the crucial questions are ones of sufficiency. Is the Bible sufficient as the saving revelation of God. Evangelicals say "yes" to this

---

[196] J. I . Packer, *The Evangelical Anglican Identity Problem: An Analysis*, Latimer Studies 1 (Oxford: Latimer House, 1978), 17-18.

question; non-evangelicals have supplemented the Bible with human reason, church pronouncements, private visions, dreams, and prophetic statements. Is Jesus' death sufficient to deal with our sins and secure our relationship with God? Evangelicals answer "yes" again; non-evangelicals argue that the ministrations and rituals of the church play a role in this. Is faith sufficient as the appropriate response to the offer of forgiveness? Evangelicals answer in the affirmative; non-evangelicals answer in the negative and impose works, ceremonies, and second experiences.[197]

CONCLUSION

It was Gisbert Voetius (1589-1676), a Dutch Reformed theologian, who coined the expression *semper reformanda*, "always being reformed." He believed, no doubt, that in ongoing reformation lay the secret for the healing of the church.[198] Some may ask, "Do we in the Brethren assemblies really need reforming?" I would answer yes for three reasons: First, there is the question of numbers. Most observers admit that the assemblies are in decline. Second, to reform is true to our history as Brethren. The Brethren movement began as a kind of reform movement. Let us remind ourselves of the boldness of Groves, Darby, Müller, Craik, Newton and others who were not afraid to confront the unbiblical traditions of their churches and to seek a better way. To oppose calls for renewal is to show that were we alive in 1828 we would have vigorously opposed the heroes that we so deeply venerate today. Third, to reform is biblical. The watchful Christ calls upon the Ephesian church to "remember...from where you have fallen, and repent." (Rev. 2:5). Likewise he calls upon Pergamum to repent or He will "make war" with the rebels in her midst (Rev. 2:16). The Thyatirans are threatened with sickness and destruction because of their lack of repentance and renewal (Rev. 2:22-23). Sardis, too, is called upon to "remember" and "repent" (Rev. 3:3). The church at Laodicea is also challenged to turn to the Lord for the spiritual riches and spiritual clothing she needs (Rev. 3:18-20).

What is the principle of reformation and renewal? It is the principle of the Reformation of the 16th century and the principle of the early Brethren, viz., *sola scriptura*, the Scripture alone. Outside of the Bible there is in this world no true source of renewal.

---

[197] Thompson, "Saving the Heart of Evangelicalism," 39-40.

[198] Alfred Kuen, *I Will Build My Church*, trans. Ruby Lindblad (Chicago: Moody, 1971), 314. For a number of the thoughts expressed in this conclusion I am indebted to Kuen.

I would therefore suggest that what is needed first of all is the re-establishment of the authority of the Bible in our churches.[199] We need to commit ourselves to the plan of the Word of God in the structure of our churches. Where Scripture speaks we must listen, and where Scripture is silent we should be silent. The Scriptures, not tradition or cultural preferences, must be the norm by which renewal must be measured. And we need to encourage the disciplined reading of the Bible among the people and the careful exposition of the Bible by our teachers. We need to come to the place where the Word of God gains "complete ascendancy" over us.

---

[199] Disheartening but insightful is this observation by a New England student: "My own concern for the Brethren movement is that they start to read the Bible again. The general ignorance of Biblical theology and content is appalling to say the least. ...This lack of Bible study is leading to the powerlessness of many assemblies. Our Lord's description of the Sadducees in Matt. 22:29, that they 'knew neither the Scriptures or the power of God,' is chillingly close to being accurate of many Assemblies today" (James Berney, "Some Inadequacies of Present-Day Brethren," *CBRF Journal* 25 [September 1973], 17). Every year Emmaus Bible College administers a Bible knowledge exam to its incoming students—students who come from conservative and middle-of-the-road assemblies. For several years we have noticed a steady decrease in the grades on the exams, indicating a steady decrease in Bible knowledge. Happily, they score much better after their time at the college. A few years ago an elder in Minneapolis challenged the members of his assembly to read the Bible through in one year. He offered to take everyone who successfully met the challenge to dinner. I used the same "bribe" on my twelve-year-old daughter, and, I'm happy to say, we went out to dinner a year later!

THE NATURE OF
THE UNIVERSAL CHURCH

BY CHARLES T. GRANT[1]

THE IMPORTANCE OF THE CHURCH

The doctrine of the church (ecclesiology) is one of the great subjects of systematic theology. It is primarily a New Testament doctrine; the word *church* does not occur in the Old Testament. The historical development of ecclesiology can be traced back to ancient writers such as Irenaeus, Cyprian, and Augustine.[2] These men stressed the external unity of the church. However, much of our understanding of the universal church was developed much later, during the time of the Reformation.

In his introduction to the subject, Charles Ryrie observes[3]

> The importance of the church can scarcely be overstated. It is that which God purchased with the blood of His own Son (Acts 20:28). It is that which Christ loves, nourishes, and cherishes (Eph. 5:25, 29), and which He shall present to Himself blameless in all her glory one day (v. 27). Building His church constitutes Christ's principal work in the world today (Matt. 16:18) through His giving of spiritual gifts (Eph. 4:12). Thus the exercise of those gifts by believers aligns us with what Christ is doing today.

---

[1]Ted Grant is a practicing physician in Minneapolis, Minnesota. For many years he has served as an elder at Long Lake Community Church [formerly Sunnyside Bible Chapel]. He is widely respected as a Bible teacher and conference speaker.

[2] R. P. Lightner, *Evangelical Theology* (Grand Rapids, Michigan: Baker, 1986). For a historical review of the doctrine of the church see pp. 218-27.

[3] C. C. Ryrie, *Basic Theology* (Wheaton, Illinois: Victor Books, 1986), 393.

THE MEANING OF THE WORD CHURCH

THE ENGLISH WORD

The English word *church*, like the German *Kirche* and the Scottish *kirk*, is derived not from the Greek word for church, but from the Greek *kyriakon* which means "belonging to the Lord." The English dictionary gives a variety of meanings of the word *church*. It may refer to a building (e.g., "the Baptist church at the corner of Fifth and Main"), or to the congregation which meets regularly in such a building. It may describe congregations in a particular locality (e.g., the church in St. Louis); or a national entity, such as the Church of England, or the Church of Scotland. It may denote a particular confession such as the Lutheran Church or the Roman Catholic Church. The word *church* may also be used to designate the clerical in contrast to the secular (e.g., "the separation of church and state"). None of these meanings, however, encompasses the meaning implied by the topic of this paper, the universal church. In order to fully appreciate the significance of this expression, we need to examine the development of the word "church" in the writings of the New Testament.

THE ETYMOLOGICAL MEANING

The word in the Greek text which is translated "church" in the English Bible is ἐκκλησία (*ekklēsia*). It is derived from the prefix ἐκ (*ek*) meaning "out of" and the verb καλέω (*kaleō*), "to call." So the etymological meaning of the word is "a person, or persons called out of." However, the lexical meaning (the meaning in actual usage) of a word is frequently different from its etymological meaning.[4] In order to determine the meaning of a word, we need to examine its connotation in an actual context.

THE CLASSICAL MEANING

In non-biblical Greek *ekklesia* originally signified the regular assembly of citizens summoned out of their homes for the discussion of public issues. These assemblies were composed of citizens of the autonomous Greek city-states and were held for the purpose of conducting public business. By the time of the New

---

[4] For example, the word *wardrobe* is derived from *ward* meaning to keep and *robe* or clothing. So the etymological meaning is a place where clothes are kept. However, the connotational meaning of the word in contemporary English is quite different.

Testament, however, the word had acquired a much broader meaning and referred to any kind of assembly or meeting. In order to see how and why it acquired its specific New Testament meaning, it is instructive to trace the history of the word in both Greek and Jewish usage.

In the Greek language *ekklesia* soon lost its meaning of summoning citizens out of their homes. In Athens it referred to a constitutional assembly which had scheduled meetings without requiring a specific summoning, and the word generally came to mean any assembly, regardless of how it was convened.[5]

THE SEPTUAGINT

The Septuagint was the Greek translation of the Hebrew Old Testament. It was the Bible of the early church and as such it is important for understanding the meaning of many New Testament words. The scholars who completed the translation were fluent in both languages and their choice of *ekklesia* significantly influenced the subsequent New Testament usage of the word.

In the Septuagint *ekklesia* always translates the Hebrew קָהֵל (*qāhāl*) or a word with the same root. This Hebrew word has no technical meaning in the Old Testament and refers to any kind of gathering. Its broad meaning is reflected by the fact that it is translated by seven different Greek words[6] and it refers only to the actual meeting and not to the congregants when they are not assembled. A related Hebrew word, עֵדָה (*ēḏāh*), may refer to the congregants when they are not assembled, but it is never translated by ἐκκλησία (*ekklēsia*),[7] but rather by συναγωγή (*synagōgē*), whose distinctly Jewish reference precluded its acceptance as a word to describe a specifically Christian assembly. In those instances where *qāhāl* is translated by *ekklesia*, it always refers to an actual meeting or assembly. Therefore in the Septuagint *ekklesia* has no technical meaning.[8]

THE NEW TESTAMENT

By the time of the New Testament writings, the word *ekklesia* had already had a long classical and secular history. So clearly *ekklesia* was not invented by the

---

[5] A. T. Robertson, *A Grammar of the Greek New Testament in the Light of Historical Research* (Nashville: Broadman Press, 1934), 28.

[6] E. D. Radmacher, *The Nature of the Church* (Portland: Western Baptist Press, 1972), 117.

[7] Radmacher, *The Nature of the Church*, 119.

[8] Radmacher, *The Nature of the Church*, 122.

authors of the New Testament, but they certainly provided it with new meaning. In studying its New Testament usage we can trace its gradual change from its non-technical use referring to any kind of assembly to its technical usage signifying the people of God in Christ.

The overwhelming majority of the one hundred fourteen occurrences of *ekklesia* in the New Testament have a technical meaning in that they refer specifically to a Christian assembly. However, there are five instances of the non-technical usage of the word. For example, in Acts 19:23-41, we have an example of the secular use of *ekklesia*. It is used twice to refer to a disorderly mob (vv. 32, 41) as well as to designate a lawfully constituted assembly (v. 39). The word is also used in the Septuagint sense of the gathering of God's people in Acts 7:38 and Hebrews 2:12. The first refers to **"the *ekklesia* in the wilderness"** on the occasion of the receiving of the law and the second is a quote from the Septuagint (Ps. 22:22). None of these usages are related to the New Testament concept of the church.

In the New Testament the vast majority of occurrences of *ekklesia* refer to the local church, that is, to a local assembly of believing followers of Christ (e.g., 1 Thess. 1:1). The plural form is used to designate a group of churches in a particular area (Gal. 1:22).[9] But in its most significant deviation from classical usage *ekklesia* also designates what has come to be known as the church universal. In this sense, the word designates not an actual meeting, but instead refers to the spiritual unity of all believers in Christ even though they are not physically assembled. Believers continue to constitute "the church" even when they are dispersed in various localities (Acts 8:1-3).[10]

Concerning this technical usage of *ekklesia*, Saucy notes:

> The *ekklesia* was therefore all those spiritually united in Christ, the Head of the church. There is no concept of a literal assembly in this sense of *ekklesia*, nor does the New Testament, as will be seen later, have any organizational structure for the church universal. The unity is that of the Spirit in the body of Christ (Eph. 4:4).[11]

The universal church represents the aggregate, not of local churches, but of believers in the Lord Jesus. At times it is difficult to distinguish between

---

[9] R. L. Saucy, *The Church in God's Program* (Chicago: Moody Press, 1972), 16.

[10] The English word "community" is often used in a similar way. For example, "the law enforcement community," "the medical community."

[11] Saucy, *The Church in God's Program*, 17.

the local and universal usages in the New Testament (e.g., Acts 2:47, 5:11), but the technical use of *ekklesia* is limited to these two meanings and does not refer to the many other meanings of the word *church* in contemporary English.

THE PROPHECY OF MATTHEW 16:18

In the first occurrence of *ekklesia* in the New Testament Christ promises His disciples, "I will build my church." These five simple words of Christ lay the foundation of the doctrine of the universal church.

First, the church is the work of Christ; He is the builder of the church. Others may share in the work of building,[12] but Christ is the chief architect. Secondly, although "will" may have a volitional aspect in this context, the future tense of the Greek verb is unavoidable. As Jesus spoke these words, the church was still a future entity, and Christ's proclamation is a prophetic utterance. Thirdly, the church is an entirely new entity. It will be built, not rebuilt. Fourthly, the church belongs to Christ; it is His church. And finally, the word church (*ekklesia*) is used here in its technical sense designating the universal church.

THE FOUNDATION OF THE CHURCH

The context of Jesus' proclamation of the church in Matthew 16 is His question to His disciples, "What about you? Who do you say I am?" Peter's response was "You are the Christ [i.e., the Messiah], the Son of the living God." In response to Peter's confession in Matthew 16:17, Jesus asserts that "you are Peter, and upon this rock I will build my church."

The Identity of the Rock on which the Church is Built

Different views. There has been much controversy over the meaning of the statement, particularly over the identity of "this rock." In the view of the Roman Catholic Church Peter as the first bishop of Rome is that rock, and therefore no church without a Petrine foundation can have any claim to legitimacy. The Roman Church regards Peter as the first bishop of Rome and the following bishops of Rome (i.e., Popes) as Peter's historical successors. From its interpretation of verses 18 and 19 the Roman Church concludes that (a) it is the only legitimate church,

---

[12] E.g., 1 Cor. 3:10.

since it alone can trace its lineage back to Peter, and (b) verse 19 establishes the infallibility of the Pope and the Church.

The Protestant reaction to the Roman claim, is to assert that the rock has nothing to do with Peter and is in fact Peter's confession. Others reject both views by appealing to those passages that affirm that Christ is the foundation. For example, in 1 Corinthians 3:11, Paul asserts that "no one can lay any foundation other than the one already laid, which is Jesus Christ" (NIV). But no one of these three solutions is entirely satisfying and as Kuen points out, that there is an element of truth in each of the three explanations.[13]

Peter as the foundation. First, it must be pointed out that the conclusions which the Roman Catholic Church draws from the identification of Peter as the rock on which the church is built are not supported by either biblical or historical evidence.

1) There is no evidence that Peter was the "bishop of Rome," or even that he had ever been to Rome.

2) The text says nothing about Peter's successors. In fact, the entire idea of an apostolic succession is a contradiction in terms. An apostle is defined in Acts 1:21-22 as one who had been with Jesus since the beginning of His ministry and who had been an eyewitness of the resurrection. Therefore in that sense the apostles did not, and could not, have any successors.

3) There is no evidence that Jesus, or the remaining apostles, or anyone else for that matter regarded Peter as infallible. In fact, in the following paragraph, Jesus rebukes Peter in the strongest terms (Matt. 16:23). Paul did the same thing in their dispute about the evangelization of the Gentiles (Gal. 2:11).

Nevertheless, the Roman Catholic view is surely correct in identifying Peter as the rock in verse 18 upon which the church is built. It is well recognized that Jesus was using a pun in that verse. Unfortunately, the pun cannot easily be translated into English. The language Jesus spoke was Aramaic, the Semitic language of Palestine at that time, in which the words for Peter and rock are identical. That word is *kepha.* So Jesus' assertion is "You are *Kepha* and upon this *kepha* I will build my church."

Kepha was not Peter's name; his name was Simon[14]. *Kepha* was a nickname

---

[13] A. Kuen, *I Will Build My Church* (Chicago: Moody Press, 1971), 112.

[14] In his response to Peter's confession, Jesus calls Peter by his given name: "Blessed are you Simon Barjona" (Matt. 16:17). Simon was a common name and it has frequently been assumed that Barjona, which means son of Jonah, was Peter's surname. However, this is unlikely for the

given to him by Jesus (John 1:42). In Matthew 16:18 Jesus is using Simon's nickname in a pun. We can attempt to convey the sense of this pun into English by translating *Kepha* as "Rocky." "You are Rocky, and upon this rock I will build my church."

The New Testament was written in Greek in which it is equally difficult to translate this pun.[15] The Greek word for "rock" is *petra*, which is feminine and therefore cannot be used as a masculine name, so Matthew translates the first *Kepha* as *Petros*, the masculine form of *petra*. But *petros* means stone, not rock, and was not used as a name at that time. In fact, each occurrence of *Petros* in the New Testament refers to Simon's nickname (that is, Peter, or *Kepha*, or Rocky).

The truth of Peter's confession as the foundation. So it is clear that Jesus intended to identify Peter as the rock. However, there is considerable truth in the Protestant reaction to the Roman Catholic claims. After all, Peter was hardly a rock-like person. He was unstable, wavering, and impetuous, and in a moment of extreme weakness he even denied knowing Jesus. But the context of verse 18 informs us that the rock is not Peter the unstable person, but Peter the confessor of Jesus as the Messiah. The rock on which the church is built is not Peter the

---

following reasons: 1) The name of Peter's father was John, not Jonah (John 1:42, contra KJV). 2) There is no evidence that Jonah was used as a man's name at the time of Christ. 3) It would be unusual to address a man as the son of his physical father. R. H. Gundry, *Matthew, A Commentary on his Literary and Theological Art* (Grand Rapids: Eerdmans, 1982), 332.

The expression "son of" means "displaying the characteristics of" or "being a follower or disciple of" as in "the sons of the prophets" (Gundry, *Matthew*, 332). This is the third time in this passage that we encounter that expression. Jesus refers to Himself as the Son of Man and Peter confesses Him as the Son of the living God. In response to that confession Jesus calls Peter the son of Jonah. Matthew has already introduced Jonah in the beginning of the chapter (16:1-4) with his discussion of the sign of Jonah. The sign of Jonah is not so much Jesus' death and resurrection as it is the proclamation of the truth about Jesus. F. F. Bruce, *The Hard Sayings of Jesus* (Downers Grove: InterVarsity, 1983), 94-98.

So in what sense was Peter the son of Jonah? First and foremost, as Jonah was a prophetic voice of God's message, Peter was a proclaimer of the truth about Jesus (Matt. 16:16, Acts 2:14f). Second, as Jonah was a prophet to the Ninevites, Peter was the apostle who helped to open the door of the gospel to the Gentiles (Acts 10). Finally, Jonah's success as a prophet was clearly not the result of his preaching skills, but of divine power; similarly, Peter's confession was not a result of his own spiritual insights, "not flesh and blood, but my Father who is in heaven" (KJV). By his bold proclamation of the truth about Jesus Peter had shown himself to be in truth "the son of Jonah."

[15] As Bruce points out, the pun works in French, where the word *pierre* means both "Peter" and "rock." In the French New Testament Jesus says to Peter, "Tu es *Pierre*, et sur cette *pierre* je bâtirai mon église." Bruce, *The Hard Sayings of Jesus*, 143.

unsteady person who denied the Lord, but Peter who affirmed that Jesus was the Christ the Son of the living God. As Bruce observes, "what matters is not the stature of the confessor but the truth of the confession."[16]

Christ as the foundation. But how do we interpret those passages which refer to Christ as the foundation of the church? Jesus describes Himself as the chief cornerstone (Matt. 21:42; Mk. 12:10) and Peter confirms that identification (1 Pet. 2:7). Such passages do not contradict Jesus' description of Peter as the foundation of the church in Matthew 16:18. Biblical metaphors are used in a variety of ways and they have to be interpreted in their specific context.[17] For example, in Matthew 16 Jesus is the builder, but in 1 Corinthians 3, Paul is an "expert builder." In the former context, Peter is the rock on which the church is built, whereas in the latter, Christ is the foundation. In still another context (Eph. 2:20), Paul states that the church is built upon the foundation of the apostles and prophets, as we will discuss below.

The foundation of the apostles and prophets. These different ways of describing the foundation of the church are neither logically nor mutually exclusive. In one sense the person and work of the Christ remains the foundation of the church. But in another sense Peter's confession of Jesus as the Messiah is the basis for the existence of the church. When Paul states in Ephesians 2:20 that the church is built upon "the foundation of the apostles and prophets," he is not implying that the apostles and prophets constitute a different foundation from Christ. But the apostles exercised the authority of Christ, and it is on that basis that their work was foundational. For example, the doctrinal foundation of the church is the apostles' doctrine (Acts 2:42). What the apostles taught has the imprimatur of Christ and reflected His delegated authority.

Like the apostles, prophets in the New Testament received distinct gifts which permitted them to perform their ministry of prediction and proclamation. The purpose of the prophetic mission was the edification, exhortation, and consolation of the church (1 Cor. 14:3). There is evidence that in the New Testament, prophets sometimes received special revelation from God, which they in turn conveyed to the church. With the establishment of the New Testament canon, the need for such gifts disappeared. However, the prophetic gift still exists today in the sense of 1 Corinthians 14:3.

---

[16] Ibid.

[17] For a discussion of this point see D. A. Carson, "Matthew," in *The Expositor's Bible Commentary*, 12 vols., ed. Frank E. Gaebelein (Grand Rapids: Zondervan, 1984), 8:368.

THE HISTORICAL BEGINNING OF THE CHURCH

When did the church begin? Did it occur during the earthly ministry of the Lord, or at some earlier or later date? Some authors find the historical beginning of the church in the Old Testament, whereas others identify its historical origin as a unique event in New Testament history. Thus for some, the universal church includes all believers, including those of the Old Testament. As a result they trace the origin of the church back to the Adamic covenant. Covenant theologians, on the other hand, find the origin of the church in the covenant with Abraham.[18] For both groups, the New Testament church is not distinct from, but merely a continuation of the Old Testament assembly.

However, these points of view fail to take into account the distinctly new meaning which the word *ekklesia* acquired in New Testament literature. And although it may be argued that Jesus inaugurated a new community during His ministry, even that community was not identical with the church. It is clear that in Matthew 16:18 Jesus regarded the church as an entity still in the future. His disciples did form a new Christian community which, although not identical as the church, may be regarded as a forerunner of the true church.

A careful systematic study of the New Testament leads to the conclusion that the church had its beginning on the day of Pentecost. The argument for the Pentecostal origin for the church is based on linguistic, grammatical, and theological considerations.

The Linguistic Argument

Jesus uses the word *ekklesia* three times in Matthew 16:18 and 18:17, and these are the only occurrences of this word in the four gospels. Was Jesus using the word in the technical sense of the New Testament church or in some other sense? Of course, Jesus did not use the actual word *ekklesia* since He was speaking in Aramaic, not Greek. But it has been argued that the book of Matthew has a Jewish emphasis and that Matthew would not have translated Jesus' words with an expression which would have been unintelligible to His original audience and therefore the word must refer to an existing Jewish community. However, if this were the case, he certainly would have used *synagoge* instead, which has a more specific Jewish reference than *ekklesia*.

---

[18] D. D. Bannerman, *The Scripture Doctrine of the Church* (Grand Rapids: Eerdmans, 1955), 43, and C. Hodge, *Systematic Theology* 3 vols. (New York: Scribners, 1883), 3:549, both cited in Radmacher, 194, 195.

In fact, Matthew's very use of the word *ekklesia* has caused some scholars to question the authenticity of verses 18 and 19 of chapter 16. The other synoptic gospels record Jesus' question to His disciples and Peter's response, but they omit Jesus' response to Peter's confession.[19] But the manuscript evidence of those verses is very strong. The article on *ekklesia* in *TDNT* observes, "Neither verse [Matt. 16:18, 19] offers real textual problems. Literary criticism points out that there are no parallels to 16:18 in Mark or Luke, but it can supply no cogent arguments for the theory of interpolation (and in any case even an interpolation might rest on a genuine tradition)."[20]

But even granted the impeccable textual credentials of these verses, such criticism still raises some important questions. Was Matthew correct in using *ekklesia* to translate Jesus' remarks? And if the church was still a future entity at that time, are we correct in translating *ekklesia* as "church"? And what did the disciples make of Jesus' statement regarding the *ekklesia*?

The context of Matthew 16 provides the answers to these questions. Peter had just confessed that Jesus was the Messiah. The word Messiah in Hebrew means "the anointed One" and in Jewish thinking the Messiah would be a man chosen by God to right the wrongs which existed in the nation of Israel and in its relationship to God. Jewish theology identified two key features of the Messianic kingdom: the Messiah would gather the people of God together from their dispersion, and he would establish the rule of God on earth. This implies that the Messiah would be a king. In fact, it was believed that he would be a lineal descendant of the great king David and the rightful heir to his throne.

Therefore belief in the Messiah was closely linked with two collateral ideas, namely, the kingdom of God and the people of God. In the Hebrew Bible, the word used to describe the people of God was *qahal*. As we have seen, this word had a variety of meanings, and in those instances where it referred to the assembly of the people of God it is translated in the Septuagint by *ekklesia*.

Neither *qahal* nor *ekklesia* has a specifically ecclesiastical meaning in the Old Testament,[21] but in the context of Peter's confession, the disciples would have understood that Jesus was speaking about the Messianic community, the renewed people of God. In that sense, Matthew's translation is certainly correct. As Albright and Mann observe, "It is hard to know what kind of thinking, other

---

[19] Mark 8:27-30; Luke 9:18-21.

[20] K. L. Schmidt, *Theological Dictionary of the New Testament*, ed. G. Kittel and G. Friedrich (abridged by G. W. Bromiley), (Grand Rapids: Eerdmans/Paternoster, 1985), 400.

[21] Radmacher, *The Nature of the Church*, 121-123.

than confessional presupposition, justifies the tendency of some commentators to dismiss this verse [Matt. 16:18] as not authentic. A Messiah without a Messianic Community would have been unthinkable to any Jew."[22]

The Grammatical Argument

In response to Peter's confession of faith, Jesus asserts, "I will build my church." The verb "build" appears in the future indicative tense, οἰκοδομήσω (*oikodomēsō*). But the Greek future tense has a volitive or deliberative sense in addition to its future meaning. Moreover, the verb "build" may mean to "build up" or to "edify." So Jesus may have been merely stating His intention to build up, or edify, an existing Messianic community. However, the context of Jesus' response is His future program for this new community. Therefore the future force of Jesus' remarks is unavoidable. Jesus is stating His intention to construct an entirely new community in the future, not to rebuild an already existing one. The force of the future tense of the verb "to build" cannot be denied; Jesus is referring to an institution not yet in existence as He spoke, and still in the future. The promise to build His church was a prophetic utterance which found its fulfillment on the day of Pentecost.

The Theological Argument

The theological defense for the Pentecostal origin of the church is based on two premises. The first is that the church is formed by the Holy Spirit and the second is that the Spirit was first given on the day of Pentecost. The crucial text is 1 Corinthians 12:13, "for we were all baptized by one Spirit into one body." This implies that the baptism by the Spirit is essential for entrance into the body of Christ. This baptism was predicted by the Lord in Acts 1:5, "in a few days you will be baptized with the Holy Spirit" (NIV).

Although the advent of the Spirit in the following chapter of Acts is not described as a baptism, it is clear that the apostles regarded that event as the fulfillment of Jesus' prophecy. When Peter reported to the Jerusalem church on the coming of the Holy Spirit to the Gentiles, he recounted that "As I began to speak, the Holy Spirit came on them as he had come on us *at the beginning*. Then I remembered what the Lord had said, 'John baptized with water, but you will be baptized with the Holy Spirit'" (Acts 11:15). The expression clearly refers to the

---

[22] Quoted in Carson, "Matthew," *The Expositor's Bible Commentary*, 8:369.

events of Pentecost; and it is equally clear that Peter and his hearers regarded Pentecost as "the beginning."

These considerations lead us to the following inferences:

- The baptism of the Holy Spirit is necessary for entrance into the church (1 Cor. 12:13).

- The Holy Spirit was first given on the day of Pentecost. The Spirit had been at work in believers prior to the day of Pentecost (Mk. 12:36; Lk. 1:41,67; 2:25; John 20:22), but the baptism of the Spirit first occurred on Pentecost (Acts 1:5; 11:15-17).

- The outpouring of the Spirit in Acts 2 was a unique event which heralded the permanent indwelling of the Holy Spirit in believers and the birth of the New Testament church.

Finally, the conclusions of the linguistic, grammatical, and theological arguments may be summarized as follows:

- The linguistic argument identifies the *ecclesia* of Matthew 16:18 as the New Testament church, the new people of God.

- The grammatical argument identifies the church as a future entity not existing at the time of Jesus' prophetic pronouncement.

- The theological argument identifies the beginning of the church with the outpouring of the Holy Spirit in Acts 2.

THE NATURE OF THE UNIVERSAL CHURCH

DESCRIPTIVE TERMS

Our understanding of the universal church comes from a systematic study of New Testament teaching concerning the church. As we have seen, such a study reveals a technical meaning of the word *ekklesia* in New Testament writings which emphasizes a spiritual unity rather than a physical assembly of believers. This unity can refer either to a congregation of Christians in a particular locality (the local church), or to the unity of all believers regardless of their physical location (the universal church).

New Testament scholars have expended considerable effort in attempting to understand the nature of this new entity, and as a result a number of descriptive terms have been used to distinguish it from the more familiar concept of a local church, that is, a congregation in a particular locality.[23] For example, the universal church has been called a *spiritual* church to distinguish it from the organized church. This is appropriate since the unity encompassing all believers is a spiritual one, as is the mystical union between Christ and the church. However, this designation is not intended to imply that the local church by comparison is unspiritual. In fact, the New Testament envisions each believer as being a member both of a local assembly as well as of the universal church. And this local congregation is no less spiritual than the universal church.

Another common designation of the universal church is that of the *invisible* church. Again, this term also reveals an essential truth about the nature of the universal church, namely, that there is no outward or visible sign of the church. By merely observing a group or a congregation of people, it is impossible to discern which of them belong to the universal church and which do not. In that sense the church is invisible. But this invisibility should not be taken to imply that the universal church is in some sense unreal. The universal church is composed of visible (as well as invisible) members of the body of Christ and is no less real than a local company of believers.

The most common description of the church is the *universal* (or catholic) church. But this designation is also subject to misinterpretation. The church is not universal in the sense of including all churches or all nominal Christians. It is universal in that it embraces all those who have been baptized into the body of Christ by the Holy Spirit so that it encompasses all believers past, present, and future.

THE PEOPLE OF GOD

The church is a designation for the people of God. It consists of those whom God has chosen before the foundation of the world (Eph. 1:4). They are the elect of God (1 Pet. 1:2) or those called by God (Rom. 8:28). These were titles which previously applied to Israel and which now identify the church as the new people of God. Moreover, as we have seen, the word used in the Septuagint to translate "people of God" was *ekklesia*. Nevertheless, the New Testament never confuses Israel and the church. The historic people of God and the new people of God remain distinct, although they may play complementary roles in the plan and purpose of God.

Peter further identifies "the chosen" or "the elect" as those who have been

---

[23] Radmacher, *The Nature of the Church*, 188-92.

sanctified by the Holy Spirit (1 Pet. 1:2). The epistles to the Ephesians and the Colossians are addressed to the "saints," rather than to the churches. The saints are those who have been set apart (i.e., sanctified) by the Spirit of God in order to fulfill the purposes of God.

This fact further emphasizes the role of the Spirit in the universal church. The advent of the Spirit designates the beginning of the church (Act 2) and He indwells its members. He (the Spirit) identifies those who belong to Christ. "If anyone does not have the Spirit of Christ, he does not belong to Christ" (Rom. 8:9). He is the one who baptizes them into one body thereby assuring their unity (1 Cor. 12:13; Eph. 4:3-6) and empowers them to perform the work of God.

The New Testament describes the church not only as "a people formed by divine initiative,"[24] but also as the congregation of those who have responded to that initiative. It is the assembly of believers. A number of other terms are used in the New Testament to describe the community of believers. They are brothers, Christians, saints, and disciples.

A believer enters the church universal at the time of conversion. At that time he is baptized by the Holy Spirit (1 Cor. 12:12,13) and thereby becomes a member of the body of Christ.

THE CHARACTERISTICS OF THE CHURCH

Universality

Its universality is a key feature of the church. This universality (or catholicity) of the church is, in fact, a corollary to monotheism. There is only one God and this one God has only one Messiah, and so there can be only one Messianic community for all men. It is perhaps no accident that Jesus went to Caesarea Philippi to reveal Himself as the Messiah (Matt. 16:13).

Caesarea Philippi was in northern Palestine bordering Gentile territory. It was perhaps the northernmost point to which Jesus traveled and the farthest place from Jerusalem that He visited. Why did Jesus choose to reveal Himself as the Messiah in the most un-Jewish place He ever visited? Perhaps it was to emphasize that, although the Messiah was Jewish by race, He was a universal Messiah. He is a Messiah for all people, not just a Messiah for the Jews. Many passages in the Old Testament that are regarded as Messianic suggest this universality. For example, God's promise to Abraham was that in Abraham's seed He would bless *all* the people of the earth, not just Hebrew people (Gen. 26:4).

---

[24] R. L. Saucy, *The Church in God's Program*, 22.

Unity

The unity of the church is closely related to its universality. There is only one church. The word *church* in Matthew 16:18 is singular; Jesus is building His church, not His churches. We have seen that the technical meaning of *ekklesia* in the New Testament implies the spiritual unity of believers. Therefore, unity is an essential feature of the church, and this unity is bequeathed by the Holy Spirit. Therefore the unity of the church does not need to be created, but it must be maintained (Eph. 4:3). When Christ prayed for unity in His high-priestly prayer, He was praying not only for the unity of His disciples, but for the unity of "all those who will believe in me through their message" (John 17:20), that is, for the unity of the universal church. The unity of the church is one of its most spectacular features, transcending the mundane categories of race, sex, and social class (Gal. 3:28).

Sanctity

The church represents the people of God, and sanctity, or holiness, is God's purpose for His people.[25] As God is holy, so His people must be holy (1 Pet. 1:15, 16). To be holy is to be separated out, or set apart for God. This sanctity or holiness also represents the work of the Holy Spirit in the church and in the life of the individual believer (1 Pet. 1:2). This holiness has two aspects; one is past and completed, and the other is present and ongoing. In one sense, the members of the church have been made holy by the atoning work of Christ (Heb. 10:10). But in another sense, they are constantly being made holy by the sanctifying work of the Holy Spirit (Heb. 10:14).

Eternity

Although the church had a historical beginning on the day of Pentecost, it will never have a historical end. In Matthew 16:18, Jesus makes a bold statement concerning the church. He promises that "the gates of Hades will not overcome it." This statement is an astonishing claim because in Jewish cosmology, Hades was the place of the dead and is often translated as the grave. Jesus' confident assertion is that the church will never die; it cannot be conquered by death.

The church is an eternal church. Local congregations may come and go, but the universal church lives on. Individual members of the church may succumb

---

[25] G. W. Kirby, "The Church," in *The Zondervan Pictorial Encyclopedia of the Bible*, 5 vols., ed. M. C. Tenney (Grand Rapids: Zondervan, 1976), 1:848.

to physical death, but they continue to be members of the universal church, which can never die. This further supports the view that the *ekklesia* of Matthew 16:18 is the universal church, the holy people of the living God.

THE METAPHORICAL DESCRIPTIONS OF THE CHURCH

Our discussion so far has indicated that the writers of the New Testament applied to the Greek word *ekklesia* an entirely new meaning previously unknown in its classical and Jewish usages. In addition, they employed a variety of literary devices in order to further define the nature of the church. We will review several of these metaphors which help us to understand the complex character of the universal church. This discussion will make no attempt to be exhaustive. We will not address every metaphorical description of the church found in the New Testament, but will limit our discussion to the most common and important of these.

THE BODY OF CHRIST

In his letters, Paul frequently refers to the church as the body of Christ. Indeed, it is his favorite metaphor for the church. Although some interpret its occurrence in 1 Corinthians 12:27 (cf. Rom. 12:4,5) to refer to a local congregation of believers, it is generally not used to refer to a local church. The phrase principally describes the universal church (Eph. 1:22; Col. 1:18), which is composed of all those who are united to Christ through the baptism of the Holy Spirit (1 Cor. 12:13).

The Figurative Expression

The expression "body of Christ" is not to be taken literally, for the church is not an extension of the Incarnate Christ. Such an interpretation clearly exceeds what the New Testament intended; it has no biblical support and leads to unbiblical conclusions. One corollary of this literal interpretation of the phrase is that the church could be regarded as being invested with the authority of Christ Himself. There is no biblical support for such an inference.

In New Testament times the group of men called the apostles did have such authority, and because of this they played a unique role in the early church. The word "apostle" simply means "one who is sent," and it is infrequently used in the New Testament to designate a delegate from a church (2 Cor. 8:23; Phil. 2:25). However, the usual meaning in the New Testament refers to those who teach with the authority of Christ. It is because of this authority that the apostles' doctrine is foundational for the church (Acts 2:42; Eph. 2:20).

The apostles, however, are men who met certain qualifications (Acts 1:21,22, see above, page 70). Because of these qualifications there can be no apostolic succession in the sense of succeeding to a specific office. So although the apostles had a divinely delegated authority, such authority was not, and could not have been, passed on to the church. The recognition of the church as the body of Christ is not to be an arrogation to it of divine authority, but rather an acknowledgment of the lordship and sovereignty of the risen Christ over His body, the church.

The Significance of the Figure

In the New Testament a corollary to the description of the universal church as the Body of Christ is the depiction of Christ as the Head of the church.

(1) This figure emphasizes the pre-eminence of Christ. Although the phrase "body of Christ" emphasizes the essential unity between Christ and the church, it also affirms that He is the head of the body. He is the sovereign Lord to whom the church submits (Col. 1:18; Eph. 5:24). He exercises sovereignty not only by right of His person, but also by virtue of the fact that the church owes its very existence to Him. He brought it into being and remains the source of its life.

(2) The analogy of body and head is also used by Paul to illustrate the fact that the church receives its essential nourishment from Christ. He is its source of life and its growth is ultimately dependent on Him (Col. 2:19; Eph. 4:16).[26]

(3) In his writings Paul also uses the metaphor of the body to describe several features of the universal church. These include its diversity, its unity, and its interdependence. One of the marvels and strengths of the church is its diversity. As a physical body is composed of many diverse parts, the church is composed of members of a diversity of ethnic, social, and cultural backgrounds. In spite of this diversity, however, it maintains an essential unity which transcends geographic distances, cultural differences, and even denominational divisions. It is an essential feature of the universal church and remains the enduring work of the Spirit of Christ.

(4) In speaking of the communion, Paul says in 1 Corinthians 10:17 "**for we being many are one bread and one body: for we are all partakers of that one bread**" (KJV). This suggests an important truth about the communion loaf, namely, that it is a symbol not only of the physical body of the Lord Jesus in which He suffered for our sins, but it is also a symbol of His corporate body, the church. Therefore

---

[26] Radmacher, *The Nature of the Church*, 139.

the celebration of the Lord's Supper is a reminder not only of His atoning sacrifice, but also of the essential unity of His body, the church.

Another aspect of the unity of the body is the interdependence of its members. The parts of the body differ in function (1 Cor. 12:17), strength (v. 22), and honor (v. 23). Yet each is necessary for the function of the body as a whole and the members are interconnected with each other. When one part suffers, all the parts suffer with it, and when one part is honored all the parts rejoice with it (1 Cor. 12:26).

The essential unity of the church is an inescapable consequence of this metaphor. "We, who are many, are one body" (1 Cor. 10:17), "the body is one" and its members "form one body" (1 Cor. 12:12), "we were all baptized by one Spirit into one body" (1 Cor. 12:13). Christ has only one body, and any denial of the unity of the body is to profane the body of Christ and may have serious consequences. This is discussed further in the excursus on 1 Corinthians 11:29.

THE TEMPLE OF GOD

Although the word *ekklesia* never refers to a building, the church is described metaphorically in the New Testament as the temple of God. As with the previous figure of the body, this metaphor also helps us to understand the nature of the church and its relationship to its Lord. The two metaphors are not as incongruous as one might think, since in antiquity the body was frequently described as a building. When the church is pictured as a body, Christ is the Head of the body, the source of its life and its guiding force. In the case of the building metaphor, Christ is described as the foundation of the church. "Other foundation can no man lay than that is laid, which is Jesus Christ" (1 Cor. 3:11, KJV).

The foundation is the basis on which the building is constructed. That basis is Christ and His teaching. Hence, as we saw above, there is no conflict between regarding Christ Himself as the foundation and Paul's statement in Ephesians 2:20 that the church is "built upon the foundation of the apostles and prophets." The apostles taught with the authority of Christ, and the teaching of the apostles forms the basis of church doctrine.

A closely related figure to the foundation is that of the cornerstone. The cornerstone determines the lay of the building and Christ is described as the chief cornerstone of God's building (Eph. 2:20, 1 Pet. 2:6). The cornerstone has a prominent location and the whole structure is dependent on it. So this figure is also a picture of the pre-eminence of Christ over the church.

The picture of the temple (or building) also illustrates the unity and diversity of the church. The church is portrayed as a single building consisting of many (diverse) stones (1 Pet. 2:4). These diverse stones are "fitly framed together" to form a harmonious building. Moreover, the significance of this building is that it becomes the habitation of the living God (Eph. 2:21,22).

The Greek language has two words which are translated as temple. ἱερόν (*hieron*) refers to the temple precincts, whereas ναός (*naos*) refers to the inner sanctuary, or the holy place where God was pleased to place His name[27]. The church is called the *naos* of God, which emphasizes the truth that the church is the dwelling place of the Holy Spirit of God (1 Cor. 3:16). The Spirit of God indwells the believer and therefore the universal church becomes the figurative sanctuary of the presence of God on earth.

THE BRIDE OF CHRIST

Another picturesque simile describing the relationship between Christ and the church is that of the church as the bride of Christ. The picture of marriage as a reflection of the relationship between God and His people already existed in the Old Testament (Isa. 54:5, 6; 62:5: Ezek. 16:8; Hos. 2:7, 19, 21). In the gospels Christ is portrayed as the heavenly Bridegroom (Matt. 9:15; 25:1-12; Mark 2:19; Luke 5:34, 35) and John the Baptist calls himself "the friend of the bridegroom." (John 3:29). The most explicit references to the bride are found in the book of Revelation where the church is described as the bride of the Lamb (e.g., Rev. 19:7; 21:9).

This theme is further developed in the New Testament epistles. In his discussion of marriage in Ephesians chapter 5, Paul compares the relationship between husband and wife to that between Christ and the church. The relationship is one of love and devotion. Christ nourishes and cherishes the church (Eph. 5:29). He loved her before she loved Him (1 John 4:19) and the church responds to His love with devoted submission to Him (Eph. 5:24).

There has been considerable discussion about whether the relationship as the bride is a present or a future one. In 2 Cor. 11:2 the church is described as betrothed to Christ. This has led some to assume that the consummation of the union between Christ and the church is still in the future. However, this represents a misunderstanding of metaphorical language, in which analogies are never complete. In Ephesians 5 it is clear that the relationship is regarded as a present one. Moreover, in many cultures a betrothal is just as binding as the actual marriage; indeed, the distinction between the two is of less significance than it is in Western culture.

---

[27] G. Schrenk, s.v. "ἱερός," *Theological Dictionary of the New Testament*, ed. G. Kittel, 10 vols. (Grand Rapids: Eerdmans, 1966), 3:232.

THE PRIESTHOOD

The New Testament concept of a priest is firmly rooted in the Old Testament description of the Levitical priesthood. A priest is one who approaches God on behalf of the people and the nation of Israel still required the intercession of a priestly class in its worship. The priests were those who were sanctified, or set apart, to lead the worship of God in the sanctuary or the holy place. There they were required to offer sacrifices to God on behalf of the people.

The Old Testament priesthood was holy; its priests were those who were set apart for the service of God. So too the New Testament priesthood is a "**holy priesthood**" (1 Pet. 2:5) consisting of those who have been sanctified by the Holy Spirit for obedience to Christ (1 Pet. 1:2).

In the Old Testament, Israel is described as a kingdom of priests (Ex. 19:6) and New Testament believers are also called a "**royal priesthood**" (1 Pet. 2:9). Yet the concept of a royal priesthood was never fully realized in the history of Israel. Hebrew kings came from the tribe of Judah, and their priests were descended from Aaron and the tribe of Levi. So a kingly priest was an impossibility. Indeed, in the Old Testament there is only one person who was simultaneously a king and a priest. He was a mysterious figure named Melchizedek, described as "**king of Salem**" and "**priest of the most high God**" (Gen. 14:18).

In the New Testament Jesus is called "**a priest forever, just like Melchizedek**" (Heb. 7:17, CEV). Jesus Himself has become the High Priest of a new order of kingly priests. This new priestly order is the universal church. The veil of the temple which represented limited access to the holy place was torn in two and the individual believer is now encouraged to boldly approach the sanctuary (Heb. 10:19-22). This access to the holy place is possible because of the intercessory work of his High Priest, Jesus Christ Himself.

A further difference between the Old and New Testament priesthood is that sacrifices for sin are no longer necessary, since Christ has offered a sacrifice once for all. Rather, the Christian priest offers himself as a sacrifice to God (Rom. 12:1), and as part of his worship he offers other sacrifices such as praise to God and good works toward others (Heb. 13:15, 16).

Radmacher summarizes the difference between the Old and New Testament priesthood as follows: "In the former dispensation, Israel *had* a priesthood, but in the present dispensation, the church *is* a priesthood."[28] Each individual believer is a priest and as such enjoys access to the very presence of God through Christ and not requiring a human intermediary.

---

[28] Radmacher, *The Nature of the Church*, 227.

OTHER PICTURES OF THE CHURCH

The New Testament uses several metaphors to highlight various aspects of the nature of the church. The New Testament sees the church as the new people of God (1 Pet. 2:10) and it uses expressions which originally applied to Israel to refer to the church (1 Pet. 2:9). However, God's "new people" are defined not by race but by faith. Christian believers are "the seed of Abraham" (Gal. 3:29) and Abraham is the "father of all those who believe" (Rom. 4:11) regardless of their racial heritage.

In Galatians 6:10 the church is described as the family of God. Believers enjoy a filial relationship with God their Father and a fraternal relationship with other believers, their brothers and sisters in Christ. The church is also the pillar and ground of truth (1 Tim. 3:15); it is the place where the truth is guarded, defended and taught. The church is also a flock, whose Good Shepherd is Jesus Christ (John 10:11,16). She is a vineyard tended by God the Father (John 15:1ff). Each one of these pictures illustrates some aspect of the nature or the function of the church, of the relationship of the church to Christ or His Father, or of the interrelationship between individual members of the church.

THE RELATIONSHIP OF THE UNIVERSAL CHURCH TO THE LOCAL CHURCH

A local church consists of a local congregation of believers who assemble regularly for worship and service. Although our discussion has focused on the universal church, the vast majority of occurrences of *ekklesia* in the New Testament refer to a local church. By one estimate, of the one hundred fourteen occurrences of *ekklesia* in the New Testament, at least ninety-two refer to the local church.[29] It is used in the singular to refer to a single congregation in a specific area (cf. Acts 8:1) or to all local churches generally without regard to a particular locality (cf. Acts 12:1). In the plural it is used to denote the sum of individual local churches in a specific region (cf. 1 Thess. 2:14).

But it is clear, as we saw above, that the universal church is more than just the aggregate of all local churches for the universal church consists of all believers past, present, and future. It includes those members of the church already in heaven, those now living on earth, and even those members who are still unborn.

What then is the relationship of the local church to the universal church? The

---

[29] Radmacher, *The Nature of the Church*, 323.

birth of the church took place on the day of Pentecost, and the book of Acts describes the individuals who received the Holy Spirit on that day and on succeeding days as "the church," without specifying whether it was the universal church or a local church. From 1 Corinthians 12:13 we have learned that those who were baptized by the Holy Spirit were baptized into the body of Christ, that is, the universal church. Yet, from Acts 2:42-47 it is clear that those individuals also functioned as a local church.

Thiessen observes that "the believers acted as a corporate unit. They had a definite doctrinal standard (Acts 2:42); they had fellowship with one another as believers...; they observed the ordinances of baptism and the Lord's Supper (vss. 42,47); they met for public worship (vs. 46); and they contributed to the support of the needy (vss. 44, 45). Surely we have here the marks of an organized local church."[30]

So on the day of Pentecost (and probably for several days thereafter) the universal church and the local church in Jerusalem were identical. The new believers were simply "the church." Both the universal church and the local church had their birth at the same time. The one hundred twenty believers in the upper room in Acts 2 were the "charter members" both of the universal church and the Jerusalem church.[31] It is therefore not surprising that at times it is difficult to distinguish between the two. And, indeed, there are passages of Scripture which seem to transcend or defy that distinction (e.g., 1 Cor. 10:32).

Like the doctrine of the Trinity, the doctrine of the universal church is not explicitly taught in Scripture, nor does the expression occur anywhere in the biblical text. Nevertheless, we have concluded that the truth of this doctrine is firmly established by a systematic study of New Testament theology, and such a study reveals many similarities between the universal church and the local church.

Paul refers to the Corinthian believers as "the church of God in Corinth" (1 Cor. 1:2; 2 Cor. 1:1). Obviously, he was referring to the local church "in Corinth." Yet the Corinthian church was not *the* church of God, to the exclusion of other churches, so the expression also has universal implications. The Corinthian church was a local expression of the universal church.

Moreover, the metaphors used of the universal church in the epistles may on occasion also apply to the local church. For example, the Corinthian church

---

[30] H. C. Thiessen, *Introductory Lectures in Systematic Theology* (Grand Rapids: Eerdmans, 1951), 410.

[31] Thiessen, *Introductory Lectures in Systematic Theology*, 410.

is called the body of Christ (1 Cor. 12:27), the temple of God (1 Cor. 3:16, 17) and the betrothed of Christ (2 Cor. 11:3).

These figures of speech imply, as Fleming remarks, that "the local church in its function and character stands in the same relation to Christ as the universal Church. It is the Church in miniature, a replica of the whole, giving visible and temporal expression to the invisible and eternal Church."[32] Like the universal church, the local church stands under the headship of Christ. Its members are indwelt by the Holy Spirit and it enjoys a loving relationship with its Savior.

The local church is a visible manifestation of the universal church in a particular location. However, as we have emphasized, the universal church is more than the aggregate of all local churches; its members are not local churches, but individual believers who have been baptized into the Body of Christ by the Holy Spirit of God.

EXCURSUS ON 1 CORINTHIANS 11:29

DISCERNING THE LORD'S BODY

1 Corinthians 11:27-32 is a passage which has been a source of great anxiety for many believers. It urges us to examine ourselves lest we partake unworthily of the Lord's supper. It suggests that he who partakes unworthily will be guilty of the body and blood of the Lord, and further will bring judgment on himself for not discerning the Lord's body.

The passage raises a number of important questions. (1) Is it possible for a believer to eat and drink unworthily? If so, how? (2) What does it mean to be guilty of the body and blood of the Lord? (3) What is the nature of the self-examination that is required? (4) What does it mean to discern or to recognize the Lord's body?

The key to answering these questions and to understanding the passage is an appreciation of the context, which is frequently ignored. The immediate context of this passage includes verses 17 to 34. In this section of the epistle Paul is addressing the problem of divisions in the Corinthian church when the believers come together to celebrate the Lord's supper. The divisions here, however, are not identical to the divisions addressed earlier in 1:10ff ("I am of Paul," "I am of Apollos"). Here we are dealing with social and class distinctions, with the difference between the haves and the have-nots. At the Lord's table, the

---

32 P. Fleming, *The Church* (Oak Park: Midwest Christian Publishers, n. d.), 10.

latter go hungry and the former gorge themselves into a stupor (v. 21), while humiliating their less fortunate brothers (v. 22).

This is the context in which Paul begins to discuss the Lord's supper in verse 23. And these divisions which manifest themselves at the Lord's table are also the context of our passage of interest. The text emphasizes this by returning to the context of v.17ff in verses 33 and 34 ("when you come together to eat"), and the passage cannot be understood apart from this context.

For the sake of simplicity, we will limit our discussion to verses 27-29. At the center of the passage is the imperative, "Let a man examine himself" (v. 28). The word translated as "man" does not refer exclusively to a male person, so the expression could be just as accurately rendered as "each person ought to examine himself." This self-examination is an imperative for all believers.

Paul appears to give two reasons for this self-examination; one in verse 27 and the other in verse 29. The purpose of the self-examination is (1) to avoid eating and drinking unworthily (v. 27), and (2) to avoid not discerning the Lord's body (v. 29). The consequence of the former is to become guilty of the body and blood of the Lord; and the consequence of the latter is to eat and drink judgment on oneself.

However, a closer examination of the passage suggests that verse 29 is not a separate reason for the self-examination, but rather an explanation of the reason given in verse 27. In verse 29 the King James translation, based on the Received Text, inserted the word *unworthily* after "eateth and drinketh" ("eateth and drinketh unworthily") and also the word *Lord's* before "body" ("not discerning the Lord's body"). This makes verse 29 conform to verse 27; but verse 29 is not merely a repetition of verse 27; it is an explanation. In other words, the meaning of eating and drinking unworthily is the failure to recognize the Lord's body.

Therefore the key to understanding the passage is to understand what it means to recognize the Lord's body. If we know what it means to recognize the Lord's body, then the nature of the self-examination will be clear; that is, we will be able to examine ourselves to see if we are recognizing His body. And if on the basis of that self-examination, we determine that we are recognizing His body, then we can be confident that we are not eating and drinking unworthily.

So what does it mean to recognize the Lord's body? The Greek word for body is σῶμα (sōma). The word appears in both verse 27 and 29, but its meaning is different in those two verses. In verse 27 it refers to the physical body of the Lord, but in verse 29 it means His corporate body, the church. Unfortunately, the wording of the KJV tends to obscure this distinction. Bruce explains:

The Western additions (from verse 27) "unworthily" after **eats and drinks** and "of the Lord" after **body**, are epexegetic in intention. In the word of institution "This is my body" [Paul] sees a reference not merely—perhaps not even primarily—to Jesus' "body of flesh" (cf. Col. 1:22), but to the corporate unity of all who share his life: "we who are many are one body, for we all partake of the one bread" (10:17). But for certain members of the church to eat and drink their fill, in unbrotherly disregard of their poorer fellow-Christians, as some were doing at Corinth, was to eat and drink **without discerning the body**, without any consideration for the most elementary implications of their fellowship in Christ.[33]

That is, "the body" in verse 29 does not refer to the Lord's "body of flesh," but rather to the "corporate unity" of the church. This conclusion is based on the following observations.

1. In verse 27 the word "body" is closely linked to the blood of the Lord; the reference is to "**the body and blood of the Lord.**" Verse 29 refers only to His body.

2. As we have noted above, although the possessive "Lord's" (KJV) or "of the Lord" (NIV) appear in the English translations of verse 29, it is missing from the critical Greek text. Paul speaks here not of recognizing "the Lord's body," but of recognizing "the body." This expression, "the body," refers to the church in the previous chapter (10:17) and in the following chapter (12:12, 13), and it is most likely also the meaning here. As a matter of fact, that is the usual meaning of "the body" in this epistle, and the words "and blood" were probably added by the apostle Paul in verse 27 to indicate the exceptional reference to the physical body of the Lord.

3. Finally, and most convincingly, the context of chapter 11 supports the identification of "the body" with the church. It is precisely for failing to recognize the body that Paul was rebuking the Corinthians. How were they doing that? They were doing it by humiliating other believers at the Lord's table. Failure to recognize the Lord's body is to despise the church of God (v. 22). A recurring theme of this epistle is the unity of the body ("**we who are many are one body,**" 10:17; "**the body is one,**" 12:12). And any act or attitude of the believer which denies the unity of the body is a failure to recognize the body of the Lord.

There is some discussion among scholars about whether "the body" in 1 Corinthians refers to the universal church or the local church (see, e.g., 12:27).

---

[33] F. F. Bruce, *1 and 2 Corinthians* (London: Oliphants, 1971), 115.

However, it seems best to interpret the expression as referring to the universal church. Christ has only one body and it includes all believers. So any attempt on my part to exclude any member of the body is not to recognize His body. If we feel that we may eat and drink but another member of the body of Christ may not, then we fail to recognize the body of the Lord and we therefore eat and drink in an unworthy manner.

It is important to recognize that, although the apostle gave instructions earlier in the epistle for excluding offending believers from the fellowship of the church (5:1-12), this is not inconsistent with his teaching here. Someone who is guilty of public and habitual sin has, in fact, broken the fellowship of believers; so the elders of the church, by excommunicating him, are merely formally acknowledging what has already occurred in fact. Moreover, it must be remembered that church discipline should always be done in an attitude of humility and with the goal of eventual restoration of fellowship (Gal. 6:1-5).

The unity of the body of Christ is a recurring theme of the Corinthian epistle and a major concern of the apostle Paul. And the question of church discipline must be considered in this context. The offending brother, by his sin, has ruptured fellowship with his Lord and with the church. And so the goal of discipline is the restoration of that fellowship and of the unity of the body. The behavior of the Corinthian believers at the Lord's supper represented another assault on the unity of the body and so Paul addresses it in the most uncompromising terms.

The above considerations lead to the following conclusions.

1. The self-examination mentioned in this passage is not an introspective exercise to see if we are worthy to partake of the Lord's supper. A certain spiritual stocktaking is certainly advisable before breaking bread, but that is not the teaching of this passage. In this respect, the KJV choice of the word "unworthily" may be somewhat misleading, for what the passage is teaching is precisely that *all* Christians are worthy to eat and drink at the Lord's table. However, some Christians may eat and drink in an unworthy manner (NIV). They do that when they deny the unity of the body by discouraging the participation of a fellow believer.

2. This passage is not directed at unbelievers; this is clear from the context. The Lord's supper is indeed intended for believers, but there is no biblical evidence that God is displeased if non-Christians participate in it. What does displease Him, the passage tells us, is when Christians eat and drink in an unworthy manner. It is far better to allow an unbeliever to break bread, than to discourage a believer from participation in the Lord's table. For when we do that, we fail to recognize the Lord's body and therefore invite judgment on ourselves.

3. The examination in this passage is a self-examination. The text says nothing about our examining anyone else. Any impediment that we place in the path of another believer who wishes to partake of the Lord's supper contravenes the teaching of this passage. There is only one biblical criterion for eating and drinking, and that is being a member of the body of Christ. There can be no biblical basis for establishing doctrinal standards, or worse, denominational criteria for admission to the Lord's table.[34] To insist that someone meets our standards before he is allowed to break bread makes us guilty of the body and blood of the Lord, because it regards His atoning sacrifice as having no effect, and it denies the unity of His body. It is enough that a person meets God's standard, that is, that he is a believer in the Lord Jesus.

So the self-examination is neither an onerous nor a difficult task. For the Christian the "context implies that his self-examination will be specially directed to ascertaining whether or not he is living and acting 'in love and charity' with his neighbours."[35] We need only ask ourselves if there is another believer with whom we would be unwilling or unhappy to share the Lord's table. If there is, then we are not discerning the body, whose unity is a glorious work of the Lord and a crowning accomplishment of the Holy Spirit.

The bread of communion is a symbol, not only of the physical body of the Lord, but also of His corporate body and its unity (1 Cor. 10:17), the unity of the church universal. To deny that unity, particularly at the Lord's supper, is to make a mockery of that celebration. But to discern the body is to act in recognition of the truth of the words of the old hymn by James G. Deck.

> We would remember we are one
> With every saint that loves thy name.
> United to Thee on the throne,
> Our life, our hope our Lord the same.

---

[34] For example, "letters of commendation" are frequently used to identify members of a particular group of Christians. Such letters are not necessarily wrong, but their use to exclude believers from the Lord's table cannot be justified.

[35] F. F. Bruce, *1 and 2 Corinthians*, 115.

THE CHARACTER
OF THE LOCAL CHURCH

BY JAMES A. STAHR[1]

INTRODUCTION

The title and subject of this article is, "The Character of the Local Church."
While I will refer to many Bible passages, there are two which I will examine
in some detail. Neither passage mentions the church, whether local or universal.
Neither is likely to be discussed, or even quoted, in typical sermons or articles
on the subject of the church. For these reasons both passages will require careful
exposition, in context, to establish the legitimacy of their credentials and their
relevance to this topic.

The first passage, Psalm 68:5-6, a text from the Old Testament, *lays a
foundation* for the character of the local church. The second, John 13:34-36, a
New Testament text, is a well-known command of the Lord Jesus. I would like
to describe this command as *the charter of the local church*.

My subject is the character, not the characteristics, of the church. Character
can be defined as the aggregate of the characteristics of a thing or a person. Using
that definition as a starting point, I might have chosen to enumerate a series of
characteristics of the local assembly of God's people, and then to sum them up
as a statement of its character. Instead, I intend to work in the reverse direction.
I will concentrate first on the basic nature of the local church. Following that, I
will list some of the characteristics that arise from this essential nature. The
presentation will conclude with some vignettes of the local church, all drawn
from New Testament epistles and all displaying the essential character of the
assembly.

---

[1] After serving the Lord for many years in pioneer ministry in eastern Canada, Jim Stahr was
editor of *Interest Magazine* for fifteen years. He is a board member of two important ministries,
Emmaus Bible College and the Council of Biblical Manhood and Womanhood. He continues
to be actively involved in a Bible teaching and preaching ministry.

My thesis is this: *first*, the local church is designed by God and intended by the Lord Jesus to be a family. *Second*, as a family the church takes on or reflects the character of the head of the family, the Lord Jesus Christ.

Other images or illustrations of the church are better known than the family image. One quickly thinks of the three "B's," body, bride, and building. The church is well described as the *body* of Christ, as the *bride* of Christ, and as a *building* that "fitly framed together groweth unto an holy temple in the Lord" (Ephesians 2:19-22). These three images all come from Paul's letter to the Ephesians. They are also found in the Corinthian epistles. They are especially appropriate to the universal church. They may be applicable in some measure to the local church as well, but in a limited way. For example, the local assembly is not the body of Christ; it is rather a part of the body. It is not the bride of Christ, but part of the bride.

On the other hand, the local congregation *is* a family. It is a family in its own right. The church universal may also be called a family, providing one concedes that, as a family, its members have no chance of knowing each other. As a family, the universal church cannot hold a family reunion. Spread over six continents and twenty centuries, the universal church is far too large to function as a family. The local church, by contrast, is in the here and now. It is small enough that its members can know and interact with one another.

THE MIND OF GOD

The first passage we want to look at is Psalm 68, verses 5 and 6:

> A father of the fatherless, and a judge of the widows,
>   is God in his holy habitation.
> God setteth the solitary in families;
> He bringeth out those who are bound with chains,
>   but the rebellious dwell in a dry land.

A passage from the Psalms might seem an unexpected starting point for a New Testament topic. King David's Psalms were composed a full millennium before Jesus Christ announced His intention to build a church (Matthew 16:18). Nevertheless, when a statement from the Old Testament expresses the mind of God, that statement may well be revealing an eternal truth that can guide our understanding of the ways of God throughout the ages of mankind. Such is the case with the sixth verse of the sixty-eighth Psalm. In David's words, "**God setteth the solitary in families.**"

THE FAMILY IN THE PLAN OF GOD

It is and has always been the mind of God to gather people into families! That purpose was implied in Genesis 1:27, where we read that God created us "male and female."[2]

God's intention to put people into families was more fully revealed in Genesis 2. In Eden, God created a life-partner for our first ancestor, thus establishing the first human family. Genesis 2:24 then proclaimed that future generations of males would leave the families they were born into in order to form new families with female partners of their own. And so it went through the entire book of Genesis, a book that spanned at least two thousand years, fully one-third of recorded human history. Genesis contains long genealogies of fathers and sons and grandsons. It records the trials and triumphs of many fathers and mothers and of their sons and daughters. It tells occasional stories of fathers reaching out to other families to find wives for their sons in order to start new families.

Genesis is the preeminent family book of the Bible. It demonstrates the mind of God that people should be born into and grow up in families, and then start families of their own.

GOD'S CARE FOR BROKEN FAMILIES

Inevitably families are disrupted by that ancient enemy, death. Death leaves orphans, and death leaves widows. The plight of the widow and the plight of the orphan moved King David to give us our text, as we see in verse five. He wanted to tell us that God desires to step into the broken family. God wants to fill the void with His own presence. In David's words, God wants to be "a father of the fatherless, and a judge (that is, a protector) of the widows" (Psalm 68:5). Why so? Because it is His very nature to put people into family relationships. When those relationships are broken, He Himself wants to fill the gap. It is the will of God that lonely and solitary people be set in families (v. 6).

Psalm 68:6 is a wonderful text from which to preach the Gospel, especially when its final phrase is contrasted to its opening words. The first phrase is, "God gathers the solitary in families." Picture the Lord Jesus extending welcoming arms and calling lost sinners to Himself. "Come unto me, all you that labor and are heavy laden, and I will give you rest.... Learn of me; for I am meek and lowly in heart, and

---

[2] Not "male and male," nor "female and female;" if you want a biblical indictment of the homosexual lifestyle, you get it right here.

you shall find rest unto your souls" (Matt. 11:28-29). Many will respond to that invitation. Many others will turn away from Him. And so David warns in the final phrase of Psalm 68:6, "**The rebellious dwell in a dry land.**"

God wants to put us into a family, His own family. The rejecter will find himself living in a desert, a place of loneliness and emptiness. The desert here is allegorical. Whether the rebel lives in the midst of a crowded city or far out on lonely ranch land, there is ultimately no lasting satisfaction, no family companionship for him. "**There is no peace, saith my God, to the wicked**" (Isaiah 57:21).

GOD'S SPIRITUAL FAMILY

A modern translation makes the words of David in verses five and six even more vivid. "**A father to the fatherless, a defender of widows, is God in his holy dwelling. God sets the lonely in families, he leads forth the prisoners with singing; but the rebellious live in a sun-scorched land**" (NIV).

By adding that last phrase, the one about dwelling in a sun-scorched land, King David took these verses beyond the human family. He had begun by talking about widows and orphans. He had been thinking about families composed of people related to one another by blood or by marriage. When David speaks of releasing prisoners and then of rebels living in the wilderness, he is enlarging the concept of family. He is saying there is not only a biological family, but there is also a spiritual family. There is a family of people bound together by spiritual ties, by a common relationship to the living God. There is, to put it simply, a family of God, and God wants to put people into that family.

God's Spiritual Family in the Old Testament

This idea of a spiritual family was not very pronounced in Old Testament history. Israel was a nation of people united by their descent from Abraham, but often very disunited in other ways. They were divided both religiously and politically. Some of them served God, while others served pagan deities. In time there were two nations of Jews, a northern and a southern kingdom, often at war with each other. This was hardly a family! Or, even two families.

God's Spiritual Family in the New Testament

The slowness of the disciples to have a family relationship. As we come into the New Testament, we find the Lord Jesus gathering a little band around Himself. They were not a family either. Not yet! His leadership bound them together, but not much else did. They expected that very soon He would take the throne of David. His closest Apostles began to maneuver politically for high-ranking cabinet positions. Two of them, blood brothers, brought in their mother, who urged the Lord to seat her sons next to Himself, one on each side of Him at the Cabinet table (Matt. 20:20-21). For those two, the bonds of blood relationship still took precedence over any sense of a spiritual kinship with the other Apostles.

When the other ten heard about this political maneuver, "**they were moved with indignation against the two brethren**" (Matt. 20:24). None of them seemed aware that their Lord was about to introduce them to a new concept of family. Little did they realize that they themselves, with one hundred ten others, would soon form the first local church. That local church was to have the characteristics of a family.

The family character of the local church. Whether they understood it or not, that was the intention of the Lord, as we shall soon see. We might well expect it to be so, for we have already learned that it is the mind of God to put people into family relationships, especially lonely people. The Old Testament emphasized the biological family, united by ties of blood and marriage. In New Testament times we see more clearly that God provides a second type of family, that is, the local assembly of believers.

I am not suggesting that the biological family ceases to be important. We find references to it in the upbringing of Timothy. He was taught the ways of the Lord by a godly mother and grandmother (2 Tim. 1:5). We read also that to be qualified for eldership, a man must know how to rule his own home and have his own children under control (1 Tim. 3:4-5). Older women are instructed to "**teach the young women**" to love their husbands and children, to be "**keepers at home, good, obedient to their own husbands, that the word of God be not blasphemed**" (Titus 2:4-5). These passages are guidelines for the biological Christian family.

The precedence of the spiritual family over the biological family. The Lord warned us, however, that the Gospel sometimes disrupts the biological family. Jesus said:

> I am come to set a man at variance against his father, and the daughter against her mother, and the daughter-in-law against her mother-in-law. And a man's foes shall be they of his own household. He that loveth father or mother more than me is not worthy of me: and he that loveth son or daughter more than me is not worthy of me (Matt. 10:35-37).

One of the defining characteristics of modern cults is the turning of the convert against his family, and the cutting off of that convert from his parents. The true gospel does not do that. We teach young converts to honor their fathers and mothers, even when those parents oppose the Gospel. Unlike the modern cults, the alienation comes only when unbelieving parents disown, expel, or disenfranchise believing children. In such cases, the family of the local assembly is all the more important. The original family has cast out the new believer.

THE NEW COMMANDMENT

Now we must get back to the story of Jesus and His little band of competing apostles. Back in Galilee they had been disputing among themselves as to who would be the greatest in the Lord's government (Mark 9:30-34; Luke 9:46). Now again in the Upper Room, on the night before the Crucifixion, as the Lord served them the Last Supper, "there was also a strife among them, which of them should be accounted the greatest" (Luke 22:24). This strife was probably a major factor in moving the Lord in that Upper Room to define the local church as family. He did so by uttering one of the most famous statements in the New Testament. It is recorded as John 13:34-35.

> A new commandment I give unto you, that you
>   love one another;
> As I have loved you, that you also love one another.
> By this shall all men know that you are my disciples,
>   if you have love one to another.

These words of Jesus are generally given a stand-alone status. They are divorced from their context and treated as something the Lord might have proclaimed anywhere and at anytime. He might have spoken them from a mountain top, à la Moses and the Ten Commandments. Indeed, these words are sometimes called the Eleventh Commandment.

Linking this new commandment to the Old Testament law is not without problems. There is enough in the original ten to burden us down, show us our guilt, and bring us in "guilty before God" (Romans 3:19). Why should our Lord add to that already heavy load on the night before He died? Why should He add another commandment that outranks the original ten in its impossibility of human fulfillment?

A cursory reading of the Ten Commandments as recorded in Exodus 20 might suggest that fulfillment is possible. We can abstain from idolatry, adultery, profanity, murder, theft, and false testimony. We can be staunch monotheists and refuse to admit the existence of any other gods. Saul of Tarsus certainly saw himself as keeping the first nine commandments. Ultimately it was the tenth, "Thou shalt not covet," that brought him to his knees before God as a guilty sinner (Rom. 7:7).

It is the grand summation of the Commandments as quoted by our Lord that defines them as impossible for sinful humans to fulfill. When asked to choose from among the ten the one that He considered the greatest commandment, Jesus replied:

> Thou shalt love the Lord thy God with all thy heart, and with all thy soul, and with all thy mind. This is the first and great commandment (Matt. 22:37-38).

ALL thy heart? ALL thy soul? ALL thy mind? Impossible of human fulfillment! But the Lord did not stop with that insurmountable mountain. He added another: "And the second is like unto it, Thou shalt love thy neighbor as thyself" (v. 39).

No wonder the Apostle to the Gentiles would later write, "There is no difference [between Jew and Gentile]. For all have sinned and come short of the glory of God" (Romans 3:22-23).

What, then, was to be gained by adding another commandment? It did expand the command to love by adding a third category. First, love God. Second, love your neighbor. And now third, love your fellow-believer. If the Lord had left it at that, we might have understood, and tried to obey. He was simply enlarging the scope of our responsibility. However, there in the Upper Room He went further. He added a qualifying phrase that made fulfillment impossible. *"As I have loved you,* that you also love one another" (John 13:34). Impossible? Not one of us would dare to suggest that we can love each other with a love as great as His love to us.

On the other hand, we cannot contradict our Lord's own words. This is "a new commandment." He called it that. Rather than linking it with the original ten, however, we might understand it better if we join it to the context of chapter 13, to the scene in the Upper Room, and particularly to the burden that was on the heart of Christ when He spoke those famous words. We will discover, if we do this, not an eleventh commandment, but rather a commandment that is new because it is designed to fit a new situation. We will find it to be *a provision for the new conditions* His little band of followers were soon to experience. We will see that the words, "as I have loved you," are not the imposition of an impossible standard, but rather a comparison of His past relationship to them with their future relationship to each other.

In short, these words were intended to define the character of the local church. The church is to be a family. It is to be a family knit together by a love for each other, just as it had been previously held together by the Lord's love for each of them. It is to be a family in which the behavior of its members reflects the character of Christ.

In order to understand the new commandment in this light, we must first understand what went on in the Upper Room that night.

JESUS IN THE UPPER ROOM

The Example of Love and Service

Looking back to the beginning of John 13, we can trace the concern that motivated our Lord to issue this new commandment. Heavy on His heart was the awareness of His soon departure. It was not so much His impending death, although that was certainly on His mind. His burden, more precisely, was the awareness of His imminent departure from this earth.

Verse one of John 13 reads, **"Jesus knew that his hour was come that he should depart out of this world."** Why should He dread that? Was He not going back to the Father who had sent Him? Of course He was. The problem was that His little band of followers would then be left alone, lonely, vulnerable, and leaderless in a hostile world. Verse one continues, **"Having loved his own which were in the world, he loved them unto the end."** This shows us that *their* well-being, not *His* suffering, was the burden of His heart that night. Their crisis would be the immediate consequence of His departure.

The third and fourth verses of the chapter restate His concern, and portray Him as doing something about it. **"Jesus knowing that the Father had given all things into his hands, and that He was come from God, and went to God; He riseth from supper, and laid aside his garments; and took a towel, and girded himself."** He proceeded to wash the feet of His disciples. He talked with them as He did so. He taught them lessons about fellowship ("If I wash thee not, thou hast no part with me"—v. 8), and about daily cleansing ("He that is washed needeth not save to wash his feet"—v. 10), and about service one to another ("If I, then, your Lord and Master, have washed your feet, you also ought to wash one another's feet"—v. 14).

He said nothing during this foot washing about a local church. Yet in only fifty days, they would be the local church, the very first local church. These words were intended to instruct them about their behavior in that local church. Their behavior was to be modeled after His behavior. He said, "I have given you an example, that you should do as I have done to you" (v. 15). When these things happen in any local church, the character of that church reflects the character of the Lord Jesus.

"As I have done to you," were His words. The local church is to be a place of serving one another. Not only serving in physical ways like foot washing, but also in the spiritual ministries illustrated by the foot washing. In other words we are to perform for one another ministries of cleansing, removing defilement, and maintaining fellowship. That is, we are to steer fellow-believers away from temptations that will drag them down into sin. We are to guide them to confession and forgiveness when they do sin. We are to exercise a ministry of cleansing because our Lord Jesus exercises a ministry of cleansing.

"If you know these things," the Lord concluded, "happy are you if you do them" (v. 17). Those words are just as true today for every local church as they were two thousand years ago for that original local church.

The Lord of Every Circumstance

With the basin and towel laid aside, and with His outer garment put back on, the Lord resumed His place at the table. He reminded His disciples that He had chosen them and then told them that one of them would soon betray Him (vv. 18, 21). Peter motioned to John, who was right next to the Lord, asking John to find out who the Lord was talking about. Jesus identified Judas as the betrayer by passing food to him, but only John was aware of that signal. Then the Lord spoke out loud to Judas. "What thou doest, do quickly" (v. 27). The men at the table thought that Jesus was sending Judas out for groceries. John would likely have understood the real message.

Certainly Judas understood it, and what a shock that must have been to him. Until that moment, he thought he had the fate of Jesus in his own hands. It was entirely up to him to choose the appropriate moment and then to summon the soldiers to make the arrest. Then came the voice of the one he had served for nearly three years. "What thou doest, do quickly." Suddenly the initiative had been taken away from him. The Lord had taken charge. "What thou doest, do quickly. I am giving the orders now."

I wrote an article about this incident in 1971 and published it in the second issue of my fifteen years as editor of *Interest Magazine*. I titled it, "The Lord of Every Circumstance." Even at a time of disastrous betrayal into the hands of Satan, our Lord made it known that He Himself was still in charge, and that betrayal would only take place when He so instructed.

When trials and tragedy come into your life, even if they come from Satan himself, do not ever imagine that Jesus Christ has lost control. He is still "the Lord of every circumstance."

By sending Judas out, the Lord set in motion the final chain of events that would bring Him to the cross in just thirteen or fourteen hours. It was like being in a countdown that had passed its last possible hold point. So, in verse 31, He spoke of His crucifixion and resurrection as if they were already accomplished. "Now *is* the Son of Man glorified," He said, "and God *is* glorified in Him." From that perspective, with the cross already behind Him, the ascension was the next event. "If God be glorified in Him, God shall also glorify Him in Himself, and shall straightway glorify Him" (v. 32).

Teaching in Light of His Departure

That being the case, it was time to tell His disciples what was coming next. Had they really comprehended the fact that He was about to die, they might still have supposed that He would immediately take the throne after coming back to life. Not so, they learned in the Upper Room, for the resurrection was to be followed by His departure to heaven. Furthermore, they would not be allowed to go with Him or even to find Him if they searched for Him! We see this in John 13:33. "Ye shall seek Me; and as I said unto the Jews, 'Where I go, you cannot come;' so now I say to you."

Apparently this was the first time that Jesus told this to His disciples. It is true that He had implied it in a number of parables [Matt. 9:15; 25:14; Mark 13:34; Luke 10:35; 19:12], but prophecy in parable form is very different from a straightforward announcement. "I am going away! You can't come with Me!" That must have been quite a shock.

In verse thirty-six, the Lord softened the shock somewhat by promising that they could follow later on. In chapter fourteen, He amplified that promise. The "later-on" following would take the form of a rapture. In His absence He would be preparing a place for them. Then He said, "If I go and prepare a place for you, I will come again, and receive you unto Myself, that where I am, there you may be also" (v. 3).

The rapture allows the church to follow Him to where He is going and to the place He is preparing. The rapture is not a turn-around in the clouds with an immediate return to earth. He has gone away to prepare a place for us, and will come back to take us to that place.[3] That, however, is getting ahead of our story. Let me pick it up again at John 13:33, where the Lord told them He was going away, and that they could not go with Him.

We must notice one more thing in verse 33 before we reach the new commandment in verse 34. Here, for the first and only time in His ministry, the Lord addressed His Apostles as "little children" [Greek: τεκνία, *teknia*]. On one other occasion, after the resurrection, He called some of them "children," using a different Greek word. Elsewhere, He spoke of believers as children of light, children of the kingdom, and children of God.[4] He taught them that God was their Father, as in the Lord's prayer.[5] But in this scene, and in this scene only, Jesus depicts *Himself* as their father, and they as *His* little children.

> Little children, yet a little while I am with you. you shall seek me; and as I said unto the Jews, "Where I go, you cannot come;" so now I say [the same thing] to you (John 13:33).

The situation here has striking parallels to what might someday occur in our own experience. Picture a man in the last hours of life. Knowing he is about to die, his children gather at his bedside. Summoning strength and rising up on his pillows, he gives them counsel for the future, and then bids them farewell, one son or daughter at a time.

The scene is reminiscent of the last words of Jacob in the forty-ninth chapter of Genesis.

---

[3] As to the timing of the rapture of the church, the importance of our Lord's words in John 14:3 should not be overlooked. He describes His church as being transported from earth to His Father's house in heaven. This event is more fully described in 1 Thessalonians 4:16-17. It is commonly called the rapture, from the Latin word *raptus*, meaning "to carry away." The movement of the church here is an upward journey (from earth to heaven).

Someday the Lord will return to judge the nations and establish His kingdom. He will return all the way to the earth (Zech. 14:2-4), not just to the clouds (1 Thess. 4:17). This is often called the "second coming proper." At that time He will bring His saints with Him (1 Thess. 3:13; Jude 14-15; Rev. 19:11-16). This will be a downward journey (heaven to earth). Of necessity this journey must take place at a different time from the rapture, because it is impossible to travel in opposite directions at the same time. So the church waits patiently for the rapture, when it will be caught up to heaven to take residence in the place the Lord has gone to prepare (John 14:2-3). At some later time it will return with Him to the earth.

Thus the rapture and the return are distinctly different events, with some interval of time between them.

[4] Matt. 5:9, 45; 8:12; 13:38; Luke 16:8; 20:36; John 11:52; 12:36.

[5] Other religious leaders were not to be called "father"—Matthew 23:8-10.

> And Jacob called unto his sons, and said, Gather yourselves together, that I may tell you that which shall befall you in the last days. Gather yourselves together, and hear, you sons of Jacob; and hearken unto Israel, your father (Genesis 49:1-2).

The long chapter continues with a prophetic message for each of his sons, and ends with these words: "When Jacob had made an end of commanding his sons, he gathered up his feet into the bed, and yielded up the ghost, and was gathered unto his people" (v. 33).

The Lord Jesus was not speaking from a bed, nor from weakness. He was not speaking in poetic format, as Jacob did. He was not talking about death, but He *was* talking about departure. What He was saying was, "I am the father in this little family, and I am going away. But I am not leaving you alone. You have each other. The head of the family will be gone, but you still have each other. You are a family. I want you to act like a family."

God's Provision for Their Future

By calling them little children, He establishes the family relationship. They are brothers! If the owner and head of a business dies, his top employees may battle with each other to take control of the business. They are not family, but competitors. The Lord's disciples had for some days been competing with each other, jockeying for position, like politicians or like business associates. But not like brothers. Even at the last supper itself, some of this maneuvering had been going on, much to the grief of the Lord. So now the Lord says, "Cut out all that competitive stuff and start acting like a family."

Thus the new commandment becomes a provision, *a provision for the future.* I am going away, but you are not alone. You have each other. There will be tough times ahead. You will need each other. You are to serve each other just as I have served you (vv. 14-15). You are to love each other just as I have loved you (v. 34).

The "as I have loved you" part of the command is not an issue of degree ("*as much as* I have loved you") but an issue of relationship ("*in the same way that* I loved you"). When so understood, the command can be fulfilled. The Lord was saying, "Just as my love held you together in the past, so now in my absence, your love for each other must hold you together. You are family." It is in this sense that His words can be called *a charter* for the local church.

His words were *a command* because He wanted them to stop competing and start teaming up like brothers. His words were *a provision* because He knew they would need each other after He went away. They would not be alone. They would have each other. If they would stand together as brothers, they could withstand the attacks of the enemy and spread the Gospel far and wide. Their love and unity would show the world that they were His disciples (v. 35). That is, of course, exactly what happened.

There are at least two other provisions that the Lord made for the centuries of His absence. In John 14, He promised to send another Comforter (Greek: παράκλητος, *paraklētos*, Paraclete, one called along side). This is the Holy Spirit, sent to take His place beside us (vv. 16-17). In chapter 17, He prayed that God would keep them during His absence (vv. 9-15), a ministry of intercession that the Lord continues until the present day (Hebrews 7:25).

The Paraclete and the Intercessor sustain us as individual believers, apart from any local assembly connection. It is the new commandment that defines us as a family, provides us with a family, and puts us into that family. Families have always been the provision of God for human beings. "**God setteth the solitary in families.**" The local assembly is a major provision for our well-being.

THE FAMILY CHARACTERISTICS

What are the implications of the local church as a family? What are the family characteristics that the assembly displays? Or, should display? We will summarize a few of them.

LOVE AND SUPPORT

One set of characteristics has been evident already in John 13, both in the foot washing scene and in the new commandment. There is *love and support* in the family. We learn to get along with each other, to love each other, to enjoy each other, to serve each other. We learn to strengthen and encourage one another. Also, and this can be hard for some of us, we learn *to be* strengthened and *to be* encouraged, for there is a mutuality here. We are brothers and sisters.

Verse 35: "**By this shall all men know that you are my disciples, if you have love one to another.**" The family character of the local church will make it attractive to people around us. That was what attracted me, when I was a straight-A high school student, but not a good mixer, and not one of the popular kids on campus. Nor was I a follower of the popular kids. When I got drawn into an off-campus Bible club, I found a warmth that kept me coming back week after week. In time, the message of salvation brought me under conviction. Without that family welcome, this lonely kid wouldn't have been there to hear it more than once. When a church behaves like a family, people will know that our message has reality.

HISTORY AND TRADITION

There is *history and tradition* in a family. I speak of traditions in the good sense of customs handed down from generation to generation, but not in the bad sense of practices that claim an equal standing with Scripture. Paul used the term favorably in respect to teachings when he wrote: **"Brethren, stand fast, and hold the traditions which you have been taught, whether by word or our epistle"** (2 Thess. 2:15).

Let me illustrate this from biological families. Family history and family traditions help bind biological families together, more so in some cultures than others. Some families search the genealogical archives for records of their ancestors. Other families pride themselves in things they do together, whether it be camping trips, musical emphasis, or going to the public library each Sunday afternoon. We hear of families creating elaborate Christmas traditions, including preparation of special foods that are traditional in their countries of origin. In doing so, they develop in their children a sense of family.

Local churches can develop traditions, too. Things like potluck suppers on the first Sunday evening of each month, or a mid-June camping weekend for assembly families, or an annual Bible conference to which other assemblies are invited. Some churches get quite involved with a children's camp, or an inner city rescue mission, or grading Emmaus courses for the prison ministry in their state. Things like this that are "special" make for special families.

We should not overlook the role of church practices that are unique as compared to the majority of churches around us. A weekly communion service, or the ability to function without an employed pastor, are examples of things that contribute to family identity, but only if they are handled in a positive way. They should be thought of as unique things that we can contribute to the wider body of Christ, not as sectarian things or things for which we must apologize.

You will lose your children if you are negative about your local church. If you want to hold them, you must convey a sense that there are some real important reasons, something really special about being a part of your particular congregation.

Examples: We are a big church. We have outstanding music and preaching. Or, we are a small church. We get to know each other in a way folks in big churches cannot. Whatever your situation, emphasize the positive. Putting down your own assembly is just as unbecoming and destructive as publicly criticizing your own wife or husband.

Share with your children and your fellow-believers something of your great historical heritage. Make them acquainted with the leaders of the Reformation in the 1600s—men like Luther, Calvin, Zwingli, and John Knox. Include also those men and women who brought the Brethren movement into being in the early 1800s—Anthony Norris Groves, John Nelson Darby, George Müller, and Lady Powerscourt. Both of these movements were marked by wonderful recoveries of biblical truth. Both movements saw the counterattack of Satan. If you want to build a family, emphasize the recovery of truth. If you want the opposite result, focus on the divisions and failures that followed both of those recoveries.

The Jewish families were instructed by Joshua to remind their children of their glorious history. Joshua ordered his soldiers to take twelve large stones from the bed of the Jordan River, one stone for each tribe, and erect them as a cairn on the west bank. Then Joshua addressed the nation:

> When your children shall ask their fathers in time to come, saying, "What mean these stones?"Then you shall let your children know, saying, "Israel came over this Jordan on dry land. For the Lord your God dried up the waters of Jordan...as [He] did to the Red Sea,...until we were gone over" (Joshua 4:21-23).

The counterpart in the assembly family is the remembrance meeting. Jesus

> took bread, and gave thanks, and broke it, and gave unto them, saying, "This is my body which is given for you; *this do in remembrance of me.*" Likewise also the cup after supper, saying, "This cup is the new testament in my blood, which is shed for you" (Luke 22:19-20).

In many assemblies, the emphasis is shifting away from remembrance toward a worship focused more on praise. Praise is an important aspect of worship, but the loss of remembrance is ill-advised. Our faith and our unity are rooted in our family history. No part of our great heritage has more power to bind us together then remembering the death and resurrection of Jesus Christ.

DOCTRINE AND DISCIPLINE

Third, there is *doctrine and discipline* in a family. The family structure of many evangelical churches is fading because of the disappearance of doctrine and discipline. When these are gone the church becomes a loose collection of individuals, held together by music or entertainment, perhaps, but not by standards and beliefs that make a group a family.

Again, we find an example in the Jewish family. This was not true of the Jewish nation, which, as I have said, was hardly a family. Rather, we find it in the instructions Moses gave to parents for the upbringing of their children.

Deuteronomy 6 contains a doctrinal assertion called the Shema [pronounced shmah] which is the Hebrew word translated "hear."

> Hear, O Israel: The LORD our God is one LORD (6:4).

This sentence, like the first commandment, sets forth what is perhaps the most fundamental doctrine of the Bible. *There is only one God*. The next sentence links that proclamation to the nation Israel:

> And thou shalt love the LORD thy God with all thine heart, and with all thy soul, and with all thy might (6:5).

The religious life of Israel was to embody the truth of monotheism in the midst of a world given over to idolatry and polytheism. But was it Israel's mission to teach monotheism to the world? There is no such commission in Deuteronomy 6. There is a commission here for each biological family in Israel. The parents were commanded to teach these truths to their children:

> And these words, which I command thee this day, shall be in thine heart; and thou shalt teach them diligently unto thy children (6:6-7).

A family, be it the Jewish biological family or the New Testament church family, has an essential core of doctrine which must be passed on in the family from generation to generation. In 1 Timothy 3:15 we are told that the local church, "the house of God," is "the pillar and ground of the truth." Timothy himself was exhorted to take the truths he had learned from Paul and "commit [them] to faithful men, who shall be able to teach others also" (2 Tim. 2:2).

Inevitably discipline must accompany doctrine. We live in an age in which truth is relative. Whatever religious view suits your thinking, that is your truth. Today this philosophy is invading the evangelical church, and doctrine is being driven out before it. That does not change the New Testament, which tells us in more than one passage that those who fall into doctrinal apostasy must be rejected by the local church and by its members [1 Tim. 1:3-4; 6:3-5; 2 Tim. 2:16-18; 2 John 9-11]. Other passages call for the expulsion of those who turn aside into serious *moral* sin.

Hebrews 12 talks about "the chastening of the Lord" and about being rebuked by Him (vv. 5-6). This passage uses the biological family as an illustration, telling us that it is characteristic of human fathers to chasten their sons (vv. 7, 9). Does it not follow, then, that if the local church is a family, it, too, will deal with sin among its people?

In the days of the American Revolution, there was an office of exhorter in churches. The service did not end when the sermon ended. Instead the exhorter took over and began applying the word just preached to the conduct of the listeners. Not just in general terms, but individually, personally. In our culture, that would be considered an intrusion on our personal space. Even that limited form of discipline is unknown in evangelical churches today.

We have spoken of *love and support* in the assembly family, then *history and tradition*, and after that *doctrine and discipline*. These are all related to the family character of the local church. I want to add one more family-related characteristic.

LOYALTY

There is *loyalty* in a family. Brothers and sisters are loyal to each other. Husbands and wives are loyal to each other. It is a family tragedy when this is not the case. So when a brother or sister or spouse says the wrong thing to you, you might get offended, but you do not walk out on your family. You do not say to your brother, "I am not going to be your brother any more because you offended me. I am going to look for a different set of brothers. I am going to change families."

We are living in days when changing church families is far too common. The ease and frequency of switching churches arises from the loss of the concept of the church as a family. I began to be aware of this more than forty-five years ago when I had a short conversation with a woman I met in one of the New Jersey suburbs west of Newark. In Newark at that time there was a strong Bible-believing church, Evangel Baptist. I am hopeless when it comes to remembering the words of conversations, yet once in a while something hangs on in my mind. I can still hear the words of that woman as if they were spoken to me yesterday.

"What church do you go to?" I asked.
"I go to Evangel Baptist. He's a very good man."

I knew what she meant, because in my mind I could supply a middle sentence that would make her response logical and grammatically correct. "I go to Evangel Baptist. The pastor is Rev. So-and-So. He is a very good man."

People often take shortcuts like that in conversation. We should not get picky with them about logic and grammar. We understand the meaning. But did she not also, inadvertently, reveal her concept of the local church? For her the church was a place to go and hear a good preacher. Just let that church change ministers, and she might well move on to some other church.

Her way of thinking is not uncommon. Many people see the church as an auditorium where you go to hear the minister. If the next preacher is a mediocre speaker, you start looking around for another place to go.

There are other concepts of the local church that do not generate loyalty. For some the church is a theater, a place to be entertained. Or it is a classroom, where you can get a good Bible education. Hopefully good preaching, good music, and good teaching will be present in your local church. But God places lonely people into families, not into auditoriums, theaters, or classrooms. And if God puts you in a family, you do not lightly leave that family just because the talents of a professional staff no longer please you.

Some of us attend churches that have a variety of preachers, not all of them outstanding. When such is the case, it is easier to think of the assembly as a family rather than as an auditorium. With the modern tendency to hire professional staff, that may change.

From today's culture, we learn to evaluate the church by what it can do for us instead of asking what can we do to serve the church. Try to resist this attitude by developing in yourself and in your people the concept of the church as a family. Not as a social club where everyone puts their best foot forward and no one ever disagrees with you. Nor as a one-owner business, where you are the owner and everyone has to do whatever you say. Nor as a hospital, where everybody waits on you and you wait on nobody.

Have you learned to think "family" with respect to the local church? Do you understand now why I say John 13:34 can well be called the charter of the local church? There is loyalty in a family. You do not lightly walk out on your family. Brothers and sisters stand together!

Marriages do not always hold together. Sometimes divorce is unavoidable. Divorce is less likely when a man and a woman "think family" and see that God joined them together as such. Separation in assemblies will be less common when we really believe that the Lord Jesus meant for us to act like family. "**What God has joined together, let not man put asunder**" (Matt. 19:6).

Vignettes of the Local Church

Now let me illustrate the family character of the local church by quoting eight short passages from the New Testament. I call these passages "vignettes," from a French word meaning "little vines." In early books, the beginnings and endings of chapters were often decorated with small vine-like illustrations. The definition of vignette applicable to my usage is "any small, pleasing picture or view." These Bible passages, each from a different New Testament epistle, give us small, pleasing pictures of the assembly family.

Quotations here are from the New International Version. Note the frequency of phrases such as "one another" or "each other." Also observe that in four of the eight quotations, some of the words set in italics indicate that the behavior of the Christians is to be patterned after the behavior and the teaching of the Father and the Son toward us. That is, the character of the local church is to reflect the character of the Lord.

Spend some time pondering these passages. As you consider each one, visualize a healthy, happy assembly family.

1. Romans 15:5-7, "May the God who gives endurance and encouragement give you *a spirit of unity* among yourselves as you follow Christ Jesus, so that with one heart and mouth you may glorify the God and Father of our Lord Jesus Christ. Accept one another, then, *just as Christ accepted you,* in order to bring praise to God."

2. Galatians 6:1-2, "Brothers, if someone is caught in a sin, you who are spiritual should restore him gently....*Carry each other's burdens.*"

3. Ephesians 4:31-32, "Get rid of all bitterness, rage and anger, brawling and slander, along with every form of malice. Be kind and compassionate *to one another,* forgiving *each other, just as in Christ God forgave you.*"

4. Colossians 3:12-16, "Therefore, as God's chosen people, holy and dearly loved, clothe yourselves with compassion, kindness, humility, gentleness and patience. *Bear with each other,* and forgive whatever grievances you may have against *one another.* Forgive *as the Lord forgave you....*Let the peace of Christ rule in your hearts....And be thankful. Let the word of Christ dwell in you richly as you *teach and admonish one another* with all wisdom, and as you sing psalms, hymns and spiritual songs with gratitude in your hearts to God."

5. 1 Thessalonians 4:9-10, "Now about brotherly love we do not need to write to you, for you yourselves have been *taught by God to love each other.*And in fact, you do love all the brothers throughout Macedonia. Yet we urge you, brothers, to do so more and more."

6. Hebrews 10:24-25. "And let us consider how we may *spur one another on* toward love and good deeds. Let us not give up *meeting together,* as some are in the habit of doing, but let us *encourage one another*—and all the more as you see the Day approaching."

7. 1 Peter 3:8-9, "Finally, all of you, live in harmony with one another; be sympathetic, *love as brothers,* be compassionate and humble. Do not repay evil with evil or insult with insult, but with blessing."

8. 1 John 3:23, "And this is [God's] command: to believe in the name of his Son, Jesus Christ, and *to love one another as He commanded us.*"[6]

CONCLUSION

I will conclude with my two original texts, which also can be considered vignettes:

Psalm 68:6, "God sets the lonely in *families.* He leads forth the prisoners with singing; but the rebellious live in a sun-scorched land" (NIV).

John 13:33-36 "My children, I will be with you only a little longer.... Where I am going you cannot come. A new command I give you: *Love one another. As I have loved you,* so you must love one another. By this all men will know that you are my disciples, if you love one another" (NIV).

---

[6] See also: Romans 12:10-13; 14:13, 19; 1 Thess. 3:12; 5:9-11; James 5:16; 1 Peter 1:22.

THE LIFE OF
THE LOCAL CHURCH

THE STRUCTURE, MINISTRY, AND FUNCTIONS
OF THE CHURCH

BY JOHN H. FISH III

INTRODUCTION

What the church is determines what the church does. Further, the structure of the local church is determined by the nature of the church. Thus, the practical matters of the structure and functions of the local church are determined not by pragmatism, what may happen to be effective for a particular community, but by theology, what the church is by its very nature. The descriptive portions of Scripture which present the organization and practice of the church in the New Testament need to be correlated with the doctrinal sections which present the character of the church itself.

The church is the whole company of believers who are spiritually united to Christ who is the head of the church. One of the favorite descriptions of the church by the apostle Paul is "the body of Christ." Christ is the head (Col. 1:18). The church as His body is a unity. A person is made a member of that body by the work of the Holy Spirit (1 Cor. 12:13) and as a member of the body is organically related to every other member.

There is one church. Every believer from the day of Pentecost to the Rapture is a member of that church (cf. "all," 1 Cor. 12:13). The church then is the whole company of the redeemed from the time the church was formed on the day of Pentecost until Christ comes again to take His bride, the church, to Himself. This aspect of the church is often referred to as the universal church.

The universal church is not the sum total of local churches, nor is it the combination of all those who are members of local churches. The members of

Jack Fish is a faculty member at Emmaus Bible College and the editor of *The Emmaus Journal*.

the body of Christ are all individuals, not churches.[1] A local church may have individuals in it who are not true believers (cf. Rev. 3:16-17). These are not part of Christ's body. These individuals have only the external profession of being Christians, but not the inward reality.

The local church is the body of Christ particularized in a specific locality.[2] The genuineness of a local church is not determined by a required organization[3] or by certain practices. It is the reality of the relationship of individuals to Christ which determines the reality of the local church. An assembly of believers in fellowship with Christ may be imperfect in their organization and practice. They are still a true local church. A group of professing Christians who have not been born again may have the organization and practice of the New Testament church, but they are a church in name only. They are not genuine. The issue is whether Christ is in the midst or not.

THE NATURE OF THE CHURCH

CHRIST THE HEAD OF THE CHURCH

Colossians 1:18 says that Christ is the "head of the body, the church." The figure of Christ as the head and the church as His body teaches important truths about the church.

Historically the truth that Christ is the head of the church has been understood to mean that He is the sovereign Lord of the church, ruling over it and directing it according to His good pleasure. This interpretation of the term "head" has been questioned in the latter part of the twentieth century by "evangelical feminists." There are a large number of popular works which maintain that the term "head" in the Greco-Roman world did not convey the idea of "authority over" but the idea of "source."[4] It is important therefore to specify what idea is conveyed by the figure that Christ is the head of the church.

---

[1] Cf. Robert L. Saucy, *The Church in God's Program* (Chicago: Moody Press, 1972), 25.

[2] Saucy, *The Church in God's Program*, 25.

[3] The churches of Asia Minor composed of the new converts from Paul's first missionary journey existed without elders until Paul and Barnabas appointed them on their return to Antioch (Acts 14:23).

[4] These views may be traced back to the seminal study of Stephen Bedale, "The Meaning of κεφαλή in the Pauline Epistles," *Journal of Theological Studies*, n.s., 5 (1954): 211-215. The problem for the feminists is not the truth that Christ is the head of the church, but the parallel truth in Ephesians 5:23 that the husband is the head of the wife.

Wayne Grudem in an extensive study of ancient Greek sources has shown decisively that the meaning of "head" as "ruler" or "person of superior authority or rank" is quite common.[5] Furthermore, there are no instances where "head" is used in the sense of source. To say that Christ is the head of the church is not to say that He is the source of the church. Rather it is saying that He is the sovereign Lord of the church.[6]

The importance of this truth lies in the fact that Christ is the only one in the New Testament who is called the head of the church. There is no earthly head who acts in the place of Christ. There is no pastor, elder, or bishop who is the head over a local church or a group of churches. To put any man in that place is to usurp the position and authority of Christ Himself. In the New Testament His authority as head has not been conferred to a vice-regent who rules in His place and under His direction. The church is directly responsible to Him as the sovereign Lord of the church.

Further, each individual local church is responsible to Him. There is no

---

[5] Wayne Grudem, "Does ΚΕΦΑΛΗ ('Head') Mean 'Source' or 'Authority over' in Greek Literature? A Survey of 2,336 Examples," *TrinJ*, 6 NS (1985): 38-59. (Reprinted from the appendix of *The Role Relationship of Men and Women*, by George W. Knight III (rev. ed., Chicago: Moody Press, 1985), 49-80.

See the continuing debate in *Trinity Journal* in Richard S. Cervin, "Does Κεφαλή Mean 'Source' or 'Authority Over' in Greek Literature? A Rebuttal," *TrinJ* 10 NS (1989): 85-112; Wayne Grudem, "The Meaning of Κεφαλή ('Head'): A Response to Recent Studies, *TrinJ* 11 NS (1990): 3-72. This is also printed as an appendix in *Recovering Biblical Manhood and Womanhood: A Response to Evangelical Feminism*, ed. by John Piper and Wayne Grudem (Wheaton: Crossway Books, 1991), 425-468.

[6] Against the meaning "source" are the following arguments:

1) Usage: The word "head" never means source in the sense of origin of. The source of a river is called the head of the river in the sense that it is one of the extremities of the river. The mouth or outlet of a river is also called the head, but it is not the river's source.

2) While it is true that the woman in Genesis 2 was created from the man, this is not the idea conveyed by the term "head."

a) The parallel in 1 Corinthians 11 is that Christ is the head of the man and the head of Christ is God. This does not mean that God the Father is the source or origin of God the Son. The Son in His deity is eternal and self-existent. He is not a derived or secondary divinity. 1 Corinthians 11:3 is saying that God is the head of Christ in the sense that the Son in His office as Mediator and Savior has submitted Himself to the will of God the Father. ("Behold, I have come, in the roll of the book it is written of Me, to do Thy will, O God" [Heb. 10:7]). This has to do with His office and His work, not with His essence and nature.

b) In Ephesians 5:23-24 there is a direct correlation between Christ being the head of the church and the church being submissive to Him. The church is to be submissive because He is the sovereign head of the church, not because the church is derived from Him.

association of churches, or council of churches, or leaders outside the local church to which the individual church is accountable.[7] When believers in the church gather in His name, He Himself is in the midst (Matt. 18:20). He exercises His rule and the church is accountable to Him alone.

THE CHURCH THE BODY OF CHRIST

The truth of the church as the body of Christ emphasizes the unity of the church as well as the mutual interdependence of the members of the body.

Ephesians 4:4 says that there is one body. The oneness of the body emphasizes the unity of the church which is not to be broken by division or faction (cf. 1 Cor. 1:10-17). The tendency in the history of the church is to follow men (Paul, Apollos, Cephas, Luther, Calvin, Wesley), or a form of church government (Presbyterian, Congregational), or particular practice (Baptist), or a particular location (Church of England, Church of Rome). These are all denials of the oneness of the body of Christ, and this tendency should be resisted.

This makes it difficult for the believer today who wants to follow Scripture in its simplicity. The name Christian (Acts 11:26) has come to signify any who are associated with Christendom, including those whose beliefs and practice deny the essential truths of the Christian faith and who manifest no desire to please God. On the other hand it is possible to take no denominational name and yet have a denominational or sectarian attitude. If I do not receive or welcome as a brother or sister anyone who is received by Christ (Rom. 15:7) and who is in fellowship with Him, then I am sectarian in attitude and practice.

THE GOVERNMENT AND MINISTRY OF THE LOCAL CHURCH

THE GOVERNMENT AND ORGANIZATION OF THE CHURCH

The Universal Church

The New Testament does not have any organizational structure for the church universal.[8] There was, however, a unique place occupied by the apostles in relation to the whole church. They were chosen by Christ, they had a unique

---

[7] Acts 15 is no exception. The church at Antioch consulted with the apostles and the elders in the church at Jerusalem because it was appropriate to look to the apostles who had a unique relationship to Christ, and also because the ones stirring up trouble in the church in Antioch were from Judea (Acts 15:1).

[8] Cf. Saucy, *The Church in God's Program*, 17.

relationship to Him during His earthly ministry, and they were commissioned by Him to make disciples of all men. Paul says that they were part of the foundation of the church (Eph. 2:20). Because of this they had a unique position of authority. The writings of the apostles were recognized as authoritative, and apostolicity was the primary test for recognizing a book as inspired and canonical. Yet even among the apostles there was a division of labor. In Galatians 2:7-8 Paul is recognized as the apostle to the Gentiles and Peter as the apostle to the Jews. The other apostles are not mentioned in this regard. The significant point, however, is that there were no others that had a position of authority over more than one church. Further there is no indication that the position of apostle was passed on to the next generation. There were no successors to the apostles. This seems evident from the unique qualifications of the apostles. They were with Christ throughout His earthly ministry from the time of John the Baptist. They were eyewitnesses of the resurrection. (Acts 1:21-22). Paul himself was an exception who had not been with Christ. He was "untimely born" (1 Cor. 15:8) and was the last one to whom Christ in His resurrection body appeared (1 Cor. 15:8). The New Testament does not know of any other exceptions. The gift of apostleship ceased with the twelve.[9]

The Organization of the Local Church

The view that no organization is taught in the New Testament. Is there an organizational structure for the local church taught in the New Testament? Some say no. They maintain either that the New Testament is not clear, or it does not command any particular structure. There is liberty for Christians to choose any organization for the church which is practical and profitable. This view is based on the following arguments:

1) There is no pattern taught in the New Testament.[10] The New Testament practice is fluid and varied. Some see a congregational pattern in certain passages, a presbyterian system in others, and an episcopal system in others. It is argued that there is no single standard practice.

2) God never intended to give us a blueprint for the organization of the

---

[9] There are others called apostles in the New Testament, but not in the same sense as apostles of Christ. They were apostles of the churches, sent out by a specific church to fulfill a particular task. Cf. 2 Corinthians 8:23 where the literal translation would be, "as for our brethren, they are apostles of the churches." 2 Corinthians 8:19 shows that they had been appointed by the churches to handle the financial matters of the collection for the saints in Jerusalem.

[10] George Ladd, *A Theology of the New Testament*, ed. Donald A. Hagner (rev. ed., Grand Rapids: Eerdmans, 1993), 579.

church which we should follow. It is wrong to insist on one type of organization or government as being correct when the New Testament never does.

3) God has given great freedom for varied organizational structures in the church depending on different circumstances, different situations, and different cultures through the centuries. We may choose what is best for us.

The view that there is an organization taught in the New Testament. I would suggest that the evidence is by no means so ambiguous and unclear as is insisted above. There was a consistent pattern in the New Testament where each local church had a plurality of elders who were responsible to oversee the church as shepherds in their care and guidance of the church. The existence of such elders in the New Testament is recorded in relation to numerous churches over a widespread geographical area. Instruction is given concerning their qualifications and their responsibilities.

There is evidence of a second group of leaders who are called deacons, but the mention of them is not as frequent or as widespread as is the reference to elders. The qualifications for deacons are given in 1 Timothy 3:8-12, and they are mentioned in Philippians 1:2. This twofold leadership is the only leadership mentioned in the New Testament for the local church. There is no evidence that any other leadership would ever be needed or wanted.

What is the evidence that there was a consistent pattern of organization in the churches of the New Testament which is meant to be normative for us? Particularly, what is the evidence that there was a consistent pattern of a plurality of elders in each local church?

It is important to note that the pattern of a leadership group of elders for a local church existed in the New Testament over a widespread area and among culturally diverse groups.

1) Elders are mentioned in the churches in Judea (Acts 11:30) and specifically in the church in Jerusalem (Acts 15:2, 4, 6, 22, 23).

2) On Paul's first missionary journey he appointed elders in the churches in Asia Minor in the cities of Derbe, Lystra, Iconium, and Antioch (Acts 14:23).

3) Elders are mentioned in western Asia Minor in the city of Ephesus (Acts 20:17).

4) Peter writing to churches in northwestern Asia Minor exhorts "the elders among you" (1 Peter 5:1).

5) Paul writes to the overseers and deacons in Philippi (Phil. 1:1).

6) Writing to Timothy in Ephesus, Paul gives the qualifications of overseers (1 Tim. 3:1-7). He specifically says at the end of the chapter that he is writing these

things in order that if he is delayed in coming himself "you may know how one ought to conduct himself in the household of God, which is the church of the living God, the pillar and support of the truth" (1 Tim. 3:15).

7) Titus in Crete is instructed "to appoint elders in every city" (Tit. 1:5).

8) In Thessalonica there was a group of those who "diligently labor among you, and have charge over you in the Lord and give you instruction" (1 Thes. 5:12). These are not specifically called elders or overseers, but they are clearly a group of leaders in that church who have the same function as elders.

It may be noted from these verses that not only is there the descriptive practice of Paul's appointing elders in every church (Acts 14:23), there is also the prescriptive command to Titus to appoint elders in every city (Tit. 1:5). Further, the qualifications of elders given in 1 Timothy 3 and Titus 1 come from two of the last epistles of the apostle Paul when he was nearing the end of his ministry. This suggests that he is giving directions for the organization of the church which will continue to be perpetuated after he is gone.[11]

Elders

Elders and overseers. This same group is called indifferently elders or overseers. This is seen in Titus 1:5-7 where Titus is instructed to appoint elders in every city in verse 5. But then verse 7 says, "For the overseer must be above reproach." The same officials are called both elders and overseers. Also in Acts 20 when Paul called the *elders* of the church at Ephesus to meet him (Acts 20:17), he addressed them and said, "Be on guard for yourselves and for all the flock, among which the Holy Spirit has made you *overseers*." It is further to be noted that in Philippians 1:1 Paul only mentions two groups, overseers and deacons (not overseers, elders, and deacons).

The view that there was only a single elder or overseer. By the second century instead of two groups, overseers and deacons, there were three. One of the overseers or bishops became the chief overseer who presided over the group of elders. There was thus a single bishop along with the elders and deacons. Some have attempted to see the pattern of a single pastor of the church not only in this second-century practice, but in the New Testament itself. It is suggested

---

[11] It should also be noted that the epistles to Timothy and Titus were not written to them as individuals. They were authoritative instructions for the churches. 1 and 2 Timothy conclude with the words, "Grace be with you." The "you" is plural in Greek (ὑμῶν, *hymōn*). Titus ends, "Grace be with you all."

that Peter or James was the chief elder or the president among the elders. Timothy is also considered by some to be the individual pastor of a local church. In addition the angel of each individual church addressed in the letters to the seven churches in Revelation 2–3 is often considered to be the pastor of that church.

There is a danger of reading later church practice or present church practice into the New Testament itself. Peter and James were leaders in the church in Jerusalem. They were classed as apostles (Gal. 1:19). Peter was often a spokeman among the apostles, but there is nothing to indicate that he was over the other apostles. James was also one of the pillars of the church in Jerusalem, but not the only one (Gal. 2:9). At the council in Jerusalem in Acts 15 the church at Antioch consulted the apostles and elders in Jerusalem (Acts 15:2, 4, 6, 22, 23). While Peter and James spoke up, the decision was the decision of the group. There is no indication that either Peter or James was the pastor of the church in Jerusalem. In fact James seems to have occupied a unique position in the church because of his relationship to the Lord as his brother (Gal. 1:19). But it is a mistake to take the unique position of the apostles whose position was not perpetuated in the church and make it the model for the pastor of the church today.

Timothy also did not have the position of local church pastor as it is usually thought of. He was a special representative of the apostle Paul and therefore an apostolic delegate. He would be sent to individual churches on behalf of Paul and minister to them under the apostle's direction. The identity of the angels of the churches in Revelation 2-3 is unclear. It may be that there are literal angels associated with and ministering to individual churches. The term *angelos* is not used of Christian leaders in the New Testament, and they are never rebuked in the letters to the seven churches. But even if they were human messengers, there is no indication that they occupied the position of being the sole leader or even the main leader of their church. They could have been the messengers who carried or even received the letters. The commentaries on Revelation are by no means agreed on the identity of the "angel," and it would seem a tenuous basis to rest the modern office of pastor on such an obscure passage.

The concept of the house-church is also used by some scholars to reject the teaching of multiple elders in the local church. It is clear that the church did often meet in the houses of believers (Rom. 16:5; 1 Cor. 16:19; Col. 4:15; Philemon 2). It is suggested that while there may have been a plurality of elders in each city, there may have also been a plurality of house-churches in each place with one pastor presiding in each. These pastors collectively were the elders of the citywide church.

This hypothesis is ingenious, but it is in fact pure speculation. There is no evidence at all that there was a single elder presiding over an individual house-church. There is no reason why there could not be a plurality of elders in these individual assemblies. The hypothesis is built on the fact that there must have been a large number of believers in a city like Ephesus and that they must have met in numerous buildings. The fact is that we do not know how the singular church at Ephesus met with its group of elders exercising pastoral oversight. But this hypothesis overlooks the fact that there were small churches which also had a plurality of elders. Paul appointed a plurality of elders in the young, recently evangelized churches of Lystra, Iconium, and Antioch (Acts 14:23). The church of Thessalonica was less than a year old when Paul wrote 1 Thessalonians and yet there was a plurality of leadership (1 Thes. 5:12).

The function of elders. The name "elder" describes the person as one who is older and mature, while the name "overseer" describes the work. Overseers exercise oversight in the church. They preside over the assembly as a husband and father presides over his own house (1 Tim. 3:5; cf. 5:17). They are instructed to shepherd the church as a pastor shepherds his flock of sheep (Acts 20:28; 1 Pet. 5:1-2). This refers to caring for the total welfare of the flock. This would include feeding the flock, leading the flock, and protecting the flock.

The elder must feed the flock. This is why the overseer must be "able to teach" (1 Tim. 3:2; cf. 5:17). Paul says that he must be sound in his doctrine so that he "may be able to exhort in sound doctrine and refute those who contradict" (Tit. 1:9).

The elders must lead the flock. The good shepherd goes before his sheep and they follow him (John 10:4). The elders who rule well are to be considered worthy of double honor (1 Tim. 5:17).

The elders must protect the flock. Paul knows that after his departure there will be false teachers who will be a great threat to the flock (Acts 20:29-30). It is the responsibility of the elders to be on guard and on the alert (Acts 20:28, 31). They must be able to refute those who teach false doctrine (Tit. 1:9). In Acts 15 the elders in Jerusalem joined with the apostles in dealing with the doctrinal issue which arose when Judaizers insisted that Gentiles must be circumcised and keep the law in order to be saved.

1 Timothy 5:17 indicates some division of labor among the elders. "Let the elders who rule well be considered worthy of double honor, especially those who work hard at preaching and teaching." All elders "rule" or "preside." This is the same word that is used in 1 Timothy 3:4-5 (προΐστημι) to indicate the primary responsibility of elders in overseeing the assembly. But some elders especially

labor in the Word and teaching. This would be because their spiritual gift lies in the area of teaching.

Conclusion. The pattern of a plurality of elders governing the local church in the New Testament is not only widespread geographically (Jerusalem, Judea, various parts of Asia Minor, Europe, Crete), it includes churches which are mainly Jewish as well as those which are mainly Gentile. Even more significantly, the instructions concerning elders in 1 Timothy 3 and Titus 1 indicate that this was the government of the church which the apostle expected to be perpetuated. It is the instruction given so that you might "know how one *ought* (δεῖ, *dei*) to conduct himself in the household of God, the church" (1 Tim. 3:15).

Alexander Strauch notes that there are more instructions given in the New Testament regarding elders than on other important church subjects such as baptism, the Lord's Supper, or the Lord's day.[12] In the history of the church this instruction concerning church organization has often been ignored and the secular models of monarchy (episcopal), oligarchy (presbyterian), and democracy (congregational) have been followed. The greatest danger followed when a single elder began to preside and ultimately became the chief authority. One person became *the* bishop of the church. With the threats to the church it was more efficient for one individual to make decisions, guard the doctrine of the church, and exercise discipline over false teachers or believers causing disturbances. When this kind of authority was combined with an autocratic spirit, it became a great detriment to the church. But the practice of the church in later centuries is not our authority for the practice of the church today. When the New Testament gives us a consistent pattern and couples that with specific instructions concerning the qualifications and practices of elders, why should this area of Scripture be less authoritative for us than others?

Deacons

The fact of deacons in the church. The evidence for deacons in each church is much less. Paul writes to the saints which are in Philippi "along with the over-seers and deacons" (Phil. 1:1). In 1 Timothy 3:8-13 we also have the qualifications of deacons. In verse 10 Paul says that they are to be examined and then "let them serve as deacons, if they are beyond reproach." Thus, it is clear that there was an official group of deacons who served in the church.

---

[12] Alexander Strauch, *Biblical Eldership* (revised and expanded, Littleton, CO: Lewis and Roth, 1995), 103.

The term διάκονος (*diakonos*) means "servant" and is frequently used in an unofficial sense for anyone who ministers or serves. Paul refers to himself as a *diakonos* (Rom. 15:8; 1 Cor. 3:5 [along with Apollos]; 2 Cor. 3:6; 6:4; 11:23; Eph. 3:7; Col. 1:25). He was a *diakonos* in a general or unofficial sense. He was faithfully *serving* or *ministering* for Christ. Others who are called *diakonoi* are Phoebe (Rom. 16:1), Tychicus (Eph. 6:21; Col. 4:7); Epaphras (Col. 1:7), and Timothy (1 Tim. 4:6). Whether these are called *diakonoi* in the official or unofficial sense is not always clear. The fact that Phoebe is called a *diakonos* and "women" are included in the list of qualifications of deacons in 1 Timothy 3:11 suggests to many that there were women deacons. But the Greek word "women" (γυναῖκες, *gunaikes*) is also the normal word for "wives" and commentators differ as to whether 1 Timothy 3:11 is talking about women deacons or wives of deacons. One must conclude that the evidence is not clear enough to decide definitely.

The one remaining passage that might have a bearing on deacons is Acts 6 where the "seven" were chosen to assist the apostles in the daily service of food to the widows in the church. There was a dispute between the Hellenistic (Greek-speaking) Jewish Christians and the Hebrew (Aramaic-speaking) Christians concerning the treatment of widows. The seven were chosen to deal with these matters so that the apostles might devote themselves to prayer and the ministry of the word (Acts 6:4). Were these seven the first "deacons?" They are commonly considered such. But the term *diakonos* is not used in the passage. It is said that the apostles would devote themselves to prayer and the ministry (*diakonia*) of the word. But the apostles were not deacons in the official sense. The apostles also said that "it is not desirable for us to neglect the word of God in order to serve (*diakonein*) tables" (Acts 6:2). Because the "seven" were chosen for that "service" (*diakonia*), they have commonly been considered the first deacons. One cannot be dogmatic.

One may conclude that the New Testament church had not only elders, but also deacons who served in the leadership of the church. Whether every church had deacons is not clear. There is not enough evidence.

The function of deacons. The New Testament nowhere gives the exact functions and duties of deacons. Their responsibilities must therefore be inferred from 1) their name, 2) their qualifications, 3) their relationship to elders, and possibly 4) the description of Acts 6.

1) The word διάκονος (*diakonos*) emphasizes the work of a servant. It was used for waiting on tables (cf. Luke 17:8; John 12:2), for caring for household

needs, and for service generally.[13] It is the term used by our Lord to describe His basic work. He came not to be *served*, but to *serve* and give His life a ransom for many (Mk. 10:45). This attitude of service was to characterize His disciples. Every kind of work in the propagation of the gospel may be described as a *diakonia*. The word itself indicates that deacons are ministers, servants of the church.

2) The qualifications of deacons in 1 Timothy 3:8-13 are all spiritual. They are essentially the same qualifications as those of elders. One might infer from this that their work is a spiritual work and is similar to the work of elders.

3) Deacons in the primary references of Philippians 1:1 and 1 Timothy 3:8-11 are linked with the elders. From this one might infer that they are assistants or helpers of the elders. They do what the elders want them to do to assist them in the ministry of the church.

4) The appointment of the seven in Acts 6 has had a strong influence in the church on the role and function of deacons. They are given responsibility over the more practical matters of finances, the care of widows, the building (although there were no separate church buildings in the New Testament era), and such matters. It should also be noticed that the qualifications of the seven in Acts 6:3 are also spiritual. They must be "of good reputation, full of the Spirit and of wisdom." It may be that there was no dichotomy between the spiritual work and the practical work of the seven. They not only cared for the widows of the assembly and their daily serving of food (the serving of tables, Acts 6:2), but Stephen in Acts 6–7 and Philip in Acts 8 were active in preaching and evangelism.

The work of deacons is a spiritual work as they assist the elders in their ministry in the assembly.

THE MINISTRY OF THE CHURCH

What the church is determines what the church does and the place of the individual in the ministry of the church. 1 Corinthians 12:13 indicates that the church is the body of Christ. By the baptizing work of the Holy Spirit each believer is joined to the body of Christ. The church is not a building, an organization, or an association of individuals. It is an organism. Each member is joined to Christ and is not only related to Him, but is also related to every other

---

[13] K. Hess, "Serve, Deacon, Worship," *The New International Dictionary of New Testament Theology*, ed. by Colin Brown, 3 vols. (Grand Rapids: Zondervan, 1978), 3:545.

member. Each person in the body has a vital function to perform. Each has a necessary ministry to the other members of the body. What that is is seen in the New Testament teaching on spiritual gifts.

SPIRITUAL GIFTS

What is a Spiritual Gift

In 1 Corinthians 12:4-6 Paul uses three words for spiritual gifts which help us understand what they are. In verse 4 he uses the word *charisma*. In verse 5 he uses the word *diakonia*, and in verse 6 he uses the word *energēma*. *Charisma*, from which we get the word charismatic, is related to the word *charis* which means grace. Spiritual gifts are *charismata* because they are abilities graciously given by God to minister in the church. They are not earned, deserved, or merited. They are *diakoniai*. The word means service or ministry. The spiritual gifts are functions or ministries. They are not offices which a person holds. A minister in a church does not occupy a position but performs a function. They are *energēmata*. This word means "effect" or "operation." The verbal form of this word is always used in the New Testament of a supernatural working or operation. The spiritual gifts are abilities given by God so that He can work through the gifted believers to perform His work.

We can see from the different words describing spiritual gifts that they are supernatural abilities given by God to believers for service in the body of Christ. The word "supernatural" does not mean that this is the ability to do the supernatural, but rather the source of the ability is from God. The ability is to do a work for God. The strength and power come from God. The strength of the church is not in its members or in superior men or women. It comes from the Holy Spirit working through those who have been given a special ability to minister in the church. In the words of Zechariah the ministry of the church is "Not by might, nor by power, but by My Spirit, says the Lord of hosts" (Zech. 4:6).

Spiritual gifts are more than natural abilities. This does not mean that there is no relationship between spiritual gifts and natural abilities. God fits the vessel for its use. In Galatians 1:15 Paul indicates that God had separated him from his mother's womb. Through his background in Tarsus, his home life and upbringing in Judaism, and his education under Gamaliel God prepared him to be the apostle to the Gentiles and the writer of thirteen books in the New Testament. But it was not until Christ appeared to him on the Damascus road that he was converted and called to be an apostle (cf. Acts 26:16-18). He did not have the gift of apostleship before he became a Christian.

Who Has a Spiritual Gift?

1 Corinthians 12:7 indicates that every believer has a spiritual gift. "But to each one is given the manifestation of the Spirit for the common good." The word "each one" is emphatic in the Greek. Verse 11 in the same chapter reiterates, "But one and the same Spirit works all these things, distributing to each one individually just as He wills." Ephesians 4:7 in the context of spiritual gifts says, "But to each one of us grace was given according to the measure of Christ's gift."

This means that there is no believer who does not have a spiritual gift. Women not only have the spiritual gifts, they have all of the gifts that men have today. With the exception of the fact that there were no women apostles, women could have any of the spiritual gifts. Philip's daughters had the gift of prophecy, which 1 Corinthians 14:1 says was one of the greater gifts. In Titus 2:4-5 the older women were to teach the younger women. Paul mentions many women who labored with him in the gospel and who therefore presumably had the gift of evangelism. Any restrictions on the place the gift may be exercised do not argue against the fact of the gift (cf. 1 Cor. 14:34-36; 1 Tim. 2:11-12).

If every believer has a spiritual gift, this means that Christians who are only ten years old also have their spiritual gifts. Their gifts may need to be developed, but if every Christian has a spiritual gift, there can be no exceptions. We may also say that while one believer may have several spiritual gifts, no one has all of them. This is the implication of the illustration of the body in 1 Corinthians 12:12-30 where there are many different members in the body.

What Is the Purpose of the Spiritual Gifts?

1 Corinthians 12:7 says that "each one is given the manifestation of the Spirit for the common good" (NASB). The phrase "common good" is an interpretive translation. The Greek phrase πρὸς τὸ συμφέρον (pros to sympheron) literally means "for [someone's] benefit." But it does not specify for whose benefit. Is it for the benefit of the individual who has the gift, or for the benefit of the assembly, or both? The translation "for the common good" takes spiritual gifts as being for the benefit of the assembly. The following reasons support this interpretation.

1) 1 Corinthians 14:12 says "since you are zealous of spiritual gifts, seek to abound for the edification of the church." Gifts are given that the church may be edified.

2) This is also the teaching of the figure of the body in 1 Corinthians 12:12-26. Each member in the body does not exist for its own benefit, but for the benefit of the whole body. It functions not for itself, but for the body.

3) 1 Peter 4:10 says "as each one has received a special gift, employ it in serving one another, as good stewards of the manifold grace of God." The gifts are given for us to minister to one another.

4) In the next verse, 1 Peter 4:11, Peter says that all of our gifts and all of our service is that God Himself might ultimately be glorified.

5) The one verse that is often interpreted to mean that the gifts are for the individual's own personal benefit is 1 Corinthians 14:4, "One who speaks in a tongue edifies himself; but one who prophesies edifies the church." To conclude that the purpose of the gift of tongues was self-edification is to confuse purpose with result. Self-edification is a result or a by-product of the exercise of one's spiritual gift. But that does not mean it is the purpose of the gift. One may say that the person who exercises the gift of evangelism and who sees fruit from his labor will be edified and blessed. But one would hardly conclude from that that the purpose of the gift of evangelism is self-edification. The biblical teaching on spiritual gifts drives us away from the individualism and self-centeredness which characterize so many Christians and gets our focus on our ministry to others and the way we may benefit them.

The Types of Spiritual Gifts

There are four passages in the New Testament which discuss spiritual gifts: 1 Corinthians 12, Romans 12, Ephesians 4, and 1 Peter 4. No passage contains a complete list of the spiritual gifts and the scope of this article does not allow us to discuss each individual gift. There is one fundamental distinction that is made in 1 Peter 4:11 which should be noted. After saying in verse 10 that each one has received a special gift, Peter says, "Whoever speaks, let him speak, as it were, the utterances of God; whoever serves, let him do so as by the strength which God supplies." There is a distinction made here between speaking gifts and serving gifts. Teaching, evangelism, exhortation would be examples of speaking gifts. Helps, administration, mercy, and giving would be serving-type gifts.

A person who has a serving-type gift should not feel compelled to have a speaking-type ministry. Nor should a person with a speaking gift feel compelled to do many of the necessary works and chores which would take him away from exercising his gift. The important thing is for each person to find his or her particular niche and do one's work for the glory of God.

There is another distinction among the spiritual gifts which should also be recognized. Some of the gifts given to the church were temporary. They were intended only for the early period of the church and are no longer given today. The charismatic movement has questioned this assumption, but it should be obvious that at least one spiritual gift was temporary, the gift of apostleship. It is clear from 1 Corinthians 12:28-29 and Ephesians 4:11 that the apostle had a special spiritual gift of "apostleship." One of the requirements to be an apostle was to have seen the risen Christ (1 Cor. 9:1). Another was to have been with Christ from the time of the baptism of John the Baptist until the resurrection (Acts 1:21-22).[14] No one today meets these requirements and the very nature of them precludes apostles today.[15]

Two types of gifts seem to have been temporary, foundational gifts and sign gifts. Paul says in Ephesians 2:20 that the church was built on the foundation of His holy apostles and prophets. These gifts were for the initial period of the church when apostles and prophets were inspired by God to give new revelation. With the completion of the New Testament revelation the foundation was completed and the gifts are no longer manifested.

The purpose of the sign gifts is seen in Hebrews 2:3-4. "**How shall we escape if we neglect so great a salvation? After it was at the first spoken through the Lord, it was confirmed to us by those who heard, God also bearing witness with them, both by signs and wonders and by various miracles and by gifts of the Holy Spirit according to His own will.**" This says that God was bearing witness to the message of the apostles with mighty miracles. Miracles were always subservient to the Word. They were designed to get attention and to attest God's messenger. They are not found frequently throughout the Bible, but rather especially at times of new revelation. They are found at the time of Moses, of Elijah and Elisha, and the time of Christ and the apostles. With the full revelation of God in Scripture, that is with the completion of the New Testament, these kinds of miracles ceased. God is still a God of miracles, but we should not look for miracle workers. These gifts were temporary.

MINISTRY IN THE CHURCH

The Authority for Ministry

If each believer is gifted by the Holy Spirit to minister in the church, then this gives

---

[14] The apostle Paul was conscious that his apostleship was unique in that he did not fit this requirement. He was one "untimely born" (1 Cor. 15:8). But he was directly called by Christ (Gal. 1:1) and was recognized by the other apostles as the apostle to the Gentiles (Gal. 2:8; cf. Rom. 11:13).

[15] Those who were commissioned by individual churches to perform a specific task were "apostles of the churches" (see note 9 above), but this was not the spiritual gift. The spiritual gift which was listed as the most important gift (1 Cor. 12:28) was restricted to the twelve along with Paul. The brethren in 2 Corinthians 8:23 were sent by the churches to watch over the collection for

each one of us not only the responsibility to minister, it also gives us the authority for ministry. The authority to teach, pastor, evangelize, administer, or help in the assembly does not come from having a certain kind of education or from any human ordination or licensing. It comes from God the Holy Spirit who has gifted us and called us to exercise that gift for the benefit of others and for His glory.

In a body each member is different, and each member is important. This is the teaching of 1 Corinthians 12:12-26. We do not choose our spiritual gifts. They are given to us sovereignly by the Holy Spirit who "**distributes to each one individually just as He wills**" (1 Cor. 12:11). That means that we must function in the body as we are, as God has made us, not as we would prefer to be. We must accept our place in the body and not envy someone else who has a different gift. The fact is that it is the uniqueness of each one of us and the uniqueness of our gift and function in the body that gives us our place of importance. We have a unique ministry that only we can perform. There should be no sense of rivalry in the church any more than there should be a sense of rivalry between the ear and the foot in the body. Each part is important and each has a unique function to perform. When any member does not exercise his gift, the whole body suffers.

The Ministers in the Church

Who are the ministers in the church and to whom do they minister? The teaching of 1 Corinthians 12 is that each believer is a minister and each believer is ministered to. The individualism that characterizes the church of the twentieth century is foreign to the church of the New Testament. There is an interdependence in the body of Christ which makes each one of us our brother's keeper.

Any concept of the ministry of the church which conceives of the ministers as the few and the ministered to as the many is fundamentally deficient. The problem where there is one minister in the church is that the gifts of all of the other ministers in the church are neglected. Each of us is called by God to edify and bless others. There is a limit to the amount of work one person can do and there is a limit to the ability of one individual. One person may be a gifted evangelist, but that does not mean that he is the person who can teach and build up the saints. Another may be a great teacher, but not a pastor or counselor. Another may be a great pastor, but he is very unorganized. He does not have the gift of administration. Further, different people with different needs respond to different individuals in the assembly.

---

the saints in Jerusalem so that there could be no question of impropriety (cf. 8:19-21). They were "apostles of the churches" as opposed to an "apostle of Christ Jesus" (1 Cor. 1:1; cf. Gal. 1:1).

The work of the ministry is the work of each believer in the assembly. This is seen in Ephesians 4:11ff. The risen Christ has given gifts, particularly gifted individuals to the church. He has given some as apostles, some as prophets, some as evangelists, and some as pastors and teachers (Eph. 4:11). But the purpose of the apostles, prophets, and so on is the equipping of the saints for the work of the ministry (πρὸς τὸν καταρτισμὸν τῶν ἁγίων εἰς ἔργον διακονίας, *pros ton katartismon tōn hagiōn eis ergon diakonias*, Eph. 4:12). The work of the ministry is not the work of the apostles, prophets, evangelists, and pastors and teachers. It is the work of the saints. They are the ministers. The goal of this ministry of the saints is the building up of the body of Christ. The church has greatly impoverished itself by restricting its ministry to the few rather than allowing each member of the body to exercise its divinely bestowed spiritual gift. The church as a collective whole is to reach the maturity of a full-grown man. This can only be done by the ministry of every member of the body.

OFFICE AND MINISTRY

A fundamentally different concept of ministry has developed where the concepts of office and gifts have been confused. Elders (or overseers) and deacons have positions of leadership in the church. It is often assumed that these leaders are the ministers in the church. The elders or pastors, or as is most often the case, the single pastor or elder does the work of the ministry. He may wind up teaching, preaching, evangelizing, pastoring, administrating, driving the Sunday school bus, and filling the baptistery. It is the work of the few to the many.

But this is not the concept of ministry that is taught in the New Testament. The ministry in the local church is not the work of one person, or the work of a few, it is the work of each believer in the church. Ministry in the church should not be confused with office in the church. Each person in the body has a spiritual gift and is to minister in the church. But not everyone is an overseer. There is no specific gift that an elder must have. An elder may have any of the spiritual gifts and must exercise that gift as a member of the body. But he had the spiritual gift and should have exercised it long before he was recognized as an elder. Thus a person may have the gift of teaching and should be teaching in the church even though he may not be an elder. A person may have the gift of pastor, but that does not automatically make him an elder. Gifts must be developed and the individual must grow and mature before he is qualified to be an overseer. An elder must be able to teach and he is to shepherd the flock, but that does not mean that this is the area of his spiritual gift any more than it means Timothy had the gift of evangelism just because he was to do the work of an evangelist (2 Tim. 4:5).

THE FUNCTIONS OF THE LOCAL CHURCH

THE GOAL OF THE CHURCH IN DIFFERENT SPHERES

What the church is to do and how it functions is to be seen first in relation to God, then in relation to the world, and finally in relation to believers.

In Relation to God

The goal of the church in relation to God is to glorify Him. Looking at the work of God in blessing the church, Paul says that it is to the praise of the glory of His grace (Eph. 1:6, 12, 14). The Westminster Shorter Catechism says that "man's chief end is to glorify God, and to enjoy him forever."[16] This is not only the goal of each individual Christian, it is the goal of the church itself. All that the church does, whether in worship, in evangelism, or in the mutual ministry of believers to one another, is to glorify God. "Whatever you do, do all to the glory of God" (1 Cor. 10:31).

In Relation to the World

The goal of the church in relation to the world is to preach the gospel. The great commission was to go into all the world and make disciples of all men (Matt. 28:19). The disciples were commanded to be witnesses to Christ "in Jerusalem, and in all Judea and Samaria, and even to the remotest part of the earth" (Acts 1:8). As a result of persecution in Jerusalem, all of the believers except the apostles were scattered throughout Judea and Samaria (Acts 8:1). But those who were scattered "went about preaching the word." They went out to a lost world taking the gospel to them.

In Relation to Believers

The goal of the church in relation to believers is for each one to minister to the others to build up the body of Christ (Eph. 4:12). The further goal is for all of us to "attain to the unity of the faith, and of the knowledge of the Son of God, to a mature man, to the measure of the stature which belongs to the fulness of Christ" (Eph. 4:13). Paul says that he proclaimed Christ "admonishing every man and teaching every man with all wisdom, that we may present every man complete in Christ" (Col. 1:28).

---

[16] Cf. Philip Schaff, ed., "The Westminster Shorter Catechism," *The Creeds of Christendom*, 3 vols. (reprint ed., Grand Rapids: Baker Book House, 1983 [= 1931]), 3:676.

The Church and Evangelism

The work of evangelism is one of the central ministries of the church. Even believers who do not have the gift of evangelism like Timothy are to "do the work of an evangelist" (2 Tim. 4:5). The young church at Thessalonica was commended because "the word of the Lord has sounded forth from you, not only in Macedonia and Achaia, but also in every place your faith toward God has gone forth, so that we have no need to say anything" (1 Thes. 1:8). The church in the book of Acts was constantly growing because believers were preaching the gospel.

But nowhere in the New Testament is there any indication that the church met to preach the gospel. Rather the church met to worship, to teach the word, to pray, to have fellowship. The meeting of the church was to edify believers and to glorify God. But it was not to preach the gospel to unbelievers. Rather the saints went out into the world to preach the gospel.

Even the evangelist in Ephesians 4:11 equipped the saints for the saints to do the ministry of evangelism. They were equipped *in* the church to preach *outside* the church. Where did they find unbelievers? It might be in the temple (Acts 3), in the midst of the Sanhedrin (Acts 4, 5, 7), in the synagogues (this was the place where Paul often went, cf. 9:20; 13:5; etc.), on a road in the desert (Acts 8:26), in a private home (Acts 10:23-48), in the market place, on the Areopagus in Athens, in prison, etc. They preached the gospel wherever they found unbelievers.

The practice of preaching the gospel in the church meeting developed when many unbelievers started attending church. It was a convenient time to present the claims of Christ. But there is no biblical mandate for an "evangelistic service" when the church comes together. There is a mandate to equip the saints to preach the gospel. The work of Christians is not to invite unbelievers to church so that they might hear the gospel. It is to preach the gospel themselves. There are many saints who reject the concept of one-man-ministry but have adopted the practice of one-man-evangelism. Instead of preaching the good news to unsaved friends and neighbors, they invite them to hear the evangelist or the preacher. This was not the biblical practice. This does not mean that the gospel should not be clearly presented in the church. But it should be taught to believers in a way that will make them more effective communicators. The book of Romans is the great New Testament treatise on the gospel. But it was written to Christians to teach them, not to the unsaved to lead them to Christ.

Some churches cling to the gospel meeting even when there are no unbelievers who attend. The biblical mandate to preach the gospel has been taken to mean preach the gospel in church. This means that the work of evangelism is not really done, and it also means that the saints are not built up to do the work that they are to do. Tradition has replaced Scripture in determining our church practice, and the work of the church is not done.

THE ACTIVITIES AND PRACTICES OF THE CHURCH

What is it that the church should do? This can be seen from the descriptions in the book of Acts as to what the church actually did and from the commands as to what the church is to do.

Baptism

The New Testament practice. The first thing that happened in the New Testament when a person believed was that he was baptized. This was the command of Christ to His disciples. "Go therefore and make disciples of all the nations, baptizing them in the name of the Father and the Son and the Holy Spirit" (Matt. 28:19). This was the uniform practice of the early church. When a person believed, he was baptized (cf. Acts 2:38, 41; 8:12, 36-38; 9:18; 10:48; 16:15, 38; 18:8; 19:5). There was no delay. There was no such thing as an unbaptized Christian.

The reason for baptism is simple. It is the command of Christ. The church in the New Testament was not disobedient to the Lord in this command.

The subjects of baptism. Those who were baptized in the book of Acts were all believers. They heard the gospel, they responded in faith, and they were baptized. This is true of those who were saved on the day of Pentecost (Acts 2), the Samaritans (Acts 8), the Ethiopian eunuch (Acts 8), Cornelius and his house (Acts 10), Lydia and her house (Acts 16), the Philippian jailer and his house (Acts 16), and the Corinthians (Acts 18). The only ones who were baptized were believers.

It has been argued on the basis of the reference to the households of Lydia, the Philippian jailer, Crispus, and Stephanas that the baptism must have also included the infant children of the believers (Acts 16:15, 33; 18:8; 1 Cor. 1:16). This is a gratuitous inference which is nowhere found in these texts. In Acts 16:33 Paul spoke the word to the jailer with all who were in his house. Crispus, the leader of the synagogue, believed in the Lord with all his household (Acts 18:8).

The households were baptized because the households believed. There is no reason to believe that the case of Lydia and Stephanas was any different. There is certainly no specific indication that infants or any who did not believe were baptized.

The meaning of baptism. Baptism is a symbolical act. The word "baptize" is a transliteration rather than a translation of the Greek word βαπτίζω (*baptizō*). *Baptizō* means "to dip, immerse."[17] The immersion in water symbolized the washing and cleansing of sin. Because baptism was the initial act of the new believer after coming to faith in Christ it was also a public act of confession of faith. A believer identifies himself with Christ by the act of baptism.[18]

The significance of baptism is also seen in the relationship of water baptism to the baptism of the Holy Spirit. Some would sharply distinguish water baptism and Spirit baptism on the basis of the words of John the Baptist. "I baptize you with water; He will baptize you with the Holy Spirit." But Ephesians 4:5 says that there is "one Lord, one faith, one baptism." If there is one baptism, then water baptism and Spirit baptism are not two completely different things. The one is the picture of the other. The baptism of the Holy Spirit is the reality. The Spirit joins us to Christ so that we are united with Him. "For by one Spirit we were all baptized into one body, whether Jews or Greeks, whether slaves or free, and we were all made to drink of one Spirit" (1 Cor. 12:13). The Spirit in His baptizing work identifies us with Christ so closely that we are united to Him. The baptism in water pictures this truth.

In Romans six Paul says that "all of us who have been baptized into Christ Jesus have been baptized into His death" (6:3). He also says, "We have been buried with Him through baptism into death, in order that as Christ was raised from the dead through the glory of the Father, so we too might walk in newness of life" (6:4). Through baptism we have been identified with Christ in His death and resurrection. Is this referring to water baptism or the baptism of the Holy Spirit? Ephesians 4:5 says that there is only one baptism. Romans 6 is speaking of the reality of our union with Christ so that we died to sin with Him, were buried with

---

[17] "βαπτίζω," *BAGD*, 130. The meanings "plunge, sink, drench, overwhelm" are also cited as other meanings found in non-Christian literature.

[18] "Identification" seems to be the meaning of the word in 1 Corinthians 10:2 where it says of Israel when they passed through the Red Sea, "All were baptized into Moses in the cloud and in the sea." They were identified or associated with Moses through this act which is described as being baptized into Moses.

Him, and rose with Him. That reality is the work of the Holy Spirit. Water baptism cannot produce that reality, but it does picture the reality.[19]

Thus baptism is an initiatory rite which pictures our cleansing from sin and our identification with Christ in His death, burial, and resurrection. As such those who put their faith in Christ were appropriately baptized in the New Testament. Those who argue for infant baptism have a problem here, for they must say that when infants are baptized, their baptism means something different than it means for all who were baptized in the New Testament. Unless one accepts the Roman Catholic view of baptismal regeneration, it does not mean that they have been cleansed from sin. It does not symbolize the fact that they have been united to Christ in His death, burial, and resurrection so as to walk in newness of life. What does baptism mean for a paedobaptist? Does it signify that this child is going to be cleansed and united to Christ in the future? That would not be accurate because there is no certainty. Infant baptism is more of a pledge by Christian parents that they will raise their children to fear the Lord and they will teach their children the gospel in order that they might come to know Him. But that is a fundamentally different notion of baptism. It is a view of baptism which is nowhere taught in the New Testament.[20]

Is baptism necessary for salvation? Some have said that baptism is necessary for salvation. This is the position of Roman Catholics who say that the water in John 3:5 refers to baptism. "**Unless one is born of water and the Spirit, he cannot enter into the kingdom of God.**" They also find support in Titus 3:5 (the washing of regeneration) and Ephesians 5:26 (Christ cleansed the church by the washing of the water by the word). Others say that Acts 2:38 and Mark 16:16 indicate that baptism is required for salvation. "**Repent, and let each of you be baptized in the**

---

[19] The parallel passage in Colossians confirms that the reality spoken of here is that of the baptism of the Holy Spirit. Colossians 2:12 says, "having been buried with Him in baptism, in which you were also raised up with Him through faith in the working of God, who raised Him from the dead." The baptism in verse twelve is parallel with circumcision in verse eleven. But the circumcision in verse 11 is not ritual circumcision. It is the circumcision "made without hands." So the baptism in verse 12 is not the ritual, but the reality.

[20] The primary argument for infant baptism is from the analogy of circumcision. Infants (male infants) were circumcised in the Old Testament as a sign of their entrance into the covenant community. But there is a fundamental difference between the old covenant and the new covenant. One became a member of the nation of Israel by physical birth. The church is the fellowship of those who have been born again. Even foreign servants were circumcised in the Old Testament (Gen. 17:10-13). Only those who believed were baptized in the New Testament.

name of Jesus Christ for the forgiveness of your sins" (Acts 2:38). "He who has believed and has been baptized shall be saved; but he who has disbelieved shall be condemned" (Mk. 16:16).

The following considerations indicate that baptism is not a requirement for salvation:

1) The clear teaching of the New Testament is that salvation is by faith alone. "For by grace you have been saved through faith; and that not of yourselves, it is the gift of God; not as a result of works, that no one should boast" (Eph. 2:8-9). "'Sirs, what must I do to be saved?' And they said, 'Believe in the Lord Jesus, and you shall be saved'" (Acts 16:30-31). "For we maintain that a man is justified by faith apart from works of the Law" (Rom. 3:28). If baptism is necessary for salvation, then all of these verses which only mention faith are misleading. The Philippian jailer in Acts 16 was not given the whole gospel.

2) Even more serious, a human work is added to faith as a requirement for salvation. This contradicts all of the verses which say that salvation is by faith apart from works. It distorts the gospel so that there is a different kind of gospel. This is the precise point Paul makes in the book of Galatians. The Galatian opponents were saying that the ritual of circumcision was necessary for salvation (cf. Acts 15:1). Paul says that this is a different kind of gospel which is not really another gospel (Gal. 1:6). Those who rely on works are "under a curse" (Gal. 3:10).

3) In 1 Corinthians 1:13-17 Paul says that he had baptized very few of the Corinthians in order that no one could say that he was making converts to himself. But he concludes by saying, "For Christ did not send me to baptize, but to preach the gospel" (1 Cor. 1:17). Paul could never have said that if baptism was an essential part of the gospel necessary for salvation.

4) The dying thief (Luke 23:43) was promised paradise in the presence of the Lord. But he never had the opportunity to be baptized.

5) John 3:5; Titus 3:5; and Ephesians 5:26 are not pertinent because they are not talking about baptism at all. Titus and Ephesians are talking about the spiritual cleansing from sin. The background of John 3:5 is found in Ezekiel 36:25-27. "Then I will sprinkle clean water on you, and you will be clean; I will cleanse you from all your filthiness and from all your idols. Moreover, I will give you a new heart and put a new spirit within you; and I will remove the heart of stone from your flesh and give you a heart of flesh. And I will put My Spirit within you and cause you to walk in My statutes, and you will be careful to observe My ordinances." The water of John 3:5 is the spiritual washing by which we are cleansed from all filthiness.

6) Acts 2:38 and Mark 16:16 mention baptism along with faith not because baptism was necessary for salvation, but because faith in Christ was immediately accompanied by baptism. It was a symbol of the reality which took place when a person believed. But salvation comes from the reality, not from the symbol. It is significant that in the Mark passage the negative statement is "he who has disbelieved shall be condemned." It says "the one who has disbelieved." It does not say "the one who has not been baptized."

We conclude then that in the New Testament baptism was the initiatory rite by which all believers in obedience to Christ signified their identification with Him. It also signified the fact that they had been cleansed from sin, had died to all they were before in Adam, and now were alive to walk in newness of life.

There is a summary statement at the end of the section on the day of Pentecost which gives a description of the activities of the new church (Acts 2:42-47). Verse forty-two is a key verse because it mentions four primary activities of the church. "And they were continually devoting themselves to the apostles' teaching and to fellowship, to the breaking of bread and to prayer."

The Apostles' Teaching

The importance of the apostles' teaching. The teaching of the apostles was central in the life of the early church. In Matthew 28:19-20 the Lord commissioned His disciples, "Go therefore and make disciples of all the nations, baptizing them in the name of the Father and the Son and the Holy Spirit, teaching them to observe all that I commanded you; and lo, I am with you always, even to the end of the age." The apostles were to teach what Christ commanded. They were the ones who were the link to the teaching of the Lord Himself. They were the foundation of the church (Eph. 2:20) because they were the ones commissioned by Christ, taught by Christ, and authorized by Christ to teach His message.

At first the teaching of the apostles was given to the church orally through their preaching and teaching. Gradually that teaching was written down so that we now have the apostles' teaching in the New Testament Scriptures. The New Testament writings were accepted as Scripture and recognized as authoritative because they were apostolic. The apostles were the ones authorized by Christ. He had promised them the Holy Spirit who would guide them into all truth (John 16:13). They were inspired in their teaching. "Which things we also speak, not in words taught by human wisdom, but in those taught by the Spirit, combining spiritual thoughts with spiritual words" (1 Cor. 2:13). Their writings were prophetic scriptures (Rom. 16:25-26).

The apostles' teaching was accepted as the Word of God and was taught in the church from the outset. In the book of Acts growth in the Word is practically synonymous with growth in the church. "And the word of God kept on spreading; and the number of the disciples continued to increase greatly in Jerusalem" (Acts 6:7; cf. 12:24; 13:49; 19:20). In Acts 6 when the apostles found that waiting on tables took too much of their time, they found others to perform that work. "We will devote ourselves to prayer, and to the ministry of the word" (Acts 6:4). They were determined that nothing would take precedence over the ministry of the Word.

The reason for the importance of the apostles' teaching. The apostles' teaching was accepted as Scripture.[21] Because it is Scripture it is inspired and therefore 1) able to give the wisdom that leads to salvation, and 2) is "profitable for teaching, for reproof, for correction, for training in righteousness; that the man of God may be adequate, equipped for every good work" (2 Tim. 3:15-17). The Word of God is the divine means of changing lives.

The extent of the teaching. The teaching of the apostles was comprehensive and thorough. Paul said to the elders of the church at Ephesus that he "did not shrink from declaring to you anything that was profitable" (Acts 20:20). "I did not shrink from declaring to you the whole purpose of God" (Acts 20:27). This included hard doctrines as well as easy. It included unpopular truths as well as popular ones. There were no truths which Paul avoided, because everything God has revealed to us is important for us to know.

The goal of the teaching. The goal of the apostles' teaching was first of all to make disciples (Matt. 28:19). It was not enough just to make converts. The young Christians needed to be nurtured, guided, and brought to maturity and stability through the ministry of the Word.

The goal of the teaching was not just to have the truth terminate with the individual, but to be passed on to others. "The things which you have heard from me in the presence of many witnesses, these entrust to faithful men, who will be able to teach others also" (2 Tim. 2:2).

The goal of the ministry of the teachers in Ephesians 4:11 is that they might equip the saints for the saints themselves to do the work of the ministry. Thus, the goal of the apostles' teaching is to have mature believers, stable in their

---

[21] For the acceptance of New Testament books as Scripture see 1 Timothy 5:18 (Luke) and 2 Peter 3:15-16 (Paul's letters).

Christian lives, following Christ in obedience, and serving Him in ministering to others.

Fellowship

The word "fellowship" means sharing something in common. It was a common word and described a wide variety of relationships from business partnerships, to the common life shared by marriage partners. It was used of philosophers who shared a common view of life and of Plato's ideal society where property was shared in common.

The fellowship of believers in the New Testament was dynamic and exciting. Religious, political, and social barriers were broken down so that there was a real sense of unity, care and concern for one another, and bearing one another's burdens. It was a fellowship which began when the Lord called the disciples to Himself. "And He appointed twelve, that they might be with Him, and that He might send them out to preach" (Mark 3:14). Their relationship to Christ brought them into relationship with each other. John said in his first epistle that he is writing what they have seen and heard "that you also may have fellowship with us; and indeed our fellowship is with the Father, and with His Son Jesus Christ" (1 John 1:3). The fellowship on the vertical level with the Father and the Son created the fellowship on the horizontal level with one another. Those in fellowship with Christ are going to be in fellowship with one another just as a hundred pianos tuned with the same tuning fork are going to be in tune with each other.

The expressions of fellowship. The fellowship of the believers can be seen in the summary sections of Acts 2:43-47 and 4:32-37. In Acts 2:44 "those who had believed were together, and had all things in common." They met together (2:46; 5:1), they ate together (2:46), they worshipped together (2:42, 47), they shared their material goods (2:44-45), and they worked together in the propagation of the gospel. The two summary passages in Acts 2 and Acts 4 indicate the remarkable unity and love that existed among the believers. They had all things in common (Acts 2:44; 4:32). They were willing to sell their possessions and share with those in need (Acts 2:45; 4:34-37). The key is in the phrase "one heart and soul." They were of one mind. They shared their material possessions, not because this was demanded or legislated. It was a completely voluntary action. It was the spontaneous generosity of believers who had a genuine love for one another.

The barriers and differences which would have separated them in the past disappeared. Matthew the tax collector should have been at odds with Simon the

Zealot. The Zealots were an intensely patriotic and anti-Roman party which was violently opposed to any involved in the tax system which collected money for the Roman government. Yet Simon and Matthew were together because of their common relationship to Christ. The disciples had quarreled before the crucifixion as to who was the greatest (Luke 22:24-30). But that self-centeredness had disappeared, and there was a true sense of fellowship. The greatest barrier, that between Jew and Gentile, was also broken down in the same way. In Ephesians 2:11-22 peace was first established with God for those who had once been far from Him, and then peace was established between those who were reconciled to God. The barrier which divided them collapsed.

The nature of fellowship. It is clear that that which binds Christians together is God's Son. In many cases the only thing that those from widely differing backgrounds share in common is Christ. But that is the essential. **"God is faithful, through whom you were called into fellowship with His Son, Jesus Christ our Lord"** (1 Cor. 1:9). Because we share in Christ we share the things of Christ with each other. Christians today often have difficulty developing this kind of fellowship. G. Campbell Morgan says:

> It has become very difficult for Christian people to talk of the things of Christ to each other. They meet together in ordinary life, and they talk of everything except the deepest things of their spiritual life; and that not because they have not deep experience, not because they are unfamiliar with the things of God and His kingdom, but because they have never learned how to help each other in mutual converse concerning them. These early Christians talked together of the things of their spiritual life, and there is no surer way to conserve and strengthen Christian life than that of such fellowship.[22]

Fellowship is not an option for believers but is a necessary part of the life of the individual and the life of the assembly. Christians are meant to live their lives in the community of the church as well as in the midst of the world. Children learn many things from their parents without a word ever being spoken. We also learn many of the most important truths of the Christian life from seeing that truth embodied in the life of another believer. William Kelly observes, "For 'teaching', however valuable, is not enough without 'fellowship'; and few weigh how much

---

[22] G. Campbell Morgan, *The Acts of the Apostles* (Westwood, NJ: Fleming H. Revell Company, n.d.), 92-93.

they owe to the presence and living commentary on the truth which sharing it all together in practice furnishes."[23]

The Breaking of Bread

The names of this act. Acts 2:42 says that the disciples were continually devoting themselves to the breaking of bread. This ordinance has been known by a number of different names. From Acts 2:42 and 20:7 it has been called "the breaking of bread." ("On the first day of the week, when we were gathered together to break bread"). From 1 Corinthians 11:20 it has been known as "the Lord's Supper." ("When you meet together, it is not to eat the Lord's Supper"). Because the Lord gave thanks before He broke the bread and passed the cup it has been called "the Eucharist" (1 Cor. 11:24; Matt. 26:27; Mk. 14:23; Lk. 22:17). The Greek word "to give thanks" is εὐχαριστέω (*eucharisteō*). From 1 Corinthians 10:16 it has been called "the Communion Service" ("The cup of blessing which we bless, is it not the communion of the blood of Christ? The bread which we break, is it not the communion of the body of Christ?" KJV).

The reason for breaking bread. The reason why the church regularly breaks bread is the same reason why the church baptizes believers. It was the command of Christ and it was the practice of the New Testament church. In Matthew and Mark it is not clear whether the Lord was commanding the disciples to eat the bread and drink the cup on that occasion or whether they were to do it as a continuing ordinance. There is a hint in Luke 22:19 as to the repeated nature of the command, "Do this in remembrance of Me." The command "do this" is in the present tense in Greek (ποιεῖτε, *poieite*) which signifies a repeated or a habitual action. It is even clearer in 1 Corinthians 11:24-25 where Christ says, "Do this, as often as you drink it, in remembrance of Me."

It was also the practice of the New Testament church to celebrate the Lord's Supper. In Acts 2:42 they were continually devoting themselves to the breaking of bread. In Acts 20:7 they came together to break bread. There were a number of disorders in the meeting of the church at Corinth so that Paul says, "When you meet together, it is not to eat the Lord's Supper" (1 Cor. 11:20). But this shows that the purpose of their coming together should have been to eat the Lord's Supper in a proper way (cf. 1 Cor. 10:16-17).

---

[23] William Kelly, *An Exposition of the Acts of the Apostles* (3d ed. London: C. A. Hammond, 1952 [= 1914]), 29.

The significance of the Lord's Supper. The meaning of the Lord's Supper is to be seen in the words of Christ at its institution. "The Lord Jesus in the night in which He was betrayed took bread; and when He had given thanks, He broke it, and said, 'This is My body, which is for you; do this in remembrance of Me.' In the same way He took the cup also, after supper, saying, 'This cup is the new covenant in My blood; do this, as often as you drink it, in remembrance of Me.' For as often as you eat this bread and drink the cup, you proclaim the Lord's death until He comes" (1 Cor. 11:23-26).

1) The bread and the cup are symbols of the body and the blood of Christ. This is the normal way of taking the words of Christ, "This is My body." "This cup is the new covenant in My blood."[24] They are symbols which are meant to remind us of Christ. "Do this in remembrance of Me" (1 Cor. 11:24, cf. v. 25). The word "remembrance" (ἀνάμνησις, *anamnēsis*) means "a reminder, a calling to mind." The symbols remind us of Christ and are designed to bring Him consciously to our mind. The bread specifically represents His body. It is that body which He assumed at the incarnation when He became man. It therefore refers to His complete human nature. It was the body in which He bore our sins on the cross (1 Pet. 2:24). The eternal Son became mortal man in order that He might be subject to death so as to die for our sins (cf. Heb. 2:14-15).

The cup, or specifically the contents of the cup, represents His blood which was shed as a ransom price for our sins (Eph. 1:7; 1 Pet. 1:18-19). It is that blood

---

[24] Roman Catholics take these words literally. They hold to a doctrine of transubstantiation where the bread and wine are transformed by the consecration of the priest into the literal body and blood of Christ. They retain the sensory characteristics of bread and wine, but in reality they are no longer bread or wine. They are the actual body and blood of Christ. Lutherans also hold that the sacrament is literally the body and blood of the Lord. They do not say that the bread and wine are changed and cease to be what they were before. But the true body and blood of Christ are present in, with, and under the bread and wine so that the participant literally eats Christ's body and drinks His blood. This has been referred to as consubstantiation.

The symbolical nature of the Lord's word should be manifest in several ways. 1) The Lord's body was there at the institution clearly separate from the bread. His hand was holding the bread. 2) Even Roman Catholics and Lutherans do not attribute the same literalness to the words concerning the cup. "This cup is the new covenant in my blood" (1 Cor. 11:25). The cup is not changed into the new covenant nor is the cup the new covenant. The contents of the cup represent His blood. But His blood is not itself the new covenant. Rather His shed blood is the foundation for the new covenant. But if one insists that the words, "This is my body," be taken literally, then the words concerning the cup must also be taken literally. 3) The words, "this is my body," are figurative just as many other expressions of Christ are figurative. "I am the vine." "I am the door." "I am the light of the world." The fact that these words are figurative seems obvious, and the words at the Lord's Supper should be taken in the same way.

shed for us that secures the forgiveness of sins (Eph. 1:7) and is the foundation of the new covenant which is grounded on the forgiveness of sins (Jer. 31:34).

The primary significance of the Lord's Supper must be seen in these words, "Do this in remembrance of Me." These are the specific words used by our Lord at the institution of the supper. The symbols are to remind us of Christ. It does not say that believers are to be occupied with their salvation, but with Christ Himself. It is in remembrance of *Me*. Further it is not Christ as a teacher or benefactor, but as a sacrifice. The Corinthians were treating the Lord's Supper as an ordinary meal. They needed to reflect on the Lord's death and the implications of it for them. As one reflects on the person of Christ and His sacrificial death for us, the appropriate response is that of thanksgiving, praise, and worship.

2) It is an announcement of the basic facts of the gospel. Paul says that "as often as you eat this bread and drink the cup, you proclaim (καταγγέλετε, *katangellete*) the Lord's death until He comes" (1 Cor. 11:26). The word "proclaim" is often used in the book of Acts for preaching the gospel (Acts 4:2; 13:5, 38; 16:17; 17:3, 13, 23; 1 Cor. 2:1; 9:14; Phil. 1:18; Col. 1:28). The breaking of the bread and the drinking of the cup are a silent proclamation of the fact and significance of the Lord's death. To whom is this proclamation made? To God, to the world, or to one another? Since the Lord's Supper was designed for the worship of believers, any unbelievers would only be there by chance. It is not likely that it was designed to be a witness to them. Rather this is the collective confession of believers to one another and to God as to the center of their faith. All centers around Christ and His substitutionary sacrifice for our sin. When He comes again and we are in His presence, there will no longer be any need for reminders. This is therefore a temporary ordinance, lasting only until the end of this age, "until He comes." Charles Hodge says:

> "As the Passover was a perpetual commemoration of the deliverance out of Egypt, and a prediction of the coming and death of the Lamb of God, who was to bear the sins of the world; so the Lord's Supper is at once the commemoration of the death of Christ and a pledge of his coming the second time without sin unto salvation."[25]

3) The eating of the bread and the drinking of the cup are symbols of our faith in Christ. John 6:53-55 is a passage which has an indirect bearing on the

---

[25] Charles Hodge, *An Exposition of the First Epistle to the Corinthians* (1864, reprint ed., Grand Rapids: Eerdmans, 1969, 229-30.

Lord's Supper. Our Lord says, "Truly, truly, I say to you, unless you eat the flesh of the Son of Man and drink His blood, you have no life in yourselves. He who eats My flesh and drinks My blood has eternal life, and I will raise him up on the last day. For My flesh is true food, and My blood is true drink." This is not a passage which is talking primarily about the Lord's Supper. He says in verse 53 that "unless you eat the flesh of the Son of Man and drink His blood, you have no life in yourselves." The requirement for salvation is not the performance of a ritual, but faith in Christ. In the discourse in John 6 where Christ says that He is the bread of life He uses a very strong figure. Eternal life comes from the spiritual nourishment which is obtained by feeding on Christ, eating His flesh and blood. This refers to partaking of Him spiritually by faith.

John 6 is not referring to the Lord's Supper per se. But in the supper when we eat the bread and drink the wine, we symbolize the fact that we are feeding on Christ in the sense of John 6. We are trusting in Him to give us life and sustain us in that life. Faith in Christ is not just a momentary, one time thing. It continues, and we symbolize in the Lord's Supper our continuing trust in Christ for our salvation.

4) The Lord's Supper also symbolizes the unity of the body of Christ. 1 Corinthians 10:16-17 says, "Is not the cup of blessing which we bless a sharing in the blood of Christ? Is not the bread which we break a sharing in the body of Christ? Since there is one bread, we who are many are one body; for we all partake of the one bread." Each individual breaks a fragment of the bread for himself and taking it indicates his individual fellowship with Christ on the grounds of His sacrificial death.[26] There is communion with Christ. But the fact that all of the believers do this in partaking of the one loaf is an indication of the oneness of the body of Christ. There is a vertical fellowship with Christ, but there is also a horizontal fellowship with one another.

It is a great tragedy in the history of the church that the ordinance which is supposed to symbolize the unity of the body of Christ has become a means of its division. Some believers are not allowed to have communion with other believers. One church will not accept those who come from a different group. Unless we "accept one another, just as Christ also accepted us to the glory of God" (Rom. 15:7), we disobey the Lord and deny the unity of the body of Christ. Any

---

[26] The "we" in these verses is not the "we" of the apostles or certain church leaders. It is the "we" of all believers who partake of the Lord's Supper. Each believer breaks the bread for himself. There is no hint that a minister or clergyman is the one who dispenses the elements to the others. Each one partakes himself.

believer who is in fellowship with the Lord Jesus Christ should also be in fellowship with us (unless we are the ones out of fellowship with Him). How can Christ invite one of His own to His table and be willing to sit with him and have fellowship with him, but we are not willing to sit at the same table?

The frequency of the Lord's Supper. How often the church should celebrate the Lord's Supper is only suggested in the New Testament. There is no specific commandment. As stated before, the command to "do this" in the present tense indicates that this is to be done repeatedly. The statement "**as often as you eat this bread and drink the cup**" likewise indicates that the Lord's Supper is to be celebrated repeatedly. But neither indicates how often. Acts 2:42 says that "**they were continually devoting themselves to...the breaking of bread**" which would indicate that this was not only repeated, but frequent. Acts 2:46 says that "**day by day continuing with one mind in the temple, and breaking bread from house to house, they were taking their meals together with gladness and sincerity of heart.**" This indicates a daily breaking of bread, but the problem here is that the same expression is used both for the Lord's Supper and for the daily meals. Both were indications of the fellowship in the early church. There is no way of proving which is in view in Acts 2:46. Acts 20:7 says, "**On the first day of the week, when we were gathered together to break bread.**" Here the specific purpose of gathering was to break bread. This shows the emphasis placed on this ordinance. The verse suggests that the first day of the week was the time when believers met to break bread. But again one cannot prove that this was done every first day of the week. 1 Corinthians 11:18ff. is actually one of the most pertinent passages for this. Paul criticizes the Corinthians for the way they were wrongly celebrating the Lord's Supper and he instructs them as to its proper observance.[27] He says that because of abuses "**when you meet together, it is not to eat the Lord's Supper.**" This would imply that when they do meet, it should be to eat the Lord's Supper. The Lord's Supper was a proper part of their gathering each time they met together. This implies that if the church met weekly on the first day of the week, then the Lord's Supper was also celebrated then. In fact the observance

---

[27] It is clear from 1 Corinthians 11:21-22 that the Lord's Supper was celebrated at Corinth as part of a full meal which was called a love feast (cf. Jude 12). But instead of sharing the food which they brought with others, some who had more food were selfishly keeping it to themselves. Some who had little were hungry, while others were overindulging and even became drunk. The love feast itself was not intended to be a normative practice which was required in the church. Paul says in 1 Corinthians 11:22 and 11:34 that the normal meal can be eaten in one's own home. What is important for the church is that which the Lord commanded to be observed. It is to be observed according to His instructions and in a decent and orderly fashion.

of the Lord's Supper on a weekly basis (and in some cases even daily) prevailed in the church until the time of the Reformation.

Prayer

The disciples met together in constant prayer in Acts 1 waiting for the fulfillment of the promise of the Holy Spirit (1:14). In Acts 2:42 they were continually devoting themselves to prayer. Individual prayer is seen in the life of Christ and the apostles. But it was also the practice of the church to pray corporately. They were instructed by Paul to pray continually (1 Thes. 5:17). They were to pray for all the saints (Eph. 6:18) and even for all men everywhere (1 Tim. 2:8). They were to pray in their times of care and anxiety that God would meet all their needs (Phil. 4:6). They prayed for Peter's release from prison, and Paul asks for prayer for his deliverance from unbelievers when he was in danger, in prison, or under attack (Rom. 15:30-31; Phil. 1:19; 2 Cor. 1:11). Paul frequently asks for prayer concerning his preaching of the gospel that he would be fearless, that he would preach clearly, that there would be an open door for the message, and that it would spread rapidly (Eph. 6:19-20; Col. 4:4; Col. 4:3; 2 Thes. 3:1). The church prayed when seeking guidance (Acts 13:3), and those who received a financial gift from other Christians naturally prayed for those who gave to them (2 Cor. 9:14).

Prayer is the act of believers who recognize their needs and their own insufficiency. The assembly that is at ease and is self-satisfied is not going to be praying. An assembly which is active and involved in the spiritual warfare which is thrust upon us as we seek to live in a hostile world is going to be characterized by prayer.

Discipline

Church discipline might seem to be an activity of the church which is of a fundamentally different character from subjects like biblical teaching, worship, prayer, and fellowship. These are positive. Yet church discipline seems to be negative, a way of punishing those who do not conform. This is a mistaken view of church discipline. Church discipline in the New Testament is always viewed as a positive thing which is designed for the benefit of the individual, the church, and the glory of God. God's discipline of Christians is for their welfare just as every father disciplines his own children whom he loves (Heb. 12:6-7). The discipline of the church is no different. It is to restore the sinning Christian (Gal. 6:1). It is for his ultimate salvation (1 Cor. 5:5). It is to keep sin from spreading in the church (1 Cor. 5:6-7). It is a warning to other believers not to fall into the same sin (1 Tim. 5:20). It is to keep the name of God from being blasphemed (cf. 1 Tim. 6:1).

The ground for discipline. The basis of church discipline is found in the character of God as holy. The first instance of discipline in the church was taken by God Himself in the case of Ananias and Sapphira (Acts 5:1-11). Because of their hypocrisy and lie in pretending to have a spirituality which was not real, God took them in death. There was no warning and no opportunity for repentance. Peter in this case did not cause the death of either. He rebuked Ananias who fell dead by the judgment of God. In Sapphira's case he announced her impending death, but it was God's act, not Peter's words which brought it about. God was teaching the young church that the free and gracious forgiveness of sins was not an encouragement to take sin lightly or a license to indulge in sin. God is holy and His church is holy. This was an object lesson which brought great fear on the whole church (Acts 5:11).

The authority for the church to exercise discipline is found in the numerous commands which are found throughout the New Testament. "Those who sin are to be rebuked publicly" (1 Tim. 5:20 NIV). "Keep away from every brother who is idle and does not live according to the teaching you received from us.... If anyone does not obey our instruction in this letter, take special note of him. Do not associate with him, in order that he may feel ashamed" (2 Thes. 3:6, 14). "Warn a divisive person once, and then warn him a second time. After that, have nothing to do with him" (Tit. 3:10). "Watch out for those who cause divisions and put obstacles in your way that are contrary to the teaching you have learned. Keep away from them" (Rom. 16:17). "But now I am writing you that you must not associate with anyone who calls himself a brother but is sexually immoral or greedy, an idolater or a slanderer, a drunkard or a swindler. With such a man do not even eat. What business is it of mine to judge those outside the church? Are you not to judge those inside?" (1 Cor. 5:11-12).

Sin is like leaven which spreads and infects and corrupts (1 Cor. 5:6). It must therefore be purged out (1 Cor. 5:7).

The attitude in discipline. The church must be very careful in this area to avoid extremes. With the church growth movement which is so popular there is a tendency to have large churches where individuals can participate in the services without being well-known. Because of the desire to get people to feel comfortable in church so that they will continue attending, care is taken to offend no one. This type of attitude is extremely reluctant to discipline.

On the other hand many have the tendency toward strictness and severity. The absolute holiness of God demands absolute holiness in the church. Every offense is a ground for excommunication. When we consider the fact that we all continue in the flesh and continue to sin, the limited and infrequent examples of discipline in the New Testament should make us cautious. God in His grace and mercy does not judge all of our hypocrisy and pretense as He did with Ananias and Sapphira. The Corinthian church had many deviations, yet only in the case of the man who was living in an incestuous relationship was the church instructed to put him out of fellowship. It is beyond our ability to keep the church completely sinless.

Scripture looks at discipline as a loving act which is done in concern for the care and welfare of the individual. "Brothers, if someone is caught in a sin, you who are spiritual should restore him gently. But watch yourself, or you also may be tempted" (Gal. 6:1). There is a humility here and a spirit of love and gentleness which the stern defenders of God's holiness overlook. The apostle Paul also recognizes that different individuals are to be treated differently. In 1 Thessalonians 5:14 he says, "And we urge you, brothers, warn those who are idle, encourage the timid, help the weak, be patient with everyone." Some who are more willful are to be warned. But there are others who are timid and weak who are to be encouraged and helped. Paul particularly urges an attitude of patience. A person who has repented needs to receive love and forgiveness (2 Cor. 2:7-8). This is different from the indefinite probation even after repentance which produces discouragement and which can be used by Satan (2 Cor. 2:7,11).

The procedure for discipline. There are two principles which are taught in the procedure of discipline.[28] 1) The knowledge of the sin should be kept to the smallest group possible. If God has not made a sin known publicly, then we do not need to. On the other hand, if He has allowed it to become a matter of general knowledge, then it needs to be dealt with openly. 2) Disciplinary measures should increase in strength until there is repentance.

The first principle is seen in Matthew 18:15-20. Private confrontation by an individual is followed by a group of two or three. This is then followed by the consideration of the church. The matter only advances to the next level if the person refuses to listen. It would seem appropriate to add, as an intermediary step between the group of two or three and the whole church, the bringing of the matter before the elders.

---

[28] See Wayne Grudem, *Systematic Theology* (Grand Rapids: Zondervan, 1994), 897.

It also seems that there were various forms of discipline depending on the type of offense. Some are to be admonished (1 Thes. 5:14), others warned (Tit. 3:10), others rebuked (2 Tim. 4:2; Tit. 1:13; 2:15). The first warning is followed by another, and then the church is to have nothing to do with that person (Tit. 3:10). In 2 Thessalonians 3:6, 14 the church is not to associate with those who are idle and disobedient. This does not seem to be the full excommunication of 1 Corinthians 5:5. It is meant to be the warning to one who is a brother (2 Thes. 3:15). When all steps have failed and the person still does not respond, "let him be to you as a Gentile and a tax-gatherer" (Matt. 18:17). Paul says that the impenitent sinner is to be removed from the midst of the church (1 Cor. 5:2, 13). Believers are not to associate with that person (1 Cor. 5:9). In verse 5 he says that such a person is to be "delivered to Satan for the destruction of his flesh, that his spirit may be saved in the day of the Lord Jesus." In putting the believer outside the church he is delivering him to that sphere where Satan rules. Paul expects that this will result in physical chastisement, sickness and even death. The world lies in the power of the evil one (1 John 5:19). The devil holds the power of death. But he can only touch the body. The purpose of God in not allowing a Christian to continue in sin is "that his spirit may be saved in the day of the Lord Jesus" (1 Cor. 5:5). He will take the believer in death rather than let him continue in sin (cf. 1 Cor. 11:30-32).

The effect of discipline. The goal of all discipline is the restoration of the sinning individual. This is seen in all of the passages which have been referred to. Discipline can cause a person to be ashamed (2 Thes. 3:14) and sorrowful (2 Cor. 2:7), but it is a sorrow which leads to repentance (cf. 2 Cor. 7:9-10). The effect of discipline on the church is warning (1 Tim. 5:20) and fear (Acts 5:11). We should also be humbled, knowing our own sinful propensity (Gal. 6:1).

The guardian of the church. The holiness of God, the sinfulness of man (even believers), and the fact that we can only judge open, manifest sin may cause some to be uneasy. How can we guard the honor and holiness of God in the church? The fact is that we cannot, and it is not our responsibility. Most sins are hidden from our eyes. Our responsibility as individuals is to judge our own hearts. "Let a man examine himself, and so let him eat of the bread and drink of the cup (1 Cor. 11:28). Sins which are clearly evident are to be dealt with by the church (1 Cor. 5:12). But the ultimate guardian of the holiness and honor of God is God Himself. When Christians are sinning secretly, partaking at the Lord's Supper in a way that dishonors Him, seemingly getting away with their disobedience, God Himself will take action. There were some at Corinth who were weak and sickly. Some even slept, that is, they died (1 Cor. 11:30). Paul says that because they did not judge themselves, they were disciplined by God. God Himself will deal with those matters which we are unable or unwilling to deal with.

The Ordinances and Their Effect

Baptism and the Lord's Supper have usually been considered in a separate way as special ordinances of the church. They are unique in that they were instituted by Christ Himself, and they both involve an outward rite which symbolizes some spiritual truth.[29]

There has been a great controversy in the history of the Christian church as to the effects of these ordinances. In Roman Catholicism they are called sacraments and are viewed as actually conveying saving grace. Through baptism a person is born again, and through the Eucharist he is spiritually strengthened and receives the forgiveness of sins.

The opposite of Roman Catholic sacramentalism would be the view that the ordinances are simply symbols and symbolical actions which represent divine truths. The Lord's Supper aids us in thinking about the significance of Christ's death for us, while baptism helps us think about our death to sin and our new life with Christ. But the spiritual reality is conveyed on the basis of the objective work of Christ through faith. The spiritual truth is valid apart from the symbolical rite.

Many of the Reformed would take a position in between. They reject the view that the sacraments magically or mechanically convey saving grace. But they also object to the symbolical view as too subjective. They say that the ordinances do not just portray something, they actually do something.

The issue is sometimes confused. The issue is not whether God uses these ordinances to strengthen and bless His people.[30] The issue is also not whether

---

[29] Roman Catholicism calls these sacraments and includes five others: confirmation, penance, extreme unction, holy orders, and marriage. Of these the first four have no basis in Scripture. Confirmation is the ratification of the baptism of infants. Penance takes the scriptural confession of sins to God and makes it an official church act where you confess to the priest and receive forgiveness through the church. Extreme unction (the last rites) has no basis in Scripture, and holy orders is taking the Old Testament priesthood into the church. In doing so the priesthood of all believers is for all practical purposes denied. The only one of these which is scriptural is marriage. But marriage is the general ordinance of God for the human race and not a specific ordinance of the church.

[30] Some would signify this by calling them means of grace.

Christ is spiritually present at the Lord's Supper.[31] The issue is whether He is present at the Lord's Supper in a different way than when He is present where two or three are gathered together in His name to listen to the teaching of the Word (Matt. 18:20). The issue is whether there is a special grace or a special blessing conveyed through baptism and the Lord's Supper that is different from the kind of blessing which we receive when we read the Word and respond to the Lord in our daily life. "Calvin was not satisfied with Zwingli's view that the Lord's Supper provides no other communion with Christ than the benefits obtained for us at the cross."[32] If the Lord's Supper only conveys the normal blessings of God, does that make it superfluous?

The trouble with these views is that no one can define clearly what that special presence of Christ is or what that special blessing or grace is which is uniquely conveyed through the ordinances.[33] God calls us to exercise faith in His Son who died as our substitute, paying the penalty for our sins. The faith that we exhibit at baptism is the same faith that we first had before we were baptized. It is because of that faith that we get baptized. But I do not look to my baptism for the assurance of salvation. I look to the Savior who died for me, and I look to Him with the same faith that I had when I first believed. When I partake of the Lord's Supper, I remember the saving work of Christ on the cross, and I renew my faith and trust in Him. The Lord's Supper calls me back to the same faith I had when I first believed. This is not to be dismissed as subjectivism. The objective reality is the saving work of Christ on the cross which reconciles us to God. The subjective means on our part through which Christ's work becomes effective for us is faith. The faith manifested in baptism and the Lord's Supper is no different than the faith which is exercised at any time by the Christian. The blessing is therefore the same in each case. The ordinances are symbols of the reality but are not the reality themselves.

CONCLUSION

We have discussed three areas of the church: the government of the church, the ministry of the church, and the activities of the church. We have argued that the local church of the New Testament was governed by a plurality of elders and

---

[31] Zwingli affirmed this as well as Calvin.

[32] G. C. Berkouwer, *The Sacraments* (Grand Rapids: Eerdmans, 1969), 226.

[33] We are not concerned here with the sacramental theology of Roman Catholicism or Lutheranism. Both of these do clearly define what they mean by the presence of Christ and the saving grace conveyed through the ordinances.

deacons, the ministry of the church was by each believer exercising his or her spiritual gifts, and the activities of the church included baptism, the teaching of the Word of God, fellowship, the breaking of bread, prayer, and church discipline. We would also conclude that these things are normative for the church and this should be the description of each local church today.

However, we have not argued that these are the marks of the church which are necessary for a church to be a true church. It is not the government of the church which makes it the church. It is not having a proper ministry. It is not certain forms of service. Wherever believers are gathered together with Christ in their midst and the gospel taught, there is the church of Jesus Christ. We would not conclude that the wide variety of church organizations, denominational divisions and structures, clerical and lay ministries, as well as liturgical and non-liturgical services are unimportant. But it would be wrong to cut off from the church those who truly belong to Christ.

Nor would we try to argue that any church which follows the organization, ministry, and activities of the New Testament church is automatically going to be a good church which is blessed by God. Things such as true devotion to Christ, the power of the Holy Spirit, true doctrine, obedience, dependence upon Christ, the fruit of the Spirit, all of these are essential to a vital, healthy, growing church. Correct outward forms cannot be a substitute for the inner realities of a vital relationship to Christ. But given the inner reality, there is blessing in following the norms of the church given to us in the New Testament.

THE AUTONOMY
OF LOCAL CHURCHES

BY JOHN A. SPENDER[1]

INTRODUCTION

Foundations are important, and they must be looked for in the right place. As the old hymn says:

> How firm a foundation, ye saints of the Lord,
> Is laid for your faith in His excellent Word.

In speaking of this foundation, Paul the apostle cautions every man to **"take heed how he buildeth upon it"**(1 Cor. 3:10). Whatever is built at the local level will be tested by constant encounters with the forces of darkness, **"the gates of hell,"** as our Lord put it. Therefore the way a congregation conducts its own internal affairs will affect its ability to stand firm over time, to relate to other congregations, and to represent the mystical church before the world.[2]

Much has been written about church polity, but a large part of it either ignores the subject of local church autonomy altogether or else treats it within a given denomination. More thought needs to be given to the biblical idea of autonomy as providing a perfect balance for that healthy intercommunion of local churches which is pleasing to God and which saints rightly desire.

The goal of this paper is to encourage an understanding of and appreciation for a truly biblical autonomy in local church government. It is one in which the churches are self-governing, self-supporting, and self-propagating. At the same time they sustain a happy, working relationship with one another, so that

---

[1] Jack Spender has been working in central Connecticut since 1972 planting new assemblies, teaching the Bible, and discipling new believers. He is currently involved in a new assembly in Waterbury, Connecticut.

[2] This refers not so much to corporate evangelism of which little is said in Scripture, but to the sense of 1 Timothy 3:15 where the church is "the pillar and ground of the truth."

individual saints are edified and the mission of the church to reach the lost world for Christ is stimulated. The overall result is that God is glorified.

LOCAL CHURCH AUTONOMY: BIBLICAL AND VITAL

DEFINITIONS: AUTONOMY AND INDEPENDENCE

The word *autonomous* comes from the Greek words αὐτός (*autos*, self) and νόμος (*nomos*, law or rule) and refers to the power and right of self-government. At first glance the word *independent* appears to be a synonym of *autonomous* meaning "not subject to the authority of another." However, there is an alternate meaning, "not affected or influenced in action or opinion by others." This has come to be the primary sense in popular usage. An independent person thinks for himself and does his own thing regardless of what other people think. When applied to the government of local churches, *autonomous* is more suitable than the broader term *independent*, which can suggest a general isolationism. In fact when referring to the fellowship of local churches, the opposite of independence should prevail. Churches should be interdependent.

Although the words *autonomy* or *autonomous* are not used in Scripture, the idea represented by them is a biblical, practical, and logical necessity.[3]

ON THE UNIVERSAL AND LOCAL CHURCH RELATIONSHIP

Before investigating the nature of church government, it is important to note that the word *church* or ἐκκλησία (*ekklēsia*) is used two different ways in Scripture.[4] It is used to refer to the whole company of God's elect from Pentecost to the Rapture. The "universal church," as it is usually called, is that great invisible company revealed through Paul to be the body of Christ. A substantial part of the church in this sense is already in heaven. By contrast the "local church" is the visible, earthly company of professing believers who gather in a particular place. The large majority of the one hundred fifteen occurrences of the word *ekklesia* in the New Testament are used in this second way.

---

[3] David Hesselgrave (*Planting Churches Cross Culturally* [Grand Rapids: Baker, 1980], 188) suggests "Christonomy" instead of "autonomy" as more accurately describing the true source of government.

[4] For an extended discussion of the meaning of the word *ekklesia* see George Johnston, *The Doctrine of the Church in the New Testament* (Cambridge, Cambridge University Press, 1943).

One reason why there are so many different views on local church government is the complexity of the relationships involved. The local church must do more than just attend to its own administrative functions. It must be loyal to Christ the Head, responsive and submissive to the Holy Spirit who indwells it, and also seek to be rightly related to the larger universal church of which it is only a part. Since each local church is a microcosm of the whole, the need for self-determination must never obscure the truth of the one body, the spiritual interconnection of all the members.

AUTHORITY IN THE CHURCH

Without authority there can be no government and all hope for order is lost. Simply stated, authority in the church comes from Christ the Head and is delegated to men called elders who are raised to function according to the authoritative Scriptures under the sovereign direction of the Holy Spirit.

At its heart church government is an authority issue, and discerning its ultimate source is not difficult, at least for Bible-believing Christians. Problems arise, however, when trying to decide the human agency through which that authority is mediated. Some see it as an unbroken chain of apostolic succession. Some allow official bodies between Christ and the local congregation. Others do not. Even within the local church there is much disagreement over where the authority resides. Volumes have been written to address the question as to whether authority is conveyed to the whole church or to its office bearers only.[5] Besides this there is the thorny matter of the names, number, selection, and function of leaders in the church.

A brief survey of the most important passages will form the next section of this study.

TRACING THE ROOTS OF THE PRINCIPLE OF AUTONOMY

ISRAEL AND THE OLD TESTAMENT THEOCRACY

There is not a single doctrine in the New Testament concerning which the Old Testament is silent, including the study of ecclesiology, the doctrine of the church.

---

[5] Cf. James Bannermann (*The Church of Christ*, 2 vols. [Edinburgh: T & T Clark, 1868], 2:260-331), who distinguishes between Presbyterian, where authority resides with office bearers only, Episcopal, who hold to apostolic succession, and Independent (as Baptists), where authority resides with congregation. A. R. Hay (*New Testament Order for Church and Missionary*

Although it does not mention the church directly, the Old Testament abounds with beautiful pictures and foreshadowings of the church which are filled with instruction. Consider some of the great distinctives of God's earthly people Israel and the parallels found in the New Testament teaching about the church.

Israel was an elect nation, called out of a foreign land, redeemed by power and by blood. As a theocracy, the supreme ruler of Israel was Jehovah, whose authority was manifested through human instruments whom He determined. The people were to be separate from the surrounding nations, and they learned that submission or rebellion in their relationship to the Lord would bring corresponding blessing or chastisement. Finally, the future of Israel was determined and settled by grace.

It is immediately apparent from this brief outline how an appreciation of the history of the nation Israel will contribute greatly to an understanding of the background in which the church was born. The influence of the old upon the new can hardly be exaggerated. Among other things Israel was not to look outside of itself for defense, resources, or form of government. The prophets spoke repeatedly against turning to Egypt for help. God had instituted a visible form of government through which He would work with His people. To look at the surrounding nations with the desire to "be like them" was a rejection of the Lord more than a rejection of His prophets.[6] The governments of surrounding nations were connected with the idols of their own making, and this produced a form of government whose authority was limited to the power of the then ruling class.

In post-exilic Israel the call of the nation back to a restored temple worship as the visible expression of God's presence was important in view of the inactivity of the royal dynasty of the line of David. During the so-called four hundred silent years many problems remained, but idolatry did not reappear, and Jehovah was acknowledged as the sovereign deity. Rome, the dominant military power, determined to maintain order in the face of prevailing fierce Jewish nationalism. Added to this were the ever increasing Messianic expectations of the time which brought a spiritual side to the question. Throughout the gospels one sees the confusion and intertwining of the religious and political thinking of the day, and these matters were often used by His enemies against the Lord.

[Argentina: New Testament Missionary Union, 1947], 132) says, "It is this doing of Christ's will through the church that gives the church its authority. It is in this way and on this ground that what is done by the Church on Earth is done in Heaven." One special contribution of brethren assemblies has been the pleasing balance of decision-making between the elders and the congregation.

[6] Cf. 1 Samuel 8:12.

As to nationality the Lord and the disciples were all Jewish. The first churches were also. The place of religious gathering in Israel was the synagogue with its elders, and the earliest Christians met both in the temple and in the synagogues. One common term used to describe the Old Testament people of God was "the assembly of the congregation of Israel," a fact to be kept in mind when trying to comprehend the words of Jesus "I will build MY *ekklesia.*" (Matt. 16:24).[7]

Therefore when the Lord, standing on Gentile soil, asked His disciples whom they did confess Him to be, the resulting dialogue was full of deep meaning and portent for the future. Following Peter's great confession, the Lord spoke for the first time of the church that He would build. The nature of it must be supernatural and universal for its conflict would not be against earthly powers, but against the gates of hell. Its triumph would be built on the revelation from the Father of who Christ really is, and its government would involve spiritual questions of binding and loosing supported by the counsels of heaven.

Yet in all of this, the church would also have a local and visible expression which could hear and preside over the smallest complaints among men. This is seen in the other gospel reference to the church (Matt. 18:15-20).

Three passages in the gospels where our Lord imparted to His disciples the authority to act in His name should be noticed in particular. In Matthew 16, after disclosing His purpose to build His church, He gave to Peter keys that would unlock doors long barred by hatred and malice and spoke to him of heaven's participation in binding and loosing. Then in Matthew 18, dealing with the subject of resolving grievances, He widened this authority to include the twelve and assured them of His presence in the midst as the true source of their authority. In John 20 He broadened the scope of the disciple's authority to represent Him in dealing even with sin. Much discussion has revolved around the nature and extent of what has been conferred, and we join with those who understand the servant to be but a channel through which the Lord Himself works these things. Nevertheless, it is evident that the church as a community

---

[7] Cf. Ex. 12:6. The Hebrew *qāhāl* is usually rendered *ekklēsia* in the LXX. See F. J. A. Hort, *The Christian Ekklesia* (London: Macmillan, 1900), 5. A. C. Headlam (*The Doctrine of the Church and Christian Reunion* [London: John Murray, 1921], 16) says, "As employed by Christianity, the word *ekklēsia* embodied a new conception for which the world was ready, which was the spiritual fulfillment of principles innate in Judaism, and awaiting development; which only came into being in the new life and revelation through Jesus Christ." J. M. Davies (*The Lord and the Churches* [Kansas City, KS: Walterick Publishers, 1967], 17-19) has a good discussion on the Hebrew and Greek background of the *ekklēsia.* He concludes, "Christ then took hold of a word in common use when He said 'My Ecclesia.'"

has been given by the Master the power and the right to do His work. This is an authority that is not civil, but spiritual.

THE DAWN OF NEW TESTAMENT AUTONOMY—THE EARLY APOSTOLIC ERA

Having briefly considered the background of the Old Testament and the Gospels, we turn to a historical survey of the book of Acts in four sections. References to the epistles will be noticed at the appropriate places.

- From Pentecost to Stephen's death, Acts 1–7.
- From the great persecution to the first missionary journey, Acts 8–12
- The three missionary journeys, Acts 13–21.
- Paul's trip to Rome to the end of the first century, Acts 22–28.

From Pentecost to Stephen's Death, Acts 1–7

On the day of Pentecost[8] the infant church of about one hundred twenty persons was suddenly swelled by the addition of three thousand new converts. We have only a slight record of what was involved in managing such numbers of people, but undoubtedly there were many needs and problems which called for decisions and decision-makers, i.e., some form of government. In this matter three things stand out in the earliest chapters of the book of Acts:

- The clear and decisive leadership supplied by the apostles with a resultant order in the community.[9]
- The sense of the Lord's real presence by His Spirit among them.[10]
- The absence of any formal governmental structure or suggestion that outside civil or religious authority should be consulted.

The church was behaving more as a body than as an organization. This was,

---

[8] The argument of A. H. Strong (*Systematic Theology* [Valley Forge, PA: Judson Press, 1907], 900) that the church was already in existence before the day of Pentecost in order to be added to (as in Acts 2:47) is weak. Through this scheme, some have held that John the Baptist was to be included in the church.

[9] The emphasis of the record is not so much on administrative ruling and decision-making, as on boldness of witness and willingness to suffer persecution. It was understandable then why people had confidence in the apostles as true leaders.

[10] The Holy Spirit is mentioned seventeen times in the six chapters between Pentecost and the death of Stephen.

of course, by design. The apostles were not officials but shepherds, able to help the new believers pursue and follow the Head, the Lord who was in their midst.[11] The idea of "government" seems almost out of place, as the emphasis was on the organic or "body life" of the church.

Nevertheless, the administrative side was not lacking as witnessed by the orderly distribution of goods and money brought to the apostles by those who had sold possessions for the poor (Acts 4:35), or the decision to delegate to chosen men the growing work of caring for the widows (Acts 6:1-7). The Acts 6 passage is historic. In a few brief verses, it is understood that:

- The church's involvement in ministries requiring administrative functions had continued to expand.
- The twelve apostles were accepted leaders having a consolidated authority and clear convictions about priorities.
- Large numbers of disciples were being involved in decision-making on significant matters.
- The actual conferring of authority to the newly-chosen deacons[12] came from the apostles, not from the multitude.

Probably the most important insights to be gained from these early records are how the apostles made decisions and how they passed on their leadership to others. It is clear from the foregoing that the process of the apostle's decision-making was handled within the local community. The next section will shed some light on how they passed on their leadership to others.

From the Great Persecution to the First Missionary Journey, Acts 8–12

Within the central chapters of the book of Acts the continuing expansion of the church is described, and it is here and in the supporting evidence of the epistles that we must study the formation of New Testament church government.

The Lord Jesus had spoken to His disciples of being witnesses throughout the world, but for a time incentive to move from Jerusalem was lacking. The church continued to expand apparently without thought of a work among the

---

[11] Acts 4:23-31 is a significant passage because the persecuted apostles reported to their own company and together turned to the Lord in prayer, as it were, instinctively taking their problems to the real source of all authority in their midst.

[12] E. M. Blaiklock (The Acts of the Apostles, TNTC [Grand Rapids: Eerdmans, 75]) calls the Seven "special officers appointed to meet a special need."

Gentiles. After the death of Stephen in Acts 7 a brief but ominous record signaled change. "At that time there was a great persecution against the church which was at Jerusalem; and they were all scattered abroad" (Acts 8:1). The seed of the gospel would now be planted throughout the countryside.

In Acts 9 the conversion of Saul of Tarsus is recorded. The fascinating story of his transformation from proud religious leader with great civil authority to humble servant with the unique authority of an apostle of Christ figures prominently in the rest of the New Testament.

Soon after this, we find reference to "the churches...throughout all Judea and Galilee, and Samaria" (Acts 9:31). Multiple churches require more leaders, and there are two provisions alluded to in this section which together would provide a natural transition to permanent local church government. The first was a widening sphere of ministry for the apostles as they moved among the young churches. We read Peter "passed throughout all quarters" (Acts 9:32) in an itinerant ministry which most likely included teaching and problem-solving.

The other provision comes with the first reference to "elders" in the church. Word had reached Jerusalem of a new working of God's grace in Syrian Antioch about three hundred miles to the north, and Barnabas was sent to investigate. If ever there was a strategic opportunity to affirm the ascendancy of Jerusalem and the submission required of daughter churches, this was the perfect occasion. But no such instruction came forth, and Barnabas rather exhorted the believers to "cleave unto the Lord" (Acts 11:23). This he did himself. The decision to go to Tarsus and seek for Saul and bring him to Antioch seems to be a matter between himself and the Lord only.

Where did Barnabas learn this principle of action? He was present in Jerusalem when the problem over proper care for the widows had arisen in the church, and those in leadership immediately developed a wise plan at the local level to solve the problem. This set an important precedent for the self-determination of the local church. Accordingly when the new Gentile church at Antioch learned of approaching famine, we read that the disciples "determined[13] to send relief....Which also they did, and sent it to the elders" (Acts 11:29-30). It is interesting that this first reference to the highest permanent office in the church is made almost in passing without further explanation. When one considers the meanings of the Greek word presbuteros, "older, mature man" and "qualified leader," it is reasonable to think that the emphasis is being placed more on the man and less on the office.

---

[13] The Greek text has ὥρισαν (hōrisan), the aorist of ὁρίζω (horizō), "to fix determinately."

The following chapters seem to anticipate the questions: "What happened to the Apostles?" and "How did the transition to elder-rule take place?" James was martyred by Herod, and Peter upon release from prison "went into another place" (Acts 12:17). An expanding work and a decreasing availability of apostles demanded a succession, either through the establishment of an enduring apostolic office or through the conferring of spiritual authority directly by the Head of the church. That the latter method was chosen by God is made clear in the next section of the Acts.[14] The divine plan for leadership in the church is confirmed by the unfolding events in history.

The Three Missionary Journeys, Acts 13–21

Within this next section of the Acts and the epistles there is enough material dealing with church government to fill a book in itself. Since the events of these chapters do not alter but only reinforce the direction already established, a brief summary of the major points will be presented.

The preaching of the Word and the gathering of converts. The missionary journeys began with a revelation of God directly through the Holy Spirit. A new ministry was being entrusted to the church through Paul and Barnabas, and all necessary communication and action took place at the local level. The Lord spoke directly to the spiritual leaders of the young church. They did not confer with Jerusalem (Acts 13:2). Students have observed the fact with interest that the first missionary endeavor of the church was launched, not from Jerusalem, but from a Gentile assembly.[15] This in itself did much to avoid reinforcing Jerusalem as the authoritative mother church, and it paved the way for events still future. As Broadbent says, "The destruction of Jerusalem by the Romans (A.D. 70) emphasized the fact that to the churches no visible head or centre on earth is given."[16]

In the record of Paul's travels set down for us by Luke his companion, only three extended speeches by Paul have been preserved: in the synagogue at Pisidian Antioch, at Mars Hill in Athens, and to the Ephesian elders at Miletus.

---

[14] "The true Apostolic succession means nothing more nor less than the continual call of men to ministerial service by Christ Himself; no ceremony avails to effect it." George Johnston, *The Doctrine of the Church in the New Testament*, 66.

[15] Blaiklock, who thinks Acts 11:22-23 implies that "the Jerusalem church was conscious of its seniority," calls Antioch "the mother of Gentile Christianity." E. M. Blaiklock, *The Acts of the Apostles*, 102.

[16] E. H. Broadbent, *The Pilgrim Church* (London: Pickering and Inglis, 1931), 7.

From the context and from statements in the epistles it is clear that the message of the gospel he preached contained an imperative and full authority to fulfill the entire commission given by the Lord to his disciples. This was not only to make and baptize new disciples, but to carry out all that pertained to observing the "all things" of the command. This is what Paul meant when he exhorted the new believers in Antioch to "continue in the grace of God" (Acts 13:43). It seems to be more assumed than expressed that the repentance and faith of which he characteristically spoke (the turning away from the old and receiving with obedience the new) must be carried beyond personal salvation and into the realm of spiritual relationships, i.e., gathering with other believers in local church fellowship. Churches sprang up throughout the Roman Empire.

The raising up of elders and other servants. While the transition to elder-rule was taking place gradually in Judea, it was almost immediate among the Gentile churches. Paul was only one person. He was also a traveling apostle, and his occasional visits, letters, and special envoys could never keep pace with the growth of the new churches and the expanding need for competent leaders. With travel and communication being slow and uncertain, they could not rely on distant boards or synods for direction, much less hope that Paul might settle in as "the pastor." God's provision lay in undershepherds, raised up from within the community itself. Paul never ceased to follow the example of self-determination in which he had participated in the young church at Antioch.

As to the question of how men are chosen to lead, two passages are of special significance: One records the appointment of elders by Paul and Barnabas "in every church" on a return visit to some of the churches of Galatia during the first missionary journey (Acts 14:23).[17] The other is in Paul's final address to the elders of the church in Ephesus during the third journey (Acts 20:28).

There has been a great deal of discussion about the nature of elder appointment in the Acts 14 passage,[18] but the critical points of the two passages are clear:

---

[17] Paul never participated in the recognition of leadership on his first visit to a city. Acts 14:21 indicates that the missionaries retraced their steps to Lystra, Iconium, and Antioch.

[18] In addition to the commentaries see the extended discussion in Roland Allen, *Missionary Methods; St. Paul's or Ours?* (London: World Dominion Press, 1927), 136f.; William Kelly, *Lectures on the Church of God* (London: G. Morrish, n.d.), 217-223; and Michael Browne, *Autonomy and Authority* (Glasgow: Gospel Tract Publications, 1988), 25. Commenting on the word "ordained" (χειροτονέω, *cheirotoneō*), Hoste remarks, "There is indeed something grotesque in the idea of Paul and Barnabas 'electing by a show of hands.'" William Hoste, *Bishops, Priests and Deacons* (London: Pickering and Inglis, n.d.), 48.

- Leadership was the sovereign work of the Holy Spirit and was to be publicly recognized in each church.[19]
- A plurality of men was raised up from within, not imported from outside.
- Older servants of Christ such as apostles might help in pointing elders out, but the elders themselves were to function in governmental autonomy. Their authority to act came from "the Lord on whom they believed."[20]

Thus, in a quiet way, the transition to elder-rule is documented through the Acts:

Beginning:	Apostles
Middle:	Apostles and Elders
End:	Elders

That the apostles themselves participated in this transition is shown by the references to both Peter and John as elders in their later years (1 Pet. 5:1; 2 Jn. 1).

When servants who could assist the apostles by working among several churches were needed, the appointment was scarcely different. Acts 16 records the account of Timothy being taken into the Lord's work based on the need and spiritual qualification.[21] Paul and the local elders evidently prayed for the young man with laying on of hands (1 Tim. 4:14; 2 Tim. 1:6). The whole matter was simplicity itself and ill befits the later complicated "ordination ceremonies" which are supposed to be derived from it.

A passage on what might be called the "personal autonomy" of workers is enlightening at this point. Paul informs the Corinthians, "As touching our brother Apollos, I greatly desired him to come unto you with the brethren: but his will was

---

[19] 1 Thessalonians 5:12, "Know them which labour among you, and are over you in the Lord." In Hebrews 13: 7, 17, 24 they are called "your leaders" (JND). Far from the honorific titles often used today, descriptives are humble and unassuming. It would be rewarding, to say the least, if every Christian worker would read the excellent section on humble, servant leadership in Alexander Strauch, *Biblical Eldership*, 3d ed. revised and expanded (Littleton, CO: Lewis and Roth Publishers, 1995), 85-98). So unassuming are the words used to describe New Testament elders that some groups of Christian brethren do not hold with a publicly recognized elder board at all.

[20] Since the authority of elders comes from God, there is no record of hands being laid on elders at the time of their appointment.

[21] The expression "full-time worker" is illustrated by this new sphere of labor for the young man Timothy.

not at all to come at this time; but he will come when he shall have convenient time" (1 Cor. 16:12). This single verse is sufficient to describe the entire chain of command among New Testament workers. The servant was directly responsible to the Lord who had called him.

Church governmental action with special reference to Acts 15. Turning to the official side of church life, what could be more interesting than a multi-church council to debate hard doctrinal questions? The Jerusalem Council of Acts 15 has called forth an immense amount of comment from expositors, probably because of its bearing on matters of authority and government in the church.[22]

Returning to Antioch from their first journey, Paul and Barnabas soon found it necessary to defend the principles of grace under which they had worked in their travels. Certain visitors from Judea were insisting on obedience to Moses' law as essential to salvation and were possibly claiming apostolic authority for their teachings. At the heart of this was the truth of the gospel and the attending questions of the unity of the churches and the apostles. Were all the churches— Jewish and Gentile—built upon the same foundation of salvation by grace alone? Did the missionaries to the Gentiles speak the same message as the apostles in Jerusalem, and did they possess the same authority? The Jewish apostles must be consulted. A group was chosen to travel to Jerusalem, and a special conference was convened. Several observations can be made.

- Although the question had far reaching implications, the dispute had arisen between two churches and had to involve them both.[23] No uninvolved parties participated.

---

[22] Cf. F. J. A. Hort, *The Christian Ecclesia*, 82; Gene A. Getz, *Sharpening the Focus of the Church* (Chicago: Moody Press, 1976), 142-46, in the section "Biblical examples of administration and organization;" Michael Browne, *Autonomy and Authority*, 30-31, lists three reasons why the council at Jerusalem was a unique and unrepeatable situation; Robert Rendall, "The Church, What Is It?," in J. B. Watson, *The Church: A Symposium* (London: Pickering and Inglis, 1949), 23, points out that doctrinal subjects might be addressed to a number of local churches grouped in a district, but "congregational affairs were never subjected to the decision of a general council or synod of churches. In each individual church, elders were raised up by the Holy Spirit and to them was committed the care of the church in which they ministered." Cf. also the appendix by F. F. Bruce, "Church History and Its Lessons," in J. B. Watson, *The Church: A Symposium*, 219 n. 12.

[23] Too often it has been overlooked that the stated reason for Antioch's appeal to Jerusalem and the counsel provided was first and foremost because "certain who went out from us have troubled you" (Acts 15:24); that is, the problem at Antioch was properly being referred back to the source from which it had come.

- The proceedings were dictated by the need and cannot fairly be otherwise described than 1) understanding the problem, 2) listening to the testimony of history and Scripture, and 3) arriving at a Spirit-led conclusion.[24] No attempt was made to institute a regular event.
- Unity was confirmed. Letters sent out describe the participants as "being assembled with one accord."[25] Jews and Gentiles are all saved by grace through faith (15:8-11). Paul and Barnabas were in harmony with the apostles at Jerusalem (15:25), and the message of salvation by lawkeeping had not been authorized by the Jerusalem apostles (15:24).
- The resulting "decrees"[26] are, to quote Dr. F. J. A. Hort, "more than advice and less than a command." He wisely concludes, "A certain authority is thus implicitly claimed. There is no evidence that it was more than a moral authority; but that did not make it less real."[27]

Supporting evidence from the New Testament epistles. This remark of Dr. Hort is vital to a proper understanding of the entire subject before us and becomes a principle that lies at the heart of the epistles written to the churches. Governmental autonomy was taken for granted because of the overriding sense of the Lord's presence with each individual church in the exercise of the authority He had entrusted to qualified men among them. It would not have occurred to the apostles and those they trained to seek permission for their actions elsewhere. If the Head spoke, no more was needed. Moral authority must be spiritually discerned and is sufficient to influence the spiritual person or assembly. Godly advice, then, and help to any congregation can be only as strong as their understanding of spiritual authority. Paul repeatedly refers to the authority that

---

[24] Dr. Hort says of James' summary, "Then again the words which begin his conclusion, 'Wherefore my judgement is,' cannot reasonably be understood as an authoritative judgment pronounced by himself independently: the whole context and what is said in v. 22 about the actual decision makes that interpretation morally impossible." F. J. A. Hort, *The Christian Ecclesia*, 80.

[25] The Greek emphasizes the process "becoming of one mind," or "having come to one accord" (Acts 15:25, γενομένοις ὁμοθυμαδόν, *genomenois homothumadon*).

[26] The word *decrees* is δόγματα (*dogmata*) in Acts 16:4. F. F. Bruce renders this "decisions" (from the Greek word δοκεῖν). F. F. Bruce, *The Acts of the Apostles*, (Grand Rapids: Eerdmans, 1951), 308.

[27] Cf. the full paragraph by Dr. Hort that begins, "The New Testament is not poor of words expressive of command,...yet none of them is used." F. J. A. Hort, *The Christian Ekklesia*, 82.

God had given him (2 Cor. 10:8; 13:10), and those he styles as "**enemies of the cross**" also attacked his apostolic position and authority (Phil. 3:18).[28]

Although the authority of the apostles was moral and spiritual rather than personal or civil, it was unique and temporary in the church. An elder had authority only in the church where he served, but apostles could move among the churches and speak or write "a word from the Lord," thus providing an element of non-autonomy in the earliest years of the church.

When the apostles wrote to the churches, they addressed the saints, not religious officials. In their letters many issues arose that bear upon the autonomous nature of local church government, but each confirms what has already been learned. They taught exactly what they practiced and reflected their understanding that local church administration is but the feeble outworking of the more dynamic processes of life between the members of the body and the Head. Lindsay is right in saying that "independence and self-government [are] evidently taken for granted and formulated in principles laid down by the apostle in his epistles."[29]

Note examples of such issues addressed in the epistles.

- Excommunicating discipline, the most serious form, did not wait for the arrival of the apostle who discerned its need and commanded its discharge. Nor was it referred beyond the local church but was carried out in all parts at the local level (1 Cor. 5).

- Disputes among believers were settled through the church, not the civil courts of law (1 Cor. 6).

- The appointment of delegates carrying funds from the church was local (2 Cor. 8:19).

- Letters of commendation were given by the local churches (2 Cor. 3:1, 2; 8:19). No other commending agency exists beside the local church.

- Ministries for the poor saints came from the local churches (2 Cor. 8–9). Again all decisions were made at the local level.

---

[28] After the 2 Corinthians 10:8 passage, Paul goes on to describe his critics as "false apostles, deceitful workers transforming themselves into the apostles of Christ."

[29] Thomas M. Lindsay, *The Church and Ministry in the Early Centuries* (London: Hodder and Stoughton, 1903), 121.

It was important that each church become grounded in its own relationship with the Lord so that each might in itself truly be called "the church in such a place," able to fully represent Him in all of its life and conduct. Rendall remarks, "The churches founded in the book of Acts were not mere outposts of a central authority."[30]

Paul's Trip to Rome to the End of the First Century, Acts 22-28

While Paul spent time in Roman imprisonments, the churches continued to benefit from his letters. Questions of spiritual authority were a constant concern. To the Ephesians he wrote of the church which is Christ's body (Eph. 1:23; cf. 2:16; 3:6; 4:12, 16, 25; 5:23) and of the great spiritual conflict with unseen rulers of darkness (Eph. 6:12). To the Colossians he gave a detailed statement of the position of Christ as "head of all principalities and powers" (Col. 2:10), head of the church (Col. 1:18), and the head from which the body derives nourishment (Col. 2:19). There follows a list of warnings about the corrupting philosophies of the day—especially those that would result in the saints "not holding the Head" (Col. 2:19). In the letters to Timothy and Titus he spells out basic qualifications for church leaders as well as some of their responsibilities. These are instructions that will help younger workers in the appointment of elders "in every city" so that things which are lacking may be set in order. (Tit. 1:5).

Browne has refuted the notion that this process of public elder recognition cannot be repeated today because the original apostles or their delegates are not available. He shows that the young man Titus had only Paul's letter, not his presence, and this was sufficient authority to act both then and now.[31]

Peter, writing to encourage scattered Jewish believers, also included a section addressed to elders. The appeal was moral rather than official, and the motivation for shepherds is neither legal nor monetary. It is the present accountability to, and future reward from, the Chief Shepherd (1 Pet. 5:1-4). John the apostle in his third epistle speaks out strongly against one Diotrephes who exalts himself to a position of "domineering ambition" in the church (3 Jn. 9).[32]

But no clearer display of local church autonomy can be found than in the seven letters sent from the risen Lord to the seven churches of Asia Minor

---

[30] Robert Rendall, "The Church, What Is It?," in J. B. Watson, *The Church: A Symposium*, 23.

[31] Michael Browne, *Authority and Autonomy*, 27.

[32] C. I. Scofield, *The New Scofield Reference Bible, KJV*, ed. by E. Schuyler English (New York: Oxford Univ. Press, 1967), 1348.

(Rev. 2-3). In sharp contrast to the well-known seven-branched candlestick of Israel, each local church appears as a separate lampstand standing on its own individual base with the Lord in the midst, presumably inspecting the light. Each is directly accountable to Him, and authority to act is conferred directly by Him. His counsel is relevant ("**I know thy works**"), but different for each church. Throughout, the responsibility is thrown back upon the church to deal with its own problems, receive its own reward, and if not, to accept the consequences. There is no hint that any but He Himself might remove the lampstand. No church is given authority to control or to disfellowship another. It is true that help and advice may be sought from other fellowships (as in Acts 15), but in the end God holds the local assembly responsible for its actions.

And so in Asia Minor anyone so inclined might profit from the instruction given to each church. "**He that hath an ear, let him hear what the Spirit saith unto the churches.**" Nevertheless, the messages are individual and personal. The Lord speaks not to a regional headquarters, but to each particular church. "**I counsel thee**" (Rev. 3:18). This personal dealing of the Lord directly with local churches which had now been in existence for many years cannot be brushed aside lightly. The warnings and commendations are not spoken as from one who is interrupting a chain of command or preempting the right of an organization. They are rather as from a Father dealing with the children of His own family.

AUTONOMY IN THE POST-APOSTOLIC AGE

As we pass into the post-apostolic era, we do well to reflect upon the condition of the church. Lindsay gives a good summary.

> Before the close of the first century the labors of apostles...had given birth to thousands of these local churches. They were all strictly independent, self-governing communities—tiny islands in the sea of surrounding paganism—each ruled by its session or senate of elders. There is no trace of one man, one pastor, at the head of any community.[33]

All this would soon change, however, and it is instructive to consider not only the fact of it, but also its cause. Dr. Edwin Hatch in his renowned work on

---

[33] Thomas M. Lindsay, *The Church and Ministry in the Early Centuries*, 155.

the organization of the early Christian churches traces what has been described as the degeneration of conditions from the original apostolic independence into the vast confederation which, in due time, persecuted the true saints of God.[34] Beginning with informal and nonbinding representative assemblies held during the course of the second century, in which he cites Cyprian (martyred in A.D. 258) as claiming "in emphatic and explicit terms an absolute independence for each community,"[35] the trend was clearly toward greater structure and control. Once Christianity was recognized by the State in A.D. 313, "such conferences tended to multiply...and to pass resolutions which were regarded as binding upon the Churches...and the acceptance of which was regarded as a condition of intercommunion with the Churches of other provinces."[36]

The process did not take place evenly throughout the Christian church and was powerfully influenced by the strength of Rome as the following quote from one within that system shows:

> If one gazes back through the vistas of the ages it is of more than passing interest to observe the state of Christendom during the fifth and sixth centuries. One notes that at that period Catholic Christendom was divided into three groups, that is to say, the church of the East whose centre was Constantinople; the church of the West whose centre was Rome; and the church of the North-west whose centre was in Ireland. The churches of the East and of the North-west had this in common, namely, each church was, as it were, composed of a group or body of local churches, each local church autonomous in itself but in intercommunion with the others....One submits that these principles of autonomy and intercommunion are not only of apostolic origin but that their observance persisted throughout the sub-apostolic age and only waned as the power of the papacy increased.[37]

Space forbids pursuing the matter except to say that as new problems and

---

[34] G. H. Lang, *The Churches of God* (London: The Paternoster Press, 1959), 22.

[35] Edwin Hatch, *The Organization of the Early Christian Churches* (London: Longmans, Green and Co., 1901), 171.

[36] Edwin Hatch, *The Organization of the Early Christian Churches*, 172. For a discussion of the gradual steps by which informal became formal and authoritative see Thomas Lindsay's chapter VIII, "The Roman State Religion and its Effects on the Organization of the Church," in *The Church and the Ministry in the Early Centuries*.

[37] Quoted in G. H. Lang, *The Churches of God*, 19.

heresies surfaced, new councils were convened and confederations proliferated, bringing the church into a prison of its own making. It is sobering to remember how this all began. The virtues of love and brotherhood as expressed in occasional conferences for fellowship and communication over matters of mutual concern were not balanced by the scriptural safeguards of local church autonomy. This is a good lesson for our generation to ponder.

In reviewing the historical record of the early church, the conclusion is justified that the acts and writings of the apostles assume local church autonomy with dependence on the Head and nonbinding interrelations with other churches. Apostolic authority was used to establish each congregation in its own relationship with the Lord, and no attempt was ever made to foster an apostolic succession.[38]

ALTERNATE MODELS AND THEIR PROBLEMS

THE ARGUMENTS FOR CENTRALIZATION

There have always been differences of opinion about how churches should relate to one another, and linking them together has usually begun for innocent reasons. But the steps from cooperation, to councils, to federations, to denominations are short ones logically. In defense, supporters often followed a line of reasoning which later came to be known as the "doctrine of development." By development is meant the growth and refinement of those principles only begun in the Scriptures by which the church should conduct itself. There is a kind of doctrinal extrapolation, implying that though Scripture may launch the ship, it cannot guide it to its final destination. Of course, development always moves in the direction of greater complexity. The resulting systems of ecclesiastical polity have multiplied beyond all measure, all the while pointing back to the early church as the root from which they have sprung. It must suffice by way of illustration to mention a few outstanding examples of attempts at centralized

---

[38] Lindsey contrasts the post-canonical succession of the male lineage of the kindred of Jesus in Jerusalem with the organization of the Gentile churches under the leadership of gifted individuals who, regardless of connection, manifested in their service "a direct gift from the Master Himself." (Thomas M. Lindsay, *The Church and the Ministry in the Early Centuries*, 120), "The absolutely irreconcilable controversy is between, on the one hand, the sufficiency and finality of Holy Scripture, and, on the other hand, either the figment of apostolic succession, and the falsehood of there being an unwritten apostolic tradition, or the assertion of the continuous inspiration of the Spirit being granted." (G. H. Lang, *The Churches of God*, 17).

control among local churches.

EXAMPLES OF CENTRALIZATION

Roman Catholicism

It does not require great spiritual acumen to discern the fallacy of the claims of Rome to be the one true church on earth, especially when her own words describing this exalted position are considered. Two examples may be noticed.

The Council of Florence (A.D. 1438) states:

> Also we decree that the Holy Apostolic See and the Roman Pontiff himself is the successor of St. Peter, the prince of the apostles, and the true vicar of Christ, and head of the whole Church, and the father and teacher of all Christians; and that to him, in the person of the blessed Peter, our Lord Jesus Christ has committed full power of feeding, ruling, and governing the universal Church.[39]

The Creed of the Council of Trent (A.D. 1564) which is still in force and is "a creedal test to which, upon demand, every faithful Catholic must subscribe"[40] includes the following:

> I acknowledge the holy, Catholic, and apostolic Roman Church as the mother and teacher of all churches; and I promise and swear true obedience to the Roman Pontiff, vicar of Christ and successor of Blessed Peter, Prince of the Apostles....I shall most constantly hold and profess this true Catholic faith, outside which no one can be saved.[41]

From its inception, Rome moved away from the biblical idea of the church as an organism, striving to become an institution of unchallenged, centralized authority with absolute control.

National Churches

The national church theory holds that all members of the church in a given country are bound together in provincial or national organization and that this

---

[39] James Bannerman, *The Church of Christ*, 2:245.

[40] John H. Leith, *Creeds of the Churches* (Garden City, NY: Anchor Books, 1963), 439.

[41] John H. Leith, *Creeds of the Churches*, 441.

[42] A. H. Strong, *Systematic Theology*, 912.

organization has jurisdiction over the local churches.[42] Davies writes, "Such expressions as the Church of England or of South India suggest an affiliation, a federation, or an amalgamation of churches which of necessity leads to a centralization of authority either in a representative group or in an individual as in the Episcopal systems."[43]

In addition to the material presented earlier, the problems of this system may be seen by a careful consideration of all those New Testament passages where churches are addressed or described. The wording is precise to the effect that there is no instance in Scripture of a church linked with a country. We find the church in the city (1 Cor. 1:2), saints of a province (2 Cor. 1:2), churches of several provinces (Acts 9:31), but no church of a district or country.

The distinction is not trivial. The nature of the church is by design local to a city, but composed of individuals from diverse national backgrounds who have been called out from former loyalties into a new sphere of life. When Paul refers to the Jews, the Greeks, and the church of God in 1 Corinthians 10:32, he distinguishes the church from nationalities.

Protestant Denominations

Every Protestant denomination has its reasons for a sectarian stand, i.e., for building an organization that is larger than the local church but smaller than the universal church. Books on the subject—both in favor and in opposition—are numerous.[44]

Bannerman, a Presbyterian, gives a typical argument for a centralized government when he lists as one meaning of the word *church* in the New Testament "a plurality of congregations connected together as one body or church by means of a common government."[45] His rationale for this definition is not convincing, since he argues from the historical fact of the large number of converts in Jerusalem to the unproved assumption of a "common ecclesiastical arrangement" over the smaller churches which he asserts must have existed.[46] Even the Baptists, for whom independence is an article of church government, have formed conferences and associations which carefully control their member-

---

[43] J. M. Davies, *The Lord and the Churches*, 25.

[44] Cf. E. H. Broadbent, *The Pilgrim Church*; Andrew Miller, *Miller's Church History* (Fincastle, VA: Scripture Truth Book Co., n.d.); and Andrew Stenhouse, *The Sin of Sectarianism* (Toronto: Christian Book Room, 1957).

[45] James Bannerman, *The Church of Christ*, 1:13.

[46] James Bannerman, *The Church of Christ*, 1:13.

[47] Speaking of Baptist principles, Strong admits, "Bodies of Christians which refuse to accept

ship, so that a truly independent church is the exception.[47]

Harold St. John has well said:

> We find the streets sprinkled with churches bearing the names of great
> Christian leaders (Wesley or Calvin), of forms of church government
> (Presbyterian or Episcopalian), of some special doctrine (Baptist), or a
> geographical region (Anglican or Roman), with many smaller societies.
> In almost every case these bodies came into existence by reason of some
> protest uttered by the Spirit of God; some truth of Scripture had been
> diluted, distorted, or denied.... It is important to see that the primitive
> church maintained intact all the doctrines and loyalties for which these
> bodies stand, but declined to use any of their party labels.[48]

Exclusive Brethren

Since the Brethren placed such emphasis on the unity of the church, one might
have expected to look in vain for such problems. Indeed things went well for a
time, and harmony prevailed. But before long the idea of a central meeting with
"as many meetings subordinate to it as grace might vouchsafe" arose.[49] When
doctrinal differences forced a split, the way was open for a "circle of fellowship"
which was ultimately based on the principle that fellowship among believers
depended upon separation from evil rather than the presence of new life in Christ.

Commenting upon J. N. Darby's role in this shift, E. H. Broadbent writes:

> His teaching abolishes the independence of congregations of believers
> and their immediate relations with the Lord, bringing in a body,
> introduction into which, or exclusion from which, by any part, is
> binding upon the whole; the Congregational principle exchanged for
> the Catholic.[50]

Later, the so-called "Needed Truth" assemblies in Ireland, consisting largely
of former Presbyterians, continued the same idea of a "united oversight" which

---

these principles we may, in a somewhat loose and modified sense, call churches; but we
cannot regard them as churches organized in all respects according to Christ's laws, or as
completely answering to the New Testament model of church organization." A. H. Strong,
Systematic Theology, 891.

[48] Harold St. John, "The Unity of the Church," in J. B. Watson, *The Church: A Symposium*, 203.

[49] Andrew Stenhouse, "The Sin of Sectarianism," 95.

[50] E. H. Broadbent, *The Pilgrim Church*, 366.

was really the synod system from which they had come.

THE UNDERLYING ERROR

At its birth, the church began under the apostles with a sort of "non-autonomy," and nothing would have been easier than to continue this direction. But the divine plan was otherwise, and underlying all of man's societies and federations are two fatal flaws which no supposed benefits can outweigh. They are at variance with the biblical teaching of the nature of the church as an expression of the one body, and they ultimately do not work out for the better in practice. As to the first of these, Thomas Lindsay put it clearly:

> The evidence for the independence and self-government of the churches to which St. Paul addressed his epistles is so overwhelming that it is impossible even to imagine the presence within them of any ecclesiastical authority with an origin and power independent of the assembly of the congregation, and the apostle does not make the slightest allusion to any such government or controlling authority, whether vested in one man or in a group of men.[51]

Indeed, there was every opportunity for the apostles to have insisted that the young churches of Judea be under the control of Jerusalem, but they did not. The epistles might have anticipated and regulated denominational tendencies, but they did not. Freedom in Christ and dependence on the Head were too important. Radmacher well says, "Such organizational alignments only serve to obscure the true nature of the church,"[52] and Michael Browne comments strongly:

> What a denial of Christ's authority and Headship and contempt for His presence and word therefore is implicit in shifting the centre of authority out of the local assembly and investing it in some person or ecclesiastical group.[53]

When we consider how perfectly opposed are the principles of unity and division, we find a consistent testimony in Scripture on the subject. The spiritual man is charged to keep in the bond of peace that unity which the Spirit has created (Eph. 4:3), while the list of works produced by the flesh includes

---

[51] Thomas M. Lindsay, *The Church and the Ministry in the Early Centuries*, 58.

[52] Earl D. Radmacher, *The Nature of the Church* (Portland: Western Baptist Press, 1972), 346.

[53] Michael Browne, *Autonomy and Authority*, 21.

"rivalries, divisions, and sects" (Gal. 5:20). The Lord's prayer for His people that they might enjoy the same oneness that He had with the Father is in bright contrast to the many warnings against the sins of pride and desire to control others by making them submit to our will. Twice He intimates that the church's ability to reach the lost will relate directly to its ability to display the loving unity that exists within the Godhead (John 17:21, 23).

Of the second concern, it is clear from history that all attempts to display the glory of these man-made systems have not been able to do so. G. H. Lang has grasped the connection between the divine goal and the practical outworking when he writes:

> Of any scheme or form of interlocking of assemblies we see no trace. Neither racial, social, geographical, nor political groupings or divisions were to be found; indeed, any such thought was wholly alien to the mind of the Lord as touching His church.[54]

> The apostles founded churches and they founded nothing else, because for the ends in view nothing else was required or could have been so suitable....No other organization than the local assembly appears in the New Testament, nor do we find even the germ of anything further.[55]

Admittedly, the problem of a fractured church has become too large for any single individual or congregation to solve given the human tendency to exclude those whom God has accepted. But neither should we fall back on the idea of some that the church is "in ruins" and give up hope. Rather, we must learn and practice the biblical instructions that apply to the nature of the church. Believers who seek to understand and apply principles of New Testament church government need solid Bible teaching and frequent reminders to look into history as regards this subject. Otherwise the blessings of "co-laboring," and "networking," and other terms meant to express the benefits of fellowship might easily become the curse of centralized control.

PRACTICAL BENEFITS OF LOCAL CHURCH AUTONOMY

Maintaining a balanced autonomy in the church will bring real practical benefits,

---

[54] G. H. Lang, *The Churches of God*, 13.

[55] Lang, *The Churches of God*, 10.

but diligence is required to ensure that self-determination is confined to the administrative functions of government. The pendulum must not swing toward isolationism on one hand, or centralized control of churches on the other so that fellowship and ministry among the saints are quenched. Some rewards and dangers are outlined in the following section.

DEPENDENCE ON THE HEAD

As unseen authority in the church, the Lord directs all aspects of the life of the community by His Word and Spirit through godly leaders He raises up. One part of this work is to teach believers dependence on Christ in their daily walk, a matter of vital importance to spiritual maturity and the well-being of the church.

Dependence must be learned, not in a vacuum, but in fellowship with others. The love of God requires sacrifice of such nature as to be really the Lord living His life out through the believer. This is only possible through moment-by-moment reliance on the indwelling Christ. Such dependent life is modeled by the older, experienced men of the assembly, called elders or overseers, and serves the twofold purpose of guiding the church according to the will of the Head and training younger believers in the same quality of life. The type of local government described in the New Testament is best suited to these two purposes, and no better plan can be contemplated than that the individual should walk in constant dependence on the Lord for guidance, strength, and fruitfulness. At the same time he functions in a harmonious relationship with his near brethren, as together they seek out direction and help from the Head. This is to be accomplished apart from outside interference which could weaken the motivation to seek the Lord. This happens when needs are met or decisions made by some distant administrative body.

Understandably, the Adversary who opposes this good work will present a thousand plausible reasons as to why some capable person or group ought to stand between a local church and the Head. Yet Scripture allows none. Paul warned the Colossian believers of the danger of giving place to spiritual intermediaries and "not holding the Head" (Col. 2:19). On the other hand, Scripture is filled with examples of the heroes of faith who learned dependence relying directly upon God. Perhaps we might paraphrase Paul's words to Timothy, "There is one mediator between God and the local church, the man Christ Jesus" (cf. 1 Tim 2:5).

THE DEFENSE OF SOUND DOCTRINE

In no area of Christian life will the enemy make greater gains than where he can corrupt the foundation of the faith, the holy Scriptures. Knowing this, Paul the apostle raised one concern above all others toward the end of his life—the urgent need for sound doctrine in the churches.[56] He warned of a day when men would exchange the conviction and correction of truth for the pleasurable sensation of a "tickled ear" (2 Tim. 4:3). To Titus he pressed the need for faithful elders who could feed the flock and silence those who undermine families with their errors (Tit. 1:9-16). In his final words to the elders at Ephesus, he predicted that men with ulterior motives would arise speaking things "having been perverted,"[57] and so divide the church (Acts 20:29-30). These warnings could be multiplied and are as crucial today as when written.

Since church leadership has the primary role in defending truth and combating false doctrine, the New Testament pattern of a plural eldership, i.e., men spending time together in the Word and prayer in fellowship with the Head, points out an interesting principle: plural leadership and local church autonomy complement one another. False teachings are more likely to take root where control is in the hands of a single person or a distant organization. Always the plague of the church, false doctrine can make but slow progress among churches which individually follow the Berean pattern, "They searched the Scriptures daily, whether those things were so" (Acts 17:11). However, false teaching spreads rapidly when it takes hold within a denomination or seminary officially linked to a circle of churches. Noting how the defense of a vigorous autonomy is a safeguard against false doctrine, Davies remarks, "In this way troubles are quarantined rather than being turned into countrywide issues."[58]

But equally dangerous to healthy doctrine in the local church is an over zealous independence which closes the community off to the rest of the body. Congregations which become isolated (or isolate themselves) are not exposed to the vast resources within the body of Christ. Erroneous doctrines or teachings which are lopsided because unbalanced by correlative truths may not be identified and corrected. Since such groups tend to be exclusive in outlook, the lessons of church history are largely ignored. Often one finds that the whole counsel of God is not preached. Some subjects are worn thin, and others are neglected because of doctrinal bias or a narrow selection of "qualified" speakers. In time, an elitist intellectualism may develop which is weak in practical service

---

[56] The Greek word for "sound" is ὑγιαίνω (hygiainō), "to be healthy." Of the twelve occurrences of the word in connection with words, faith, and doctrine eight are found in Timothy and Titus.

[57] The Greek word διεστραμμένα (diestrammena) means "distorted, corrupted."

[58] J. M. Davies, The Lord and the Churches, 26.

and outreach into the world.

THE ADMINISTRATION OF LOCAL AFFAIRS INTERNALLY

The right to administer its own affairs is conferred upon the church by the Lord and taught in the Scriptures by both precept and example. Even the smallest of groups has all that is required for the proper functions of self-government, self-support, and self-propagation. The recognition of leadership, the feeding of the flock, the order of worship, methods adopted for various ministries, matters of discipline, outreach to the community, missions, and so much more need simply be subject to the Head of the church as He directs. His own presence and Spirit, the Scriptures, and such gift as is necessary to allow Him to serve His people from the midst require that the real control of the church remain local, not distant.

It is therefore important that the church take a biblical stand on matters of accountability and discipline. The prayer life of a church is a good indicator of its spiritual health, as God's people express dependence upon, and accountability to the Head in prayer. If prayers are vague or absent, and especially if they are prideful, something is wrong. The headship of Christ must not be usurped either from outside by controlling agencies or from within by autocratic individuals or groups. As those who lead are prayerfully accountable to the Head, accountability within the congregation may be more readily encouraged.

Autonomy must not become the cloak for an unbridled will, a way to excuse rampant individualism and lawlessness. The church must walk in humility and always be on guard against a dictatorial spirit that typically progresses as follows:

> "No outsider will tell us what to do."
> "No one in the church will tell us what to do."
> "No one will tell me what to do."

In extreme cases this ends in a cult. After exhorting the younger men to submit to their elders, Peter says, "Yea, all of you be subject one to another" (1 Pet. 5:5).

Of like importance is the matter of discipline within the church. Sin must be dealt with to preserve fellowship. In commenting on the phrase used at the Jerusalem Council, "it seemed good to the Holy Spirit, and to us" (Acts 15:28), F. F. Bruce notes the protecting value of autonomy on Christian fellowship. "If the mind of the Spirit be humbly sought, ascertained and followed, fellowship between churches will be promoted, as it will not if a church is subjected to the

---

[59] F. F. Bruce, "Church History and Its Lessons," in J. B. Watson, *The Church: A Symposium*, 220.

authority either of another church or of a group of churches."[59]

Of the several different forms of discipline mentioned in Scripture, both preventive and corrective, every one is exercised within the assembly and provides no appeal beyond the local church. However, autonomy can be pressed so that there is little regard for the viewpoints or disciplines of other churches. This leads to the detriment of the whole body of Christ.

Certainly no church has the right to impose its decisions on other groups, and each should remember that there is but one body and one Spirit. Much trouble and harm may be spared by respecting as much as possible the righteous judgments of the Lord as discovered and carried out in other congregations. Furthermore, discipline is based on the unity of Christ and the church and must be truly *church* discipline. Even though the procedures of discipline are exercised at the local level and the resulting decisions are not binding, they should be honored as widely as necessary within the whole Christian church.[60]

The testimony of Scripture is abundant and clear as to where the final authority in the church resides. Each local congregation is taught to wrestle with the questions of leadership, ministry, discipline, outreach, etc. on their own. One looks in vain for suggestions that the church ought to seek guidance or funding or for that matter anything whatsoever from an outside source.

Perhaps the clearest passage on this subject is found in the book of Revelation. In sharp contrast to the well-known seven-branched candlestick of Israel, each local church appears as a separate lampstand, standing on its own individual base with the Lord in the midst, presumably inspecting the light. Throughout, the responsibility is thrown back upon the church to deal with its own problems, receive its own reward, and otherwise accept the consequences. The thought of one church disfellowshipping another is never contemplated.

The picture is not always so today. Often the autonomy of a local work has been compromised by denominational affiliation. The writer remembers a conversation some years ago in which a young man lamented that his congregation could take the Lord's Supper only semiannually, since the group was small and at a distance from the main church from which an official must be sent to preside.

It is true that help and advice may be sought from other fellowships (as Acts 15), but in the end, God holds the local assembly responsible for its actions. So, in Asia Minor anyone so inclined might profit from the instructions given to each

---

[60] Anyone familiar with the vast amount of literature produced on all sides of this question by the Brethren will appreciate the difficult nature of this point.

church. "He that hath an ear, let him hear what the Spirit saith to the churches." Nevertheless, the messages are individual and personal. The Lord does not speak to a regional headquarters, but to each particular church (cf. "I counsel thee," Rev. 3:18).

Another way for churches to join in fellowship for the common good is in the exchange of letters of commendation, a practice used by early Christians and still valued by some today. Such a letter simply written communicates that "we value your help and fellowship in a matter of mutual concern." Of course, the inability of an assembly to provide such a letter is a matter which other churches disregard at their own peril.

To be independent in matters where we are told to cooperate is not a virtue. I remember one time the frustration of sitting in required silence through the meeting of a certain independent church which was debating a question at length which our own congregation had just finished researching extensively.

THE DEVELOPMENT OF MINISTRY IN THE CHURCH

One of the responsibilities of church elders is to act as stewards of God (Titus 1:7). More than any material treasure, this stewardship pertains to that great resource—people. All the blessings of gift and ministry come from Christ to the extent which and in the persons whom He wills to provide them. The church, then, is ideally a community of new creations in Christ whose potential for creativity and ministry is developing into service useful to men and a delight to God. Each member is to exercise his individual gift within the community for the benefit of the whole so that the church may fulfill its mission.

The world today is filled with greater needs and challenges than ever before, and the gospel of God's grace is the only hope. Happy is the congregation that, by its biblical design, can move quickly in times of need to respond with the gospel and practical help. In changing situations it can take advantage of original thinking and spontaneous leading. In this way the church demonstrates that the Lord desires to give good things to His people, for it is evident that spiritual gifts will arise most quickly in the autonomous church.[61] Lindsay says, "The theocratic element was not given in a hierarchy imposed upon the church from without;

---

[61] Gifted individuals may be stifled in conventional church governments if their gifts threaten the established clergy. How might a young man who has been given the New Testament gift of pastor (or shepherd) feel if he is developing in a church where one individual is constantly referred to as "The Pastor"?

[62] Thomas M. Lindsay, *The Church and the Ministry in the Early Centuries*, 33.

it manifested itself within the community."[62]

In several New Testament passages, Paul gives extended teaching on spiritual gifts and their uses. Any study of these gifts would fall outside the scope of this paper. It is worth noting, however, that the orderly use of the gifts and the controls and guidelines laid down by the Spirit of God are all under the jurisdiction of the local assembly. There is no hint that a wider circle of influence might scrutinize or control the proceedings.

In order to be effective shepherds, those who lead must guard against narrowness of vision. Being faithful to biblical principles and at the same time being open-minded toward new people, new ideas, and new opportunities for discipleship and outreach is the challenge. It is a strange thing how some who extol the quick thinking and flexibility displayed by the early Christians when their widows began to suffer neglect, or by a Hudson Taylor or a George Müller, will frown on any such creativity or flexibility when it arises closer to home. Paul's letter to the Corinthians sets a good example for church leaders to follow. While standing firm on the principles of the gospel, he was flexible in his life and work so that he might reach many (1 Cor. 9:19-27).

THE BIBLICAL INTERRELATEDNESS OF CHURCHES

The safety and blessing of the church is not through isolation, but through communion. This involves communion with the Head and communion within the body. In the early years of the church, division had not yet splintered the relationships among Christian groups, and the sense of unity and belonging to that one holy temple which was being built together as an habitation of God through the Spirit was a strong testimony before the world of the reality of the Christian message. Thomas Lindsay summarized this principle of "belonging-ness" as follows:

> It must not be forgotten that while each Christian community was a little self-governed republic, the visible unity of the corporate church of Christ was never forgotten. Although each local church was an independent society, although it was not connected with other Christian communities by any organization of a political kind, it was nevertheless conscious that it belonged to a worldwide federation of equally independent churches. Its self-containedness did not produce isolation. On the contrary, every local church felt itself to be a real part of the universal and visible church of God to which many hundreds of similar societies belonged.[63]

---

[63] Thomas M. Lindsay, *The Church and the Ministry in the Early Centuries*, 155-56.

True autonomy encourages cooperation among local churches, and the ways in which this practical interdependence may be expressed are countless because the resources within the body of Christ are immeasurable. God has put them there to draw His people together in mutual love and care. Davies reminds us pointedly:

> On the one hand, anything savoring of affiliation must be avoided, and on the other, local church autonomy should not militate against united activities for specified purposes. We must not be like the people of Laish who had "no business with any man." They were easily overcome (Judges 18:27, 28).[64]

Accordingly, it is easier to give advice or receive counsel or lend a hand if both sides are clear that the only yoke into which each has entered is with the Lord Himself and not some humanly devised organization. Every local congregation must be secure in its interaction with others that its individual conscience will not be forced, that no outside authority may intervene, that its involvement is limited to its own exercise of heart, and that even its material contributions of time and resources will be done of its own free will.

But human pride wars against balance, and through the centuries the Christian church has suffered more from the extremes of sectarianism and isolationism than perhaps any other evil. Strange to say, the key to the dilemma was given by the Lord Himself in the two great commandments. "Thou shalt love the Lord thy God...and thy neighbor as thyself" (Matt. 23:37-39). In regard to the church, autonomy says that we are responsible to the Lord, and interdependence says that, in some ways at least, we are our brother's keeper. These are two sides of the one coin of healthy church life. Growth can come when they are in balance. The church suffers when they are not.

It is sad to see some Christian groups glorying in independence when there is such great need in our day. They talk about their autonomy. They cut off every opportunity toward the world around them. They enter into a monastery of their own imagination right in the middle of a desperately needy society. Services are conducted and business is discharged in isolation and fear of contamination. If a report comes that a nearby church is seeing growth, the suspicion is immediate. They must be compromising.

---

[64] J. M. Davies, *The Lord and the Churches*, 27.

It is rare to find a church where full fellowship and warmth are extended to believers on the basis of life in Christ (rather than light on issues) that is at the same time closed to the needs, perspectives, gifts, and resources of the larger body of Christ. When the church closes its eyes and heart and arms, its sight of the Lord, its reception of the saints, and its mission in the world become crippled. Unless revival comes, this leads to a slow death. It is a constant work of spiritual leaders to promote a healthy balance of autonomy and interdependence in the Christian church and guard against things which destroy that balance.

THE CHURCH AND CIVIL GOVERNMENT

While prescribing a form of church government ideally suited to God's pilgrim people in the world, the Scriptures also sanction civil government as ordained of God. Jesus assumed the coexistence of both, and in His famous statement, "Render to Caesar the things that are Caesar's and to God the things that are God's" (Mk. 12:17), set before His people two distinct spheres of obligation. This separation of church and state, as it has come to be known, presents the challenges of honoring both authorities and guarding against the dangers of fellowship with the world. (The problem becomes even more difficult when church and state encroach on one another's domain). In its universal and mystical aspect, the church is separate, transcendent, and safe. But in its local expression, it must relate to the governments and affairs of this world, without compromising its testimony. J. Clyde Turner has warned, "There is a growing tendency on the part of the government to invade the realm of religion and impose restrictions on the churches. On the other hand, there is a persistent effort on the part of certain religious organizations to bring the church and state into partnership."[65]

It would be well if the lesson of history on this point could be learned. E. H. Broadbent condensed it to a paragraph:

> The first three centuries of the church's history prove that no earthly power can crush it. It is invincible to attacks from without. The witnesses of its sufferings, and even its persecutors, become its converts and it grows more rapidly than it can be destroyed. The following period of nearly two hundred years shows that the union of the Church and the State, even when the powers of the mightiest Empire are put into the

---

[65] Quoted in Earl D. Radmacher, *The Nature of the Church*, 347.

church's hands, do not enable her to save the State from destruction, for, in abandoning the very position which her name implies, of being "called out" of the world, and of separation to Christ, she loses the power that comes from subjection to her Lord, exchanging it for an earthly authority that is fatal to herself.[66]

The point at which different authorities intersect is the point of danger, which in turn makes a proper understanding and application of local church autonomy vital. The safest course of action is to preserve as much as possible the separation. As Forrester says, "It follows that only where the life of a church touches the civic life of a community has the civil authority any right to interfere."[67]

The applications of this position are manifold. Paul defended civil authority as ordained of God, but rebuked the Corinthians for attempts to settle brotherly disputes in civil law courts (1 Cor 6).

F. F. Bruce points out that "spiritual liberty is more likely to be preserved where the Scriptural principle of the administrative independence of each local church is maintained.... If the state be adversely disposed it can more easily paralyse a centrally organized corporation than a multitude of unfederated congregations, each independently governed and administered by its own elders and deacons."[68]

Being in the world but not of it, and using the world but not abusing it, is not an easy assignment. But preserving the mission of the church and its ability to minister effectively is worth the efforts required to maintain appropriate relationships with civil authorities. History offers many examples of those who were negligent in this matter.

THE ENCOURAGEMENT OF PIONEER AND INDIGENOUS WORKS

When there is harmony with the government and harmony within the fellowship, the church can pursue its God-given mission toward the world. New Testament church government is admirably suited to the unique opportunities that spring from the unusual cultures of other lands. The church planter who has helped in the opening of new works can appreciate the freedoms granted to both worker and congregation in the Scriptures—the freedom to labor in the place and

---

[66] E. H. Broadbent, *The Pilgrim Church*, 29.

[67] E. J. Forrester, "Church Government," *The International Standard Bible Encyclopedia,* ed. James Orr, 5 vols. (Grand Rapids: Eerdmans, 1939), 1:655.

[68] F. F. Bruce, "Church History and Its Lessons," in J. B. Watson, *The Church: A Symposium,* 191.

according to the method of his conscience before God without the fetters of institutional restrictions. He is able in this way to follow the guidance of the Lord in the many details of a new effort and to train younger workers to do the same without the constraints and regulations imposed by outside organizations. Such a course of action will encourage the early development of local leadership and the financial stewardship so indispensable for self-propagation.

This freedom must be guarded as G. H. Lang warned:

> Should the gospel message be so blessed that churches spring up spontaneously through the testimony of evangelists or other believers, then forthwith men will arise whose great business seems to be to federate these local assemblies into Fellowships, Unions, Denominations. God, on the contrary, is working today in exactly the opposite direction, towards a return to His chosen plan as recorded in the New Testament.[69]

Every saint should have confidence that the essential unity which God created remains intact.[70] He should therefore seek to reflect this oneness with other believers wherever possible by a gracious attitude toward those with whom he may differ.

In non-biblical matters the culture of the people should be respected when the functions of government in the church are established. Even in the poorest of societies the work must always be on the shoulders of the local believers. This is especially important in the financial matters of the congregation. How else but through ownership and real involvement can commitment be tested and dependence on the Head be cultivated?

The book of Acts then, is much more than the history of the early church. It is a trustworthy guidebook for Christian workers to follow wherever a new field of labor opens.

CONCLUSIONS

Bible-believing Christians have been taught to regard the Scriptures as sufficient in all matters of faith and practice. This certainly includes the church. E. H.

---

[69] G. H. Lang, *The Churches of God*, 11.

[70] F. F. Bruce calls it "irrefragable." F. F. Bruce, "Church History and Its Lessons," in J. B. Watson, *The Church: A Symposium*, 191.

Broadbent in his survey of the history of the pilgrim church has said:

> Events in the history of the churches in the time of the Apostles have been selected and recorded in the book of the Acts in such a way as to provide a permanent pattern for the churches. Departure from this pattern has had disastrous consequences, and all revival and restoration have been due to some return to the pattern and principles contained in the Scriptures.[71]

The same inspiration that wrote the history of the earliest years of the church forewarns of conditions at the end of the age. It is of more than passing interest that of all the evils which were foretold of the end times, none is more glaring than that which led to the first of all sins, namely, contempt for authority. As the days darken and signs of the approaching end of the age are seen everywhere, Christian churches face the pressures of what Paul called "perilous times." Those founded on the rock of Scripture, will have a ministry in a desperately needy world. Those built on the shifting sands of false doctrine or emotionalism will collapse.

Every disciple of the Lord Jesus must weigh again the words of the Master, "This is my commandment, that ye love one another, as I have loved you" (Jn. 15:12). Loving those with whom we agree cannot be all that He meant, for the world does this. Rather, the love of Christ extends warmth and kindness to all true saints of God though they differ on secondary matters, including questions of church administration. The love of Christ seeks to promote practical unity wherever possible.

To be specific, let those whose zeal for progress and openness may entice them toward organizing churches into controlling structures remember Paul's words which apply as well to government as to the gospel. "Stand fast, therefore, in the liberty with which Christ hath made us free, and be not entangled again with the yoke of bondage" (Gal. 5:1). May the Lord preserve us from sectarianism. And let those who look with suspicion on the widely different approaches to community within the bounds of what Scripture allows remember that we are instructed to seek "to comprehend WITH ALL SAINTS...the love of Christ" (Eph. 3:18-19). May He preserve us from Phariseeism so that we walk humbly in the fear of the Lord with love and acceptance for every true child of God.

Finally, let us be ever alert to the wiles of that one whose gates stand against

---

[71] E. H. Broadbent, *The Pilgrim Church*, 2.

the Lord and His church. Biblical autonomy is one safeguard of church unity worthy of all efforts in its defense by those who love Christ and His bride and who would share in His work to "present it to himself a glorious church, not having spot, or wrinkle, or any such thing" (Eph. 5:27). The old saying remains true: "The price of liberty is eternal vigilance."

The Interdependence of Local Churches

by Alexander Strauch[1]

Introduction

How can autonomous local churches be interdependent? This subject is complex in character, frustrating to implement, relevant to the age of ecumenicity, and volatile to discuss among conservative, bible-believing churches.

Regarding interchurch relations, all church elders walk a tightrope: they must protect their flocks from doctrinal error and at the same time express, in a horribly divided Christian community, the oneness of the Church of Jesus Christ and the love of Christ towards all Christians and local churches—a near impossible assignment I assure you. This article is designed to provide some degree of guidance and balanced perspective on an intensely vexing subject.

For ease of organization and clarity, I have divided my paper into two parts. I will first present the biblical data for autonomous local churches and their interrelatedness. We should all find general agreement with the theology of this section. In the second section I will address the far more complex issue that generates much confusion and disagreement of how autonomous local churches can interrelate with other churches in a world of false churches, true churches, dangerous churches, wacky churches, and hundreds of denominational divisions and subdivisions. It is my desire that this paper will stimulate fresh biblical thinking and help your church's attitude toward other churches be more biblical.

Autonomous Local Churches and Interchurch Fellowship

Under this first section it is our contention that (1) there is and can be only one, true Church of Jesus Christ, (2) upon earth the Church is manifested visibly in

---

[1] Emmaus alumnus Alex Strauch is a well-known Bible teacher and author. He serves as an elder and full-time worker in Littleton Bible Chapel in Denver, Colorado.

countless local churches, (3) local churches should lovingly interact with one another, providing that they are genuine churches indwelt by the Spirit of Christ, (4) local church isolationism is unscriptural, and (5) there are rich benefits resulting from interchurch relationships.

ONE LORD, ONE CHURCH

As to the doctrine of the oneness of the Church of Jesus Christ, all Christians agree: our Lord and Savior established one Church. At one of the most crucial moments in our Lord's earthly ministry, He declared to His disciples, "**I will build my Church**" (Matt. 16:18). He also said, "**There shall be one flock, and one shepherd**" (John 10:16). In John 17 He prayed that all believers would "**be one; as Thou, Father, art in Me, and I in Thee**" (17:20, 21). Paul affirms with special force in Ephesians 4:4-6 the essential unity of the Church by the use of seven *ones*, four *alls*, and the doctrine of the Holy Trinity when he writes that there is "**one body and one Spirit...one hope...one Lord, one faith, one baptism, one God and Father of all who is over all and through all and in all.**" By its intrinsic nature the Church is one. Thus Paul exhorts believers to be "**diligent [spare no effort] to preserve the unity of the Spirit in the bond of peace**" (Eph. 4:3). Peter charges all believers to "**love the brotherhood,**" that is, the worldwide Christian community (1 Peter 2:17). The oneness of the Church is a fundamental attribute of the body of Christ, the Church.

ONE CHURCH, COUNTLESS LOCAL CHURCHES

A fair and unprejudiced reading of the New Testament reveals that although Paul had a driving passion for unity among all Christians,[2] He (the master architect of the Gentile churches) never created a perpetual, organizational structure over local congregations to which all local churches must belong and submit or be considered schematic. Robert Banks sums up the Pauline evidence for us with remarkable precision when he writes:

> These scattered Christian groups did not express their unity by fashioning a corporate organization through which they could be federated with one another, but rather through a network of personal contacts between people who regarded themselves as members of the

---

[2] See the previous article by Jack Spender.

same Christian family. This is so even with respect to the foundation church in Jerusalem. Paul is eager to gain its recognition of his missionary endeavors so as to avoid any division in the Christian movement between its Jewish and Gentile wings (Gal. 2:1-10), for a denominationalism of this kind would be totally abhorrent to him. He is also concerned to gain the involvement of his Gentile churches in the collection for the poor in the church at Jerusalem (Rom. 15:25-27), so as to mark their acknowledgment that the gospel stemmed from them. Yet there is no sense in which his churches are subservient to the original Christian community or organizationally controlled by it.[3]

The local churches of the New Testament era were independent, self-governing, and complete in themselves. In the life and power of the Holy Spirit, Christ was present in each local gathering of His people (Matt. 18:20). In the mind of the New Testament apostles and writers, each local church is a visible, tangible—albeit imperfect—manifestation of the one Church of Jesus Christ. Each local church is thus to express the reality of the one, true Church of God. Addressing the local church at Corinth, Paul could write "**to the church of God which is at Corinth**" (1 Cor. 1:2; cf. 2 Cor. 1:1). The one, true Church of God was concretely and fully represented in the local church at Corinth. The Church of God as it is at Corinth is not merely a small part of the whole, a subdivision or a member of the Church belonging to it, but a true representative of the whole, the Church. It is the Church in its time and space expression, a microcosm of the whole. This cannot be said of any group or circle of churches or denomination, only of the local church. In this sense, the local church is independent.

On the other hand, each local church is truly the Church of God only as it conforms to and manifests the Church of God as defined by apostolic doctrine and practice. No local church can steer its own direction or establish its own beliefs. The Church is built "**upon the foundation of the apostles and prophets, Christ Jesus Himself being the cornerstone**" (Eph. 2:20; cf. 1 Cor. 3:11). Any local church that moves from this foundation is a counterfeit church. "The local congregation," as Ladd states, "is no isolated group but stands in a state of solidarity with the church as a whole."[4] In this sense no local church is independent. Hence Paul expects local churches to amend their practices and beliefs to other churches that follow faithfully apostolic teaching and practice (1 Cor. 14:33-36).

---

[3] Robert Banks, *Paul's Idea of Community* (Grand Rapids: Eerdmans, 1980), 48.

[4] George Eldon Ladd, *A Theology of the New Testament* (Grand Rapids: Eerdmans, 1974), 537.

Each New Testament local congregation, then, knew that it was part of a worldwide family of brothers and sisters sharing the same life in union with Christ by the Spirit, the same apostolic foundation, beliefs, and heavenly destination. They knew that their unity was guaranteed by the Spirit of God indwelling each believer. Hence, New Testament local churches expressed the oneness of the Church of God among themselves, not by one universal church leader, a pope, or a visible super-church institution, but by voluntary, loving fellowship with one another as the family of God. The New Testament beautifully harmonizes local church autonomy with loving interchurch fellowship. In his now classic work, *The Christian Ecclesia*, F. J. A. Hort skillfully summarizes this point for us:

> By itself each of these details may seem trivial enough: but together they help to show how St. Paul's recognition of the individual responsibility and substantial independence of single city Ecclesiae was brought into harmony with his sense of the unity of the body of Christ as a whole, by this watchful care to seize every opportunity of kindling and keeping alive in each society a consciousness of its share in the life of the great Ecclesia of God.[5]

We move now to explore some of the key examples of New Testament local churches interacting with one another.

NEW TESTAMENT LOCAL CHURCHES AND THEIR INTERRELATEDNESS

I can think of no better way to introduce the following survey of New Testament interchurch relationships than with this superb summary quotation by Herman Ridderbos from his magnum opus, *Paul: An Outline of His Theology*. Of all the material on this subject, and there is not much, he best captures Paul's thinking on this topic:

> In various ways [Paul] makes the local congregations also realize their fellowship among each other and wishes to promote among them as large a degree of agreement in their actions as possible. Time and again he points the churches to what is taking place elsewhere. They are to be conscious of the cosmic ('ecumenical') relationships in which the

---

[5] Fenton John Anthony Hort, *The Christian Ecclesia* (1897; repr. ed. London: Macmillan, 1914), 122.

gospel involves them (Col. 1:6, 23; 1 Tim. 3:16; cf. Eph. 1:10). What happens in other congregations must have their full interest (cf. 2 Cor. 9:2ff.; Col. 4:16); they are to participate in that which is undertaken elsewhere (1 Cor. 16:1ff.); they must allow themselves to be guided by the same directives in all the churches (1 Cor. 7:17; 4:17; 14:33); he wants them to pay heed to each other's ecclesiastical rules.[6]

Here are five major New Testament examples of interchurch fellowship.

Interchurch Relief Aid

The first account of a church providing relief aid to another church is Antioch sending an offering for the poor in Jerusalem (Acts 11:27-30). Luke records that "in the proportion that any of the disciples [in Antioch] had means, each of them determined to send a contribution for the relief of the brethren living in Judea."

Some ten years later the churches of Macedonia, Achaia, and Galatia collected and sent a large financial contribution to the poverty-stricken Christians in Jerusalem (Rom. 15:26). Paul not only considered this a gracious, sacrificial love offering but a spiritual indebtedness and responsibility the Gentile churches owed their Jewish brothers and sisters because the gospel first emanated from them. "For Macedonia and Achaia have been pleased to make a contribution for the poor among the saints in Jerusalem. Yes, they were pleased to do so, and they are indebted to them. For if the Gentiles have shared in their spiritual things, they are indebted to minister to them also in material things." (Rom. 15:26, 27). Although there is this spiritual indebtedness on the part of the Gentile churches, the offering was still a voluntary, love gift, not a required tax to the mother church or central organization for churches.

Paul also remarks that the Gentile offering to the poor in Judea was necessary as "a principle of equality...in the universal Christian fraternity," the "spirit of reciprocity," or "law of equilibrium."[7] Paul writes, "For this is not for the ease of others and for your [the Corinthians] affliction, but by way of equality." Paul believed that funds should flow from churches with plenty to churches in desperate need. This principle is operative for churches today: churches sharing their finances with churches in needy circumstances.

---

[6] Herman Ridderbos, *Paul: An Outline of His Theology* (Grand Rapids: Eerdmans, 1975), 478.

[7] Philip E. Hughes, *Paul's Second Epistle to the Corinthians*, NICNT (Grand Rapids: Eerdmans, 1962), 306.

Furthermore, the Gentile churches' contribution to Jerusalem was a marvel-ous demonstration of the oneness and *agape* love of the worldwide Christian brotherhood across racial lines. Commentator Philip Hughes concludes:

> We may be sure, further, that Paul regarded these acts of charitable giving as expressions of the organic unity of the Church, which is the body of Christ. They afforded tangible evidence to the world that in Christ the middle wall of partition between Jew and Gentile had indeed been broken down.[8]

Interchurch Communication: Greetings, News, Recommendations, and Counsel

Writing from Rome, Paul urged the church at Colossae to convey greetings from himself and Timothy to the church at Laodicea, some ten miles away in the Lycus valley. He further charged the church at Colossae with the responsibility to have the letter of Colossians read "in the church of the Laodiceans" and to procure the letter to the Laodiceans and have it read in its own assembly (Col. 4:15, 16; cf. 2 Cor. 1:1; 1 Peter 1:1; Rev. 1:4, 11; 2:23). Such detail reveals the close bond of fellowship that existed between these first churches and the desire to receive information and news from other churches and the Lord's servants. (See also Rom. 16:1-16; Phil. 4:22; Heb. 13:24; 1 Peter 5:13; 3 John 3, 6, 14)

Furthermore, letters of recommendation were used among the first churches in order to authorize and identify visiting teachers and fellow believers (2 Cor. 3:1). Correspondence among the first churches was welcomed and common.

The extant letter of Acts 15 from the church at Jerusalem with the apostles and elders to churches at Antioch, Syria, and Cilicia offered counsel and encouragement, provided doctrinal clarity, and introduced their delegates, Judas and Silas, who would in person restate the position of the apostles and elders regarding salvation apart from Jewish circumcision (Acts 15:22-33; 16:4).

Interchurch Ministry: Itinerant Teachers and Prophets

The New Testament reveals that there were a good number of itinerant teachers and prophets who traveled freely among the churches (Acts 11:27; 15:1, 3, 32). Apollos, for one, was an extraordinarily gifted teacher, apologist, and preacher.

---

[8] Hughes, *Paul's Second Epistle to the Corinthians*, 286.

Luke records that while ministering at Ephesus, Apollos felt lead to visit Corinth to help teach, hence "the brethren [at Ephesus] encouraged him and wrote to the disciples to welcome him; and when he had arrived [at Corinth], he helped greatly those who had believed through grace" (Acts 18:27; cf. 16:12). At a later period of time, after being absent from Corinth, Paul urged Apollos to visit Corinth to help in the ministry (1 Cor. 16:12). When the church at Jerusalem first heard about the establishment of the new church at Antioch, it sent Barnabas as its delegate to investigate. Barnabas encouraged the new congregation; he even helped provide leadership, teaching, and direction for the new congregation (Acts 11:22-26; cf. 8:14).

It was expected that local churches would heed such teachers and help them financially (3 John 5-8). Of course, there were false teachers who also traveled among churches creating confusion and division (2 Cor. 11:4–12:18; Gal. 5:7-12). It is disheartening to read how easily these false teachers made inroads into churches and how quickly believers embraced their teachings.

Interchurch Controversy and Deliberation

Growing Jew-Gentile fraternization at Antioch put unpleasant pressure on the church at Jerusalem from Jews both outside and inside the church (Gal. 2:12). Hence the church at Jerusalem put pressure on the church at Antioch to curtail its table fellowship with Gentile believers, which when Peter and Barnabas complied, Paul sternly rebuked them for inconsistent living and theology.

Eventually, the legalistic doctrinal problems brewing in Jerusalem spilled over to Antioch. When Jewish legalistic teachers from Jerusalem disrupted the congregation at Antioch with their false gospel, the church sent Paul and Barnabas as its representatives to Jerusalem to meet in joint counsel with the apostles and elders to discuss salvation apart from circumcision and the Law of Moses. The positive results of the meeting were written down and sent along with representatives from Jerusalem to the church at Antioch. The letter clarified the apostles' and Jerusalem elders' doctrinal position on circumcision and added some wise counsel for helping Gentiles live in peaceful coexistence with their scrupulous Jewish brethren.

It is essential to note that the decision to go to Jerusalem was a voluntary decision on the part of the church at Antioch. There is no biblical evidence to suggest that there was an established, supreme court in Jerusalem to which all Christian churches were answerable. The leaders of the church at Jerusalem needed to publicly clarify their position and policies regarding Gentile evangelization and fellowship. So, for the sake of unity among the churches, respect for

Jerusalem and the apostles, the future Gentile mission, and the defeat of the false gospel, the church at Antioch sent representatives to Jerusalem to defend their actions and to seek clarification (Acts 15:2). Antioch, not Jerusalem, initiated the conference.

Every effort appears to be made to maintain loving fellowship between the two churches. The same should be done today among churches. Churches can help other churches arbitrate disputes, give counsel, or study together.

We should note that some of the first churches experienced fears, suspicions, strains, and tensions between themselves just as churches do today (Acts 15; 21:18-26; Gal. 2:11-14). Dividing or establishing separate denominations was not an option for these first Christians.

Interchurch Modeling

Paul states that the church in Thessalonica was a positive model of courage and bold witness in the face of suffering to all the churches in Macedonia and Achaia (1 Thes. 1:7). He further says that the Thessalonians were imitating "the churches in Judea" in suffering, persecution, and endurance (1 Thes. 2:14). The love of the church in Thessalonica had spread to others in Macedonia (1 Thes. 4:10). Paul boasted to the churches in Macedonia about the Corinthians' desire to contribute to the poor in Jerusalem. In fact, Paul can honestly say, "Your zeal has stirred up most of them" (2 Cor. 9:2). Later Paul told the church at Corinth about the sacrificial contributions of "the churches in Macedonia" in order to move Corinth to action (2 Cor. 8:1-5). Thus churches learned from other churches, inspired one another to perseverance and love, and encouraged and comforted one another in hard times (1 Peter 5:9).

Several times in the letter to the Corinthians, Paul reminds the independent-minded Corinthians of standard apostolic church practices (1 Cor. 4:17; 7:17; 11:16; 14:33), appealing to them to conform to such practices.

> For this reason I have sent to you Timothy, who is my beloved and faithful child in the Lord, and he will remind you of my ways which are in Christ, just as I teach everywhere in every church (1 Cor. 4:17).

> For God is not a God of confusion but of peace, as in all the churches of the saints (1 Cor. 14:33).

> Only, as the Lord has assigned to each one, as God has called each, in this manner let him walk. And thus I direct in all the churches (1 Cor. 7:17).

> But if one is inclined to be contentious, we have no other practice, nor
> have the churches of God (1 Cor. 11:16).

> Now concerning the collection for the saints, as I directed the churches
> of Galatia, so do you also (1 Cor. 16:1).

The church at Corinth was to measure its practices by churches following
apostolic order. Among the churches, writes Herman Ridderbos, "[Paul] wishes
to promote among them [all the churches] as large a degree of agreement in their
actions as possible."[9] Churches, therefore, were to learn and be corrected by the
examples of other churches. (See also 1 Tim. 2:8; Titus 1:5.) Hort's lengthy
comment on this issue bears repeating and is a fitting conclusion to this point:

> We have varied evidence as to the pains taken by St. Paul to counteract
> any tendency towards isolation and wantonness of independence, which
> might arise in the young communities which he founded, or with which
> he came in contact. The Epistle which contains most evidence of this kind
> is I Corinthians, the same Epistle which more than any other is occupied
> with resisting tendencies towards inward division. The spirit of lawless-
> ness would evidently have a disintegrating effect in both spheres alike,
> as between the members of the individual Ecclesia, and as between it and
> the sister Ecclesiae of the same or other lands. The keynote as against
> isolation is struck in the very salutation (1:2). Without going into all the
> ambiguities of language in that verse, we can at least see that in some
> manner the Corinthians are there taught to look on themselves as united
> to "all who in every place invoke the name of our Lord Jesus Christ"; and
> I believe we may safely add that "theirs and ours" means "their Lord and
> ours," the one Lord being set forth as the common bond of union, and
> obedience to His will as Lord, the uniting law of life.[10]

THE ERRORS OF EXTREME INDEPENDENCE AND ISOLATIONISM

In light of the tendency of the churches like Corinth to isolate themselves from
other churches, we need to address the errors of extreme independence and
isolationism. A *Christianity Today* article entitled "The Independent Church

---

[9] Ridderbos, *Paul*, 478.

[10] Hort, *The Christian Ecclesia*, 119.

Myth" graphically challenges churches who pride themselves on being totally independent of other churches or ecclesiastical bodies to think again. Using his own local church as an example, Ken McGarvey writes:

> Take the congregation I pastor. Because it belongs to no denominational group, it is considered independent. Yet this church's life and witness would be greatly impoverished without the support and resources of other churches.... We do not print our own Sunday-school literature or write all our own music. Nor do we write or publish books for Bible study. We operate no radio or television station. Even the missionaries we help need support from other churches. We read periodicals, attend conferences and seminars, and even use films, tapes, and computer software produced by others. Every phase of our ministry is dependent upon others—other Christians and other churches.[11]

So from the weekly use of Sunday school curriculum to our hymnbooks, it is obvious that we depend for significant ministry help on Christians other than those who attend our own local congregation. Prideful, "rugged individualism," as McGarvey says, is not suited for the body of Christ, the Church.[12]

The fact is, every local church is born, not out of a theological or historical vacuum, but out of a history, a theology, a tradition, a culture, and a people influenced by previous churches, books, and bible teachers. Every local church has been affected by two thousand years of Christian history. We have all been affected by the councils of Nicea (A.D. 325), Constantinople (A.D. 381), and Chalcedon (A.D. 451) regarding the person of Christ and the Holy Trinity. The Reformation and its justification by "faith alone" doctrine has left its mark on all professing believers and churches. Many of us are the sons and daughters of the nineteenth-century Brethren movement. This is precisely what Paul brings to the attention of the Corinthians when he reprimands them for their individualizing and independent attitude: "Was it from you that the word of God first went forth? Or has it come to you only?" (1 Cor. 14:36).

Refusal to acknowledge a church's history or theological heritage, a common trait among highly independent churches and leaders, only causes the same old errors and failures to be repeated again and again without learning or resolving anything. A knowledge of Christian history (and the history of Israel

---

[11] Ken McGarvey, "The Independent Church Myth," *Christianity Today* (July 22, 1991): 8.

[12] McGarvey, "The Independent Church Myth," 8.

from the Old Testament) can help protect from doctrinal and practical error (Rom. 15:4; 1 Cor. 10:11). It also gives you a more realistic and humble perspective on yourself and your local church.

There is an aphorism that is well articulated by the famous Russian dissident Aleksandr Solzhenitsyn that goes: "He who forgets his own history is condemned to repeat it. If we don't know our own history, we will simply have to endure all the same mistakes, sacrifices, and absurdities all over again."[13] If you read Roy Coad's *A History of the Brethren Movement*, as I have several times, you will realize that the same debates and divisions have been reproduced today, especially among Exclusives, as their recent divisions so painfully demonstrate. History can protect a church from repeating the same ancient errors and also provide more objective appraisal of our disagreements. As King Solomon wrote, "There is nothing new under the Sun." It is to be hoped that we can establish a mind-set that seeks to resolve problems and errors rather then repeat them ad nauseam to the dishonor of our blessed Lord.

Zealously independent churches that have no interest in or even worse are suspicious of all outside their local fellowship breed all sorts of sub-Christian behavior. It bespeaks the opposite of Christian unity, oneness, and *agape* love. It is a poor and shallow witness of the global message and worldwide family of God. Moreover, highly independent churches become, as Roy Coad observes, "the happy hunting-ground of the individualist" leader-despot.[14] We at Littleton Bible Chapel, where I attend, have experienced firsthand over the past four years the spiritual abuse these loner churches inflict on the Lord's people. I have personally counseled numerous couples and individuals shattered by abusive churches and their leaders. It often takes years for these believers to deal with their anger and sense of betrayal.

Furthermore, isolationist churches produce Christian people with unChristlike attitudes. Trapped in the fortress mentality of "we are the only true and faithful people to the Bible," these believers often become self-satisfied, suspicious of all others (even those slightly different from themselves), prideful, closed-minded, biblically stagnate, and self-deceived. Their badge of distinction is that they are not like other churches. Indeed, if other churches are doing something effective for God, they wouldn't follow simply because other churches are doing it. Being distinct is more important than their shared beliefs with fellow Christians. In truth, we all need the whole body of Christ in order

---

[13] Aleksandr Solzhenitsyn, "Why Study Church History?" *Christian History*, 25 (1990): 41.

[14] F. Roy Coad, *A History of the Brethren Movement* (Grand Rapids: Eerdmans, 1968), 164.

to be balanced, wise, and awakened to our own failures and shortcomings, of which we are often totally blind.

Finally, there is a built-in desire on the part of every Christian to identify with and belong to something bigger than a local church. The reason is, we are part of a worldwide family, and we want to know and be part of the development of that worldwide family. Just as there should be no loner Christians, there should be no loner churches. Loner churches with Diotrephes-type pastors are unhealthy, deceived, deficient churches.

BENEFITS OF INTERCHURCH RELATIONSHIPS

To start with, churches can learn from other churches. Much of what we are at Littleton Bible Chapel is a result of learning from other churches. In our first years as a church we emulated Southside Bible Chapel with John Walden in Colorado Springs, Believers Chapel in Dallas, Texas, and the Fairhaven Bible Chapel in San Leandro, California. These were mentor churches to us. I can truly say that over the past thirty years we have been a learning church. We have some ideas and practices that are unique to us, but the lion's share of what we practice, we borrowed from other churches. We delight in learning from the amazing creativity of the churches of God.

In my limited travels as a preacher, I get to see what other churches are doing and how we at Littleton can learn from their strengths and creative ideas of worship, evangelism, administration, preaching, and pastoral care. So when you visit other churches, which is always an educational experience both negatively and positively, keep your eyes open and ask lots of questions. In my judgment, when people become annoyed with all your questions, you know you have done your job.

If you are with missionaries, ask them about their local churches. I have learned a great deal from missionaries. Missionaries are often very creative people. I remember years ago having a four-hour, educational lunch with Bill Deans from Zaire, Africa. I asked him hours of questions concerning the churches in Africa. I found that they were taping all their sermons years before assemblies here in the United States even owned taping equipment.

Furthermore, conferences are important because as you interact with brothers and sisters from other churches you gain new insights and ideas. We can learn from the strengths, successes, and failures of other churches. So churches can learn from one another and teach one another. Be a learning church, not a know-it-all church, or an anti-change church. All of our churches can use improvement in nearly every area of ministry.

A. T. Pierson said that Bethesda Chapel in Bristol, England, where George Müller and Henry Craik ministered, was one of the truly apostolic churches in the world in his day. Throughout the world over the past hundred years there have been churches that emulate the spirit and practice of Bethesda. You can read about Bethesda Chapel in the book *I Will Build My Church: 150 Years of Local Church Work in Bristol* by Keith and Alan Linton. You too can learn from this dynamic church.

Second, churches can use the resources and expertise of other churches. I was encouraged to hear from the small assembly I attended in New Jersey many years ago that other assemblies had provided financial help for the church's building needs. There is an assembly in Maryland that helps rebuild church buildings destroyed by tropical storms. Recently many churches united to help rebuild some of the black churches burned in the South by arsonists. Many of our churches sent blankets and money to the poor churches in Romania during the communists' reign.

Furthermore, if one church has a number of able teachers or evangelists it can share them with churches that lack competent teachers or evangelists. Churches with a small youth group need to occasionally meet with other church youth groups in order to meet more Christian young people.

One of the most exciting things happening in our church at this time is our work with churches in Mexico and Indonesia. In Tenancingo, Mexico we are helping to build a building for the church. We have sent teams to help in evangelism and a team to help build the building. We have flown two of their leaders to Denver to meet and minister to us; it has been very encouraging collaboration for both churches. People are excited to give and help their needy brothers and sisters in Mexico. Through one of our missionaries in Indonesia we have planted several churches there. We consider them sister churches. We pray for them regularly. We also support several local native workers who shepherd these churches and plant new churches. We are encouraging other churches to help with this great work in Indonesia.

The fact is, when many churches pool their financial resources, human resources, and prayer support they can do so much more than one church alone.

Third, in a unique way churches can display the oneness and love of the worldwide family of God through their cooperation with one another. When churches sacrificially help and share with one another and work together for world or local evangelism, they display the power of the gospel to a watching world. They also greatly encourage one another. It is a marvelous witness to the world of the reality of the saving gospel of Christ. In the words of our Lord, "By this all men will know that you are My disciples, if you have love for one another"

(John 13:35). I will close this first section of this paper with wise counsel from the book *A New Testament Blueprint for the Church*:

> We act more like marbles than grapes. When squeezed together we produce glass shards rather than sweet wine.
>
> If we resist a spirit of cooperation and interdependence within the Body of Christ, then we are denying the reality of the Body of Christ. If we are single-minded in intent that all ministry meetings, efforts, and resources are to be used exclusively for one local church, or at least to point believers toward membership and participation in only one church, then we are denying the reality of the Body of Christ. If we do not join hands in our communities in matters of doctrine and discipline of believers, and cooperate energetically toward that end, then we are denying the reality of the Body of Christ.[15]

Because we do act more like marbles than grapes, let us now move to the second part of this paper and suggest some biblical principles for better interchurch relations.

HOW DO LOCAL CHURCHES DISPLAY THE ONENESS OF THE CHURCH AND LOVING INTERCHURCH FELLOWSHIP IN DIVIDED CHRISTENDOM?

There is universal agreement that there is only one Church and Jesus Christ is the Founder and Head. It is also agreed that the New Testament churches lovingly interacted with one another in various ways. However, the worldwide Christian community today, representing hundreds of thousands of churches, which we will call Christendom, is divided into many denominations, some of which propagate an utterly false gospel and erroneous view of the nature of the Church. Even more disheartening is that among bible-believing churches there are denominational barriers, conflicting theological camps, and, in some cases, near impenetrable walls of division and distrust. What then is a local church to do in this disagreeable, conflicting ecclesiastical environment?

To answer this question, we first must separate false churches from true, Spirit-indwelt, gospel churches. We should all be aware that there are those who profess

---

[15] John Moore and Ken Neff, *A New Testament Blueprint for the Church* (Chicago: Moody, 1985), 87.

to be the true Church, but are in fact false professing Christians and pseudo-churches planted directly by Satan. Regarding fellowship with these churches, we have no unity to maintain. We are to separate from a false gospel and false church. Jesus warned us that "the enemy" would sow useless, annoying tares in "the world" in order to counterfeit the wheat planted by Himself (Matt. 13:24-30; 36-43). The world is full of tares that significantly outnumber the wheat planted by Christ. John the apostle also warned that there would be many antichrists and false prophets in the world (1 John 4:1-3; 2 John 7-11). Paul taught that in a large house [professing Christendom] there will be vessels of honor [godly teachers] and vessels of dishonor [false teachers]. Paul urged Timothy to separate himself from these false teachers in order to be a useful servant for God. "If a man cleanses himself from these things [vessels of dishonor, false teachers], he will be a vessel for honor, sanctified, useful to the Master, prepared for every good work" (2 Tim. 2:21).

The false teacher is the archenemy of the local church. The New Testament calls the elders to guard the local church from wolves (Acts 20:28-31) and to separate from those who perpetuate a false gospel, which is no gospel at all (2 Cor. 6:14-17; Rom. 16:17; Eph. 5:11; 1 Tim. 6:3-6; 2 Tim. 2:16-21; 2 John 6-11). Separation from false doctrine is a New Testament principle that must counterbalance seeking unity among all who profess the name of Christ. One of the most frightening verses in the New Testament is 2 Corinthians 11:14. "For even Satan disguises himself as an angel of light." Thus false teachers also are "deceitful workers, disguising themselves as apostles of Christ" (2 Cor. 11:13). The world is full of counterfeit Christian teachers, messengers of Satan, wolves in sheep's clothing. "Satan's great campaign," writes Peter Masters, "is to pollute God's churches on earth and bring them into doctrinal and spiritual chaos. He longs to see utter confusion engulf churches which have borne a powerful testimony, and he is behind all the heretical infiltration of sound congregations."[16]

In much of the literature on church unity, even among evangelicals, the New Testament's principle of separation from false doctrine is strangely absent. Some evangelicals talk as if Roman Catholicism and Eastern Orthodoxy are authentic expressions of biblical Christianity and that we can unite with them. We all agree that there are born again brothers and sisters who love the Lord in these denominations, but the systems are false, counterfeit expressions of the gospel; they give false hope of salvation to millions of people; moreover they continue to this day to persecute true believers in Christ.

---

[16] Peter Masters, "After 1900 years-the 'Conversion' of Evangelicalism," *A Sword & Trowel* (Special Issue: *Separation and Obedience*, 1983): 3.

We wholeheartedly concur with Paul when he says, "being diligent to preserve the unity of the Spirit in the bond of peace" (Eph. 4:3), but many churches and professing Christians have no part in the "unity of the Spirit" because they do not have the Holy Spirit; they are not the body of Christ. We have no "unity of the Spirit" to maintain with them. Therefore we need to lovingly warn them and tell them of the true gospel of the Lord Jesus Christ, but never unite, for what "fellowship has light with darkness" (2 Cor. 6:14)?

Now it is plain that we should not fellowship with churches built on a false gospel, but far more difficult and vexing to explain is the fact that among bible-believing Christians and churches that agree on most major doctrines, there are sinful divisions dividing churches and fellow believers. Although there are wonderful examples of unity and cooperation among churches, there are still thousands of conservative, bible-believing churches that refuse fellowship with other bible-believing churches because of doctrinal and historical reasons. Some of these doctrinal issues dividing churches are quite significant, like baptismal regeneration or women's ordination; others are as trite as mixed bathing or styles of worship.

For my part, I envision no grand plan for ending denominational divisions or tribal warfare among churches and denominations. As I picture it, however, the Lord doesn't acknowledge our man-made parties in any way. Baptist, Lutheran, Presbyterian, Wesleyan are not of His making or concern. According to Scripture, Christians should never name themselves or churches after a puny man or a pet point of theology (1 Cor. 1:12; 3:1-5, 21; 4:6). In His sight all true believers are one family born of the Spirit. The local congregation and the individual saint is still His loving, undivided focus of attention. He walks among the lampstands, not denominations (Rev. 2:1). When Christ returns He will clean up the mess we have created. At the judgment seat He will burn away prideful, misguided party loyalties. He will reward His saints for faithfulness to His Word and love for Himself and the family of God. He will be victorious in the end. He will "present to Himself the church in all her glory, having no spot or wrinkle or any such thing; but that she should be holy and blameless" (Eph. 5:27).

But what can a local church do at present that seeks to show the love of Christ and oneness of the body of Christ and yet protect itself from error within a divided Christian community? There are no easy answers. The fact is, doctrine does divide! Sinful sectarian attitudes also divide! We have to live with the consequences of our sins and divisions. So in the end, most decisions regarding association and cooperation with other evangelical churches or parachurch organizations are going to be a matter of individual or corporate conscience, and there are no simple solutions or answers for everyone.

Because, however, each local church is ideally to be a microcosm of the one, true Church of Jesus Christ, it is biblically mandated that a local church teach and model the love and oneness of the family of God. This is why Paul says that each church and individual must "[spare no effort] to preserve the unity of the Spirit in the bond of peace" (Eph. 4:3). To help us in this effort of maintaining the "unity of the Spirit in the bond of peace" in the midst of a divided bible-believing community, I have listed some practical suggestions and biblical concepts of how an individual local church can honor the Lord in this matter and also be an example to other churches of the glorious oneness of the Church of Jesus Christ.

TEACH AND MODEL THE ONENESS OF THE CHURCH AND LOVE OF CHRIST FOR ALL THE BRETHREN

As leaders, teachers, and models of God's family, overseer-elders must teach and model the importance of the oneness of the Church of Jesus Christ and the love of Christ for all our brothers and sisters. The oneness of the Lord's people is a highly significant doctrine yet many show little or no regard for it. Christians will split over minor issues, ignoring the sacredness of the unity of the body of Christ. For example, there is a very large circle of churches that have divided over musical instruments. This disagreement over musical instruments seems to be more important than the unity of the body and the testimony of the Lord. The myriad of unnecessary divisions among conservative, bible-loving churches demonstrates that something is catastrophically wrong with our doctrinal priorities. You will not find this attitude in Paul. He went to great personal and sacrificial lengths to maintain unity among the Lord's people. This is true of his dealing with the independent-minded, boastful church at Corinth and the suspicious, parochial, legalistic church at Jerusalem (Acts 21:18-26). Paul could have collected a file drawer full of reasons for starting his own denomination, but he didn't. Problems just had to be worked out in the family of God.

But teaching right doctrine about the unity of the Church is not enough; you must teach right attitudes. In the Ephesians 4 context of preserving "the unity of the Spirit," Paul enumerates the Christian virtues necessary for maintaining the unity created by the Spirit: "with all humility and gentleness, with patience, showing forbearance to one another in love" (Eph. 4:2). Without humility, gentleness, forbearance, and love, there will be no peace or unity among God's people. When Lawrence Sandy was asked about his leadership role as president of the Navigators, he made the insightful comment that one of his most important jobs as leader of leaders was "checking attitudes." The elders of the church must "check attitudes."

For an example of wrong attitudes that need checking, read Jack Van Impe's revealing book *Heart Disease In Christ's Body*.[17] The book explains why Van Impe would not conduct citywide evangelistic crusades among his fundamentalist churches for over five years. Although these fundamentalists' churches were in ninety-nine percent agreement over doctrinal and lifestyle issues, they were constantly fighting with one another, accusing one another of compromise and false doctrine, criticizing, faultfinding, talebearing, rumormongering, and hating. They displayed all the evils of fanaticism, extremism, negativism, judgmentalism, provincialism, demagoguery, and divisiveness. In the name of protecting the truth and their local churches, the most Satanic attitudes and deeds were justified by so-called godly Christian leaders. These Christians had right doctrine (or so they boasted) but wrong, sinful attitudes. Paul E. Billheimer provides the correct diagnosis for this deadly spiritual sickness. "Most controversies in local congregations are produced, not primarily by differences over essentials, but by unsanctified human ambitions, jealousy, and personality clashes. The real root of many such situations is spiritual dearth in individual believers, revealing lamentable immaturity in love."[18] The very same fanatical, unbalanced, unChristlike attitudes split the Brethren movement, as discussed in Harry A. Ironside's *An Historical Sketch of the Brethren Movement*.[19]

Again Billheimer is positively New Testament in spirit when he states that we will never have complete doctrinal unity on all details or minor matters among God's people this side of heaven. Thus, love must cover our differences (1 Peter 4:8), and our common family origin must take precedence over differences in nonessentials to salvation. "No amount of grace," writes Billheimer, "will ever enable all born-again people to agree on what formulated doctrinal system constitutes absolute conceptual truth.... [Thus] it means that love for the family will exceed devotion to one's personal opinions in nonessentials to salvation."[20]

AVOID EXCLUSIVE CHURCH GROUPS

If your church associates with a group of churches that requires exclusive allegiance to itself, you are part of a sect. Despite their boastful claims, sects do

---

[17] Jack Van Impe, *Heart Disease in Christ's Body* (Royal Oak, MI: Jack Van Impe Ministries, 1984).

[18] Paul E. Billheimer, *Love Covers: A Viable Platform for Christian Unity* (Fort Washington: Christian Literature Crusade, 1981), 34.

[19] H. A. Ironside, *A Historical Sketch of the Brethren Movement* (Grand Rapids: Zondervan, 1942).

[20] Paul E. Billheimer, *Love Covers*, 29.

not understand the New Testament doctrine of the Church. They are in error. All sects are based on half-truths, faulty reasoning, doctrinal oddities, deceptions, guilt-manipulation, and fear, which are not of the Spirit of truth and liberty. If your church denies you your Spirit-given right and privilege to fellowship with all Christ-loving, bible-loving Christians and churches, you need to obey God rather than man and free yourself and family from these unbiblical chains.

MAINTAIN AN OPEN LORD'S TABLE

The Lord's table should be the one place all true believers can fellowship together remembering and praising the Lord for His substitutionary work on our behalf. A closed table is sectarian and divisive. The bread upon the table is not only a symbol of His death, but of the "**one body**" of which we are all members (1 Cor. 10:17). Remember, it is His table not ours, and thus all His people are welcome despite our differences. The open table for all true believers centering on Christ's great substitutionary work was one of the truly great discoveries of the early Brethren movement. So make the Lord's Supper a place of unity and oneness. Ministry in the local church is another matter but worship and fellowship around the symbols of His death should be as open as possible for all God's dear children. Our attitude should reflect that of Anthony Norris Groves when he wrote his friend Mr. Caldecott, an Anglican curate, about his break with the Church of England:

> You say I quitted your communion; if you mean by that, that I do not now break bread with the Church of England, this is not true; but if you mean that I do not exclusively join you, it is quite true, feeling this spirit of exclusiveness to be of the very essence of schism, which the apostle so strongly reproves in the Corinthians. I therefore know no distinction, but am ready to break the bread and drink the cup of holy joy with all who love the Lord.[21]

MAINTAIN AN OPEN RECEPTION POLICY

Do not make entrance into your local fellowship difficult or threatening. Do not erect artificial, unbiblical barriers to your fellowship. Our rallying cry should be Romans 15:7. "**Wherefore, accept one another, just as Christ also accepted us to the glory of God.**" Drawing out the implications of this verse, Anthony Norris

---

[21] F. Roy Coad, *A History of the Brethren Movement*, 23.

Groves wrote, "The basis of our fellowship is life in the Christ of the Scripture rather than light on the teaching of the Scripture. Those who have part with Christ have part with us." William Kelly in his probing little booklet *Christian Unity and Fellowship or The Unity of the Spirit and How to Keep it* sounds much like brother Groves when he writes:

> But I will go further. Take hope of the return of the Lord Jesus. You know how very important it is for Christians to be waiting in truth and heart for Christ from heaven; but would you require that those who seek fellowship in the name of the Lord should understand and confess that hope before you receive them in the Lord? Would not this be a sect? Be it that your assertion of the Christian hope is ever so ignorant on that subject; but who authorizes you or others to stand at the door and forbid his entrance?...
>
> Is then knowledge of truth or growth in spiritual intelligence to be slighted? In no way; but it is false and vain to require either as a preliminary condition from saints who seek fellowship according to God. Help them, instruct them, lead them on in both. This is a true service, but arduous withal. The other is sectarian, and wrong.[22]

In succinct style, John Frame states our point. "The conditions for church membership should be no narrower than the Scriptures' conditions for belonging to the kingdom of God. Anyone who can make a credible profession of faith in Christ should be welcomed into the church."[23] Of course, it is understood that Christian people who are unrepentant in their sin or under discipline from another church need to be referred back to their home church for reconciliation and restoration.

Issue Letters of Recommendation

When people leave your fellowship, give them a letter of recommendation so they can pass it on to the spiritual leaders of their new church. In this small way we can help demonstrate the oneness of the body of Christ and loving, familial interchurch relations.

---

[22] William Kelly, *Christian Unity and Fellowship or The Unity of the Spirit and How to Keep it* (London: Hammond Trust, n. d.), 8, 9.

[23] John M. Frame, *Evangelical Reunion: Denominations and the Body of Christ* (Grand Rapids: Baker, 1991), 96.

HONOR THE DISCIPLINE OF OTHER CHURCHES

Always seek to honor the discipline of other bible-believing churches. If a believer under discipline from another church seeks your fellowship, contact the disciplining church for information. If you feel the discipline of the erring member is unjust, then inform the disciplining church why. If it is just, then refuse fellowship to the sinning member until the problem has been reconciled with the disciplining church.

HONOR BELIEVER'S BAPTISM FROM OTHER CHURCHES

We should honor one another's baptisms. A number of years ago, a couple from our assembly moved to the opposite side of town where they started to attend a Southern Baptist church. The church would not allow them to join or participate in ministry until they were re-baptized. They called us to ask what they should do? We told them emphatically not to be re-baptized. We told them there was only one baptism and one Church. We told them to ask the pastor if he had been crucified for them. If he had, then they should be re-baptized into his name. If he had not, tell him they were baptized in the name of the Lord Jesus Christ (1 Cor. 1:11-17), the only Savior and Lord.

COOPERATE WITH OTHER BIBLE-BELIEVING CHURCHES WHEN POSSIBLE

Participate in local community prayer meetings or community evangelistic outreaches like the Billy Graham outreach. In 1987 we had the Billy Graham citywide crusade in Denver. Hundreds of bible-believing, evangelical churches participated in the citywide crusade. Over twenty-four thousand people made professions of faith. After the crusade Billy Graham said he believed that the reason for such an enormously successful response to the gospel was because of the unity displayed among all the churches sponsoring the crusade. Such unity centering around an evangelist for the advancement of the gospel is thoroughly in keeping with the spirit of the New Testament.

If there is a local prayer meeting or fellowship meeting of bible-believing churches in your community, send a representative to meet with your local brethren for prayer and mutual encouragement.

If your church senses the need for greater cooperation with the larger evangelical community, join an interdenominational group like the National Association of Evangelicals or The World Evangelical Fellowship. Of course, you are under no biblical mandate to join any association of churches, but you are also free to join if your conscience allows and you have need to experience Christian fellowship and cooperation on a larger scale. Let me make one more suggestion. If your circle of churches is having a conference, invite a few other churches in your neighborhood to attend. Don't hide your blessings or distinctives. Others might find your conference spiritually rewarding. I know it will please the Lord.

Finally, we must keep in mind that what an individual Christian does or a preacher of the Word does in relation to other churches will be different from what a whole church does in participating with other churches. For example, I have spoken in churches as radically different as the liberal United Methodist Church to fundamentalist churches and charismatic churches. However, I certainly do not want our local church to work with some of these churches. Much more is at stake when churches associate and work together.

LEARN FROM ALL GOD'S SERVANTS

Encourage the saints to learn from all God's faithful teachers and preachers, even those outside one's own circle of fellowship. According to Ephesians 3:18 we learn about God and His eternal purposes not simply on our own but in solidarity with all of God's people. Spurgeon said that he thought it was odd that some people think so much of what God teaches them but so little of what God teaches others. The point is, we learn from the whole body of Christ, which has existed over the past two thousand years.

In a highly significant text, Paul tells the factious-minded Corinthians that "**all things belong to you**" (1 Cor. 3:21-23). What Paul is referring to is the Corinthians' tendency to idolize one favorite teacher and to shut themselves off from other Spirit-given teachers. What Paul is saying, however, is that all God's teachers belong to us, not just one favorite: Calvin, Darby, Wesley, Augustine, Bruce, Mac Donald, Luther, MacArthur, Swindoll, Hodge, Warfield, Kelly, Müller, and all the thousands of other teachers God has graced His people with. Listen to what William Kelly has to say in this regard:

> Let none fancy this is to disparage those admirable men whom the Lord used in days gone by. Cherish unfeigned respect for such as Luther, Calvin, Farel, and Zwingle, though quite allowing the infirmities of every one of them. It is childish to find fault with Tyndale and Cranmer, whilst idolising Melancthon or John Knox. They were all of like passions as ourselves; and if disposed to study their lives and labours there are ample materials not far to seek for criticism; and so with men of God in our day.[24]

All of God's servants have something to teach us about our Lord Jesus Christ.

KEEP INFORMED

Local church elders and leaders should keep informed on the theological trends and workings of God in the worldwide evangelical community. Read magazines like *Christianity Today* or *Moody Monthly* for such information. Also when able, attend conferences that are not strictly in your circle of churches. You will find such conferences will broaden your perspective of the worldwide ministry of the Spirit of God and enliven your study of Scripture.

CONCLUSION

The local churches of the New Testament were autonomous yet interrelated because they were all one worldwide family of redeemed brothers and sisters. Among the first churches there was much interaction, especially through personal contacts and letters. There was also responsibility to share financial resources with needier churches (2 Cor. 9:13), to learn and follow the example of other churches, and to resolve differences between churches (Acts 15). Therefore, no healthy local church is an island. It shares the same apostolic ground of truth and life-giving Spirit of God with all other believers. Churches thus need other churches; indeed, they can learn from and be encouraged by all true, bible-believing churches.

As to this fellowship and cooperation with other bible-believing churches of various degrees of diverse theology, each local church is autonomous and thus will decide for itself, guided by its elders, which churches it will associate and work with and to what degree there will be cooperation and fellowship. I would counsel, in the spirit of the New Testament, that each local church should be as broad, understanding, peaceable, open, and inclusive in its fellowship with other churches as possible, yet as protective and wise as possible. We cannot be naïve. This is a sinful, confused world and even our own brothers and sisters can be involved in aberrant practices and doctrines. Let us seek to be balanced like our Lord Jesus Christ through whom "grace and truth were realized" (John 1:16, 17).

In closing, remember our Lord's response to John when he informed Jesus

---

[24] John M. Frame, *Evangelical Reunion*, 14.

that he and the others had tried to stop an unknown disciple from ministering because "he does not follow along with us" (Luke 9:49, 50). Jesus, perceiving their suspicions and provincialism, said, "Do not hinder him; for he who is not against you is for you." In other words, the unknown ministering brother is a friend not an enemy! Let us not treat as enemies Christian brothers and sisters or churches that are not of our select circle of churches. The work of God is a large worldwide work, let us be large enough to appreciate it and be a part of it. The Lord help us to balance ourselves on this tightrope of unity and doctrinal purity.

ABOUT THE AUTHORS

Jack Fish was born August 7, 1941. As a result of listening to Billy Graham, Jack trusted Christ in his junior year of high school. He graduated from Brown University with a B.A. in Linguistics and went on to receive Th.M. and Th.D. degrees from Dallas Theological Seminary. For the past thirty years Jack has taught at Emmaus Bible College. He currently serves as Editor of *The Emmaus Journal* and as an elder at Asbury Community Chapel in Dubuque, IA. Nancy and Jack have four children, all of whom have graduated from or attended Emmaus.

Ted Grant was born April 29, 1941 and saved nine years later in Jamaica, West Indies. His education spans several disciplines with a B.A. from Yale, an M.S. and Ph.D. (in Physics) from Lehigh University, and an M.D. from the University of Minnesota. Not married, Ted is an endocrinologist in private practice in Minneapolis, MN, while at the same time serving as an elder at Long Lake Community Church. He is also a regular Bible conference speaker.

Dave MacLeod was born in Nova Scotia in 1944, raised in Massachusetts, and converted to faith in Jesus Christ at the age of sixteen. He holds Th.M. and Ph.D. degrees from Dallas Theological Seminary. He and his wife Linda have four children. A member of the faculty of Emmaus Bible College and Associate Editor of *The Emmaus Journal*, he has written extensively, preaches throughout North America, and serves as an elder at Asbury Road Bible Chapel in Dubuque, IA.

Jack Spender was born July 3, 1943. Jack was saved at Camp Berea in New Hampshire in July 1950. He graduated from Barrington College, Rhode Island with a B.A. and from Trinity Evangelical Divinity School in Deerfield, Illinois with an M.A. He and his wife Ruth have three children. Calling Connecticut home, Jack has a full-time church-planting and Bible-teaching ministry. He also serves as an elder at West Woods Bible Chapel.

Jim Stahr was born June 7, 1926 in the Chicago area and came to Christ in 1942 in a high school Bible study. After finishing a tour of naval duty, he graduated with a B.S. in Electrical Engineering from Rutgers University and then received his Th.M. from Dallas Theological Seminary. Two years after they were married Jim and Betty were commended to full-time ministry, first in Newfoundland and Prince Edward Island and later in the Chicago area where he served as Editor of

Interest magazine for fifteen years. Now semi-retired, Jim continues a preaching and writing ministry. He and Betty have been blessed with four children, twelve grandchildren, and two great-grandchildren. Jim's home church is Bethany Chapel in Wheaton, IL where he serves as Elder Emeritus.

Alex Strauch was born November 11, 1944 and was saved at Pine Bush Bible Camp in New York at eleven years of age. He received a B.A. in Philosophy from Colorado Christian University and a M.Div. from Denver Seminary. Alex and Marilyn have four daughters. Operating out of Littleton, Colorado, Alex is a full-time Bible teacher, author, and elder at Littleton Bible Chapel. He is perhaps most widely known for his seminal work *Biblical Eldership*.

BIBLIOGRAPHY

Allen, Roland. *Missionary Methods; St. Paul's or Ours?* London: World Dominion Press, 1927.

Armstrong, John H., ed. *The Coming Evangelical Crisis.* Chicago: Moody, 1996.

Attridge, Harold W. *The Epistle to the Hebrews.* Hermeneia. Philadelphia: Fortress, 1989.

Banks, Robert. "From Fellowship to Organisation: A Study in the Early History of the Concept of the Church." *RTR* 30 (September 1971) 79-89.

———. "Fulfilling the Promise of the Priesthood of All Believers." *CBRF Journal* 129 (December 1992) 25.

———. *Paul's Idea of Community.* Grand Rapids: Eerdmans, 1980.

Bannerman, D. D. *The Scripture Doctrine of the Church.* Grand Rapids: Eerdmans, 1955.

Bannermann, James. *The Church of Christ.* 2 vols. Edinburgh: T & T Clark, 1868.

Barnes, Albert. *Notes on the New Testament: Revelation.* Edited by Robert Frew. New York: Harper, 1851. Reprint ed. Grand Rapids: Baker, 1972.

Batiffol, Pierre. *Primitive Catholicism.* Translated by H. L. Brianceau. New York: Longmans, Green, 1911.

Berkhof, Hendrikus. *Christian Faith.* Translated by Sierd Woudstra. Rev. ed. Grand Rapids: Eerdmans, 1986.

Berkhof, Louis. *Systematic Theology.* 4th ed. Grand Rapids: Eerdmans, 1949.

Berkouwer, G. C. *The Sacraments.* Grand Rapids: Eerdmans, 1969.

———. *The Church.* Translated by James E. Davison. Grand Rapids: Eerdmans, 1976.

Berney, James. "Some Inadequacies of Present-Day Brethren." *CBRF Journal* 25 (September 1973) 17.

Billheimer, Paul E. *Love Covers: A Viable Platform for Christian Unity.* Fort Washington: Christian Literature Crusade, 1981.

Blaiklock, E. M. *The Acts of the Apostles.* Tyndale New Testament Commentaries. Grand Rapids: Eerdmans, n.d.

Bourke, Myles M. "Reflections on Church Order in the New Testament." *CBQ* 30 (1968) 493.

Broadbent, E. H. *The Pilgrim Church.* London: Pickering and Inglis, 1931.

Brown, Colin, ed. *The New International Dictionary of New Testament Theology.* 3 vols. Grand Rapids: Zondervan, 1978.

Browne, Michael. *Autonomy and Authority.* Glasgow: Gospel Tract Publications, 1988.

Bruce, F. F. *The Acts of the Apostles*. Grand Rapids: Eerdmans, 1951.

————. *The Acts of the Apostles: Greek Text with Introduction and Commentary*. Rev. ed. Grand Rapids: Eerdmans, 1990.

————. *The Epistles to the Colossians, to Philemon, and to the Ephesians*. New International Commentary on the New Testament. Rev. ed. Grand Rapids: Eerdmans, 1984.

————. *The Hard Sayings of Jesus*. Downers Grove: InterVarsity, 1983.

————. "Practice or Principle (2)." *Harvester* 68 (February 1989) 7.

Brueggemann, Walter. "Rethinking Church Models Through Scripture." *Theology Today* 48 (July 1991) 128-38.

Brunner, Emil. *Dogmatics*. 3 vols. Translated by David Cairns. Philadelphia: Westminster, 1962.

Caird, George B. *The Apostolic Age*. London: Duckworth, 1955.

Callahan, James Patrick. "Primitivist Piety: The Ecclesiology of the Early Plymouth Brethren." (Ph. D. dissertation: Marquette University, 1994).

Campbell, Donald K. *Walvoord: A Tribute*. Chicago: Moody Press, 1982.

Campbell, R. Alastair. *The Elders: Seniority Within Earliest Christianity*. Edinburgh: T. & T. Clark, 1994.

Carson, D. A. *The Gospel According to John*. Grand Rapids: Eerdmans, 1991.

Cervin, Richard S. "Does Κεφαλή Mean 'Source' or 'Authority Over' in Greek Literature? A Rebuttal" *Trinity Journal* 10 NS (1989) 85-112.

Charles, R. H. *The Revelation of St. John*. International Critical Commentary. 2 vols. Edinburgh: T. and T. Clark, 1920.

Clowney, Edmund P. *The Church*. Downers Grove: InterVarsity Press, 1995.

Coad, F. Roy. *A History of the Brethren Movement*. Grand Rapids: Eerdmans, 1968.

Craik, Henry. *New Testament Church Order*. Bristol: W. Mack, 1863.

Culver, Robert. "Apostles and the Apostolate in the New Testament." *Bibliotheca Sacra* 134 (April 1977) 136-37.

Darby, John Nelson. *The Collected Writings of J. N. Darby*. 34 vols. Edited by William Kelly. Reprint ed. Oak Park, IL: Bible Truth Publishers, 1972.

————. *Letters of J. N. Darby*. 3 vols. Edited by William Kelly. Reprint ed. Oak Park, IL: Bible Truth Publishers, 1971.

Daughters, Kenneth A. *New Testament Church Government*. Kansas City, KS: Walterick, 1989.

Davies, J. M. *The Lord and the Churches*. Kansas City, KS: Walterick Publishers, 1967.

Davies, W. D. *Christian Origins and Judaism*. Philadelphia: Westminster, 1962.

deWitt, John R. "Contemporary Failure in the Pulpit." *Banner of Truth* (March 1981) 23.

Dugmore, C. W. *The Influence of the Synagogue Upon the Divine Office*. 2nd ed., Westminster: Faith Press, 1964.

Ellingworth, Paul. *The Epistle to the Hebrews*. New International Greek Testament Commentary. Grand Rapids: Eerdmans, 1993.

Elliot, Elisabeth. *Shadow of the Almighty*. New York: Harper and Row, 1958.

Epstein, I. *The Babylonian Talmud: Seder Nezikin*. 4 vols. London: Soncino, 1935.

Erickson, Millard J. *Christian Theology*. 3 vols. Grand Rapids: Baker, 1983.

Fee, Gordon D. *The First Epistle to the Corinthians*. New International Commentary on the New Testament. Grand Rapids: Eerdmans, 1987.

————. *1 and 2 Timothy, Titus*. New International Biblical Commentary. Peabody, MA: Hendrickson, 1988.

————. "Reflections on Church Order in the Pastoral Epistles with Further Reflection on the Hermeneutics of *Ad Hoc* Documents." *Journal of the Evangelical Theological Society*, 28 (June 1985) 141-51.

Fish, John H., III. "Brethren Tradition or New Testament Church Truth." *Emmaus Journal*, 2 (Winter 1993) 135.

Fleming, P. *The Church*. Oak Park: Midwest Christian Publishers, n. d.

Frame, John M. *Evangelical Reunion: Denominations and the Body of Christ*. Grand Rapids: Baker, 1991.

Gaebelein, Frank E., ed. *The Expositor's Bible Commentary*. 12 vols. Grand Rapids: Zondervan, 1984.

Getz, Gene A. *Sharpening the Focus of the Church*. Chicago: Moody Press, 1976.

Giles, Kevin. *What On Earth is the Church?* Downers Grove: InterVarsity Press, 1995.

Grudem, Wayne. "Does ΚΕΦΑΛΗ ('Head') Mean 'Source' or 'Authority over' in Greek Literature? A Survey of 2,336 Examples." *Trinity Journal*, 6 NS (1985) 38-59

————. "The Meaning of Κεφαλή ('Head'): A Response to Recent Studies, *Trinity Journal*, 11 NS (1990) 3-72.

————. *Systematic Theology*. Grand Rapids: Zondervan, 1994.

Gundry, R. H. *Matthew, A Commentary on his Literary and Theological Art*. Grand Rapids: Eerdmans, 1982.

Guralnik, D. B., ed. *Webster's New World Dictionary of the American Language*. New York: Simon and Schuster, 1984.

Guthrie, Donald. *New Testament Introduction*. 4th ed. Downers Grove: InterVarsity Press, 1990.

Harnack, Adolf. *The Constitution and Law of the Church*. Translated by F. L. Pogson. New York: Putnam's, 1910.

Harris, Murray J. "Christian Stewardship." *Interest* (February 1979) 4-5.

Hatch, Edwin. *The Organization of the Early Christian Churches*. London: Longmans, Green and Co., 1901.

Hay, A. R. *New Testament Order for Church and Missionary*. Argentina: New Testament Missionary Union, 1947.

Headlam, A. C. *The Doctrine of the Church and Christian Reunion.* London: John Murray, 1921.

Hemer, Colin J. *The Book of Acts in the Setting of Hellenistic History.* Tübingen: J. C. B. Mohr, 1989.

Henry, Carl F. H. *The Uneasy Conscience of Modern Fundamentalism.* Grand Rapids: Eerdmans, 1947.

————. *Twilight of a Great Civilization: The Drift Toward Neo-Paganism.* Westchester: Crossway, 1987.

Hesselgrave, David. *Planting Churches Cross Culturally.* Grand Rapids: Baker, 1980.

Higgins, A. J. B., ed. *The Early Church.* Philadelphia: Westminster, 1956.

Hodge, Charles. *An Exposition of the First Epistle to the Corinthians.* 1864. Reprint ed. Grand Rapids: Eerdmans, 1969.

————. *Systematic Theology.* 3 vols. New York: Scribners, 1883.

Hoehner, Harold W. "A Chronological Table of the Apostolic Age." (unpublished class notes, Dallas Theological Seminary, 1972).

Hort, Fenton John Anthony. *The Christian Ecclesia.* 1897. Reprint ed. London: Macmillan, 1914.

Hoste, William. *Bishops, Priests and Deacons.* London: Pickering and Inglis, n.d.

Huebner, R. A. *The Ruin of the Church, Eldership, and Ministry of the Word by Gift.* Morganville: Present Truth Publishers, n.d.

Hughes, Philip E. *Paul's Second Epistle to the Corinthians.* New International Commentary on the New Testament. Grand Rapids: Eerdmans, 1962.

Inrig, J. Gary. "Ecclesiology, Cultural Relativism, and Biblical Absolutism." (written for a course at Dallas Seminary in May 1969).

Ironside, H. A. *A Historical Sketch of the Brethren Movement.* Grand Rapids: Zondervan, 1942.

Johnson, John E. "The Old Testament Offices as Paradigm for Pastoral Identity." *Bibliotheca Sacra* 152 (April 1995) 194-95.

Johnson, S. Lewis, Jr., "The First Passover." *BelieverÆs Bible Bulletin* (Sept. 27, 1981) 1.

Johnston, George. *The Doctrine of the Church in the New Testament.* Cambridge: Cambridge University Press, 1943.

Kaiser, Walter C., Jr. "The Future Role of the Bible in Seminary Education." *Concordia Theological Quarterly,* 60 (October 1996) 250.

Käsemann, Ernst. *Essays on New Testament Themes.* London: SCM, 1964.

Kelly, William. *An Exposition of the Acts of the Apostles.* 3rd ed. London: C. A. Hammond, 1952.

————. *Christian Unity and Fellowship or The Unity of the Spirit and How to Keep It.* London: Hammond Trust, n. d.

————. *Lectures on the Church of God.* London: G. Morrish, n.d.

Kirk, Kenneth E. ed. *The Apostolic Ministry* (reprint ed., London: Hodder & Stoughton, 1957).

Kittel, G. and Gerhard Friedrich, eds. *Theological Dictionary of the New Testament*. 10 vols. Abridged by G. W. Bromiley. Grand Rapids: Eerdmans/Paternoster, 1985.

Knight, George W., III. *The Pastoral Epistles: A Commentary on the Greek Text*. NIGTC. Grand Rapids: Eerdmans, 1992.

————. *The Role Relationship of Men and Women*. Rev. ed. Chicago: Moody Press, 1985.

————. "The Scriptures Were Written for Our Instruction." *Journal of the Evangelical Theological Society*, 39 (March 1996) 3-13.

Kober, Manfred E. "The Case for the Singularity of Pastors." *Baptist Bulletin* (June 1982) 8-10,19.

Kuen, Alfred. *I Will Build My Church*. Translated by Ruby Lindblad. Chicago: Moody, 1971.

Koivisto, Rex A. *One Lord, One Faith*. Wheaton: BridgePoint, 1993.

Küng, Hans. *The Church*. Translated by Ray and Rosaleen Ockenden. New York: Sheed and Ward, 1967.

Ladd, George Eldon. *A Theology of the New Testament*. Edited by Donald A. Hagner. 1974. Rev. ed. Grand Rapids: Eerdmans, 1993.

Lake, Kirsopp. *The Apostolic Fathers*. 2 vols. Loeb Classical Library. Cambridge: Harvard University Press, 1912.

Lane, William L. *Hebrews 1–8*. Word Bible Commentary. Dallas: Word, 1991.

Lang, G. H. *The Churches of God*. London: The Paternoster Press, 1959.

————. *Departure: A Warning and an Appeal*. 2nd ed. London: C. J. Thynne and Jarvis, 1926.

Lea, Thomas D. and Hayne P. Griffin, Jr., *1, 2 Timothy, Titus*. New American Commentary. Nashville: Broadman, 1992.

Leith, John H. *Creeds of the Churches*. Garden City, NY: Anchor Books, 1963.

Lewis, C. S. *Letters to Malcolm: Chiefly on Prayer*. New York: Harcourt, Brace, Jovanovich, 1963.

Lincoln, Andrew T. *Ephesians*. Word Bible Commentary. Dallas: Word, 1990.

Lindsay, Thomas M. *The Church and Ministry in the Early Centuries*. London: Hodder and Stoughton, 1903.

Lightfoot, J. B. *St. Paul's Epistle to the Philippians*. 12th ed. London: Macmillan, 1913.

Lightner, R. P. *Evangelical Theology*. Grand Rapids, Michigan: Baker, 1986.

Litton, Edward Arthur. *Introduction to Dogmatic Theology*. Edited by P. E. Hughes. 1892. New ed. London: James Clarke, 1960.

Lloyd-Jones, D. Martyn. *Preaching and Preachers*. Grand Rapids: Zondervan, 1972.

Logan, Samuel T. Jr., ed. *The Preacher and Preaching*. Phillipsburg: Presbyterian and Reformed, 1986.

Luter, A. Boyd. New Testament Church Government: Fidelity and Flexibility." *Michigan Theological Journal*, 2 (1991) 127,135.

MacArthur, John F. Jr. *The Master's Plan for the Church*. Chicago: Moody, 1991.

———. "Truth vs. Technique." *Reformation & Revival Journal*, 3 (Fall 1994) 17-42.

MacDonald, Gordon. "Ten Conditions for Church Growth." *Leadership*, 4 (Winter 1983) 45.

MacDonald, William. *Christ Loved the Church*. Oak Park: Emmaus Bible School, 1956.

Machen, J. Gresham. *Christianity and Liberalism*. 1923. Reprint ed. Grand Rapids: Eerdmans, 1972.

Manson, T. W. *The Church's Ministry*. London: Hodder and Stoughton, 1948.

Mappes, David. "The New Testament Elder, Overseer, and Pastor." *Bibliotheca Sacra*, 154 (April 1997) 169.

Marshall, I. Howard. *The Acts of the Apostles*. Tyndale New Testament Commentaries Grand Rapids: Eerdmans, 1980.

Masters, Peter. "After 1900 years-the 'Conversion' of Evangelicalism." *A Sword & Trowel* (Special Issue: *Separation and Obedience*, 1983) 3.

McGarvey, Ken. "The Independent Church Myth." *Christianity Today* (July 22, 1991) 8.

McLaren, Ross Howlett. "The Triple Tradition: The Origins and Development of the Open Brethren in North America." *Emmaus Journal*, 4 (Winter 1995) 193-208.

McRae, William J. *The Principles of the New Testament Church*. Dallas: Believers Chapel, 1974.

Miller, Andrew. *Miller's Church History*. Fincastle, VA: Scripture Truth Book Co., n.d.

Minear, Paul S. *Images of the Church in the New Testament*. Philadelphia: Westminster, 1960.

Moore, John, and Ken Neff, *A New Testament Blueprint for the Church*. Chicago: Moody, 1985.

Morgan, G. Campbell. *The Acts of the Apostles*. Westwood, NJ: Fleming H. Revell Company, n.d.

Morris, Leon. *Ministers of God*. Chicago: Inter-Varsity Press, 1964.

Moule, C. F. D. *The Birth of the New Testament*. 3rd ed. San Francisco: Harper & Row, 1982.

Mounce, Robert H. *The Book of Revelation*. New International Commentary on the New Testament. Grand Rapids: Eerdmans, 1977.

Motyer, Alec. *The Message of James*. The Bible Speaks Today. Downers Grove: InterVarsity Press, 1985.

Murray, Iain H. "The Problem of the 'Eldership' and Its Wider Implications." *The Banner of Truth*, 395-96 (August 1996) 36-56.

Murray, John. *The Epistle to the Romans*. 2 vols. New International Commentary on the New Testament. Grand Rapids: Eerdmans, 1965.

Neatby, William Blair. *A History of the Plymouth Brethren*. London: Hodder and Stoughton, 1902.

Norbie, Donald L. *New Testament Church Organization* (Chicago: *Interest Magazine*, 1955), 35-50

Orr, James. *The Christian View of God and the World* (1893; reprint ed., Grand Rapids: Eerdmans, 1954), 20.

———, ed. *The International Standard Bible Encyclopedia*. 5 vols. Grand Rapids: Eerdmans, 1939.

Packer, J. I . *The Evangelical Anglican Identity Problem: An Analysis*. Latimer Studies 1. Oxford: Latimer House, 1978.

Peel, Albert, ed. *Essays Congregational and Catholic*. London: Congregational Union of England and Wales, 1931.

Peters, George W. *A Theology of Church Growth*. Grand Rapids: Zondervan, 1981.

Piper, John, and Wayne Grudem, eds. *Recovering Biblical Manhood and Womanhood: A Response to Evangelical Feminism*. Wheaton: Crossway Books, 1991.

Postman Neil. *Amusing Ourselves to Death*. New York: Penguin, 1985.

Rackham, R. B. *The Acts of the Apostles*. London: Methuen, 1901.

Radmacher, Earl D. *The Nature of the Church*. Portland: Western Baptist Press, 1972.

Ramsey, Michael. *The Gospel and the Catholic Church*. 2nd ed. London: Longmans Green, 1956. Reprint ed. Cambridge, MA: Cowley, 1990.

Ridderbos, Herman. *Paul: An Outline of His Theology*. Grand Rapids: Eerdmans, 1975.

Robertson, A. T. *A Grammar of the Greek New Testament in the Light of Historical Research*. Nashville: Broadman Press, 1934.

Robinson, Haddon W., ed. *Biblical Sermons*. Grand Rapids: Baker, 1989.

Rowdon, Harold H. "Elders and Deacons: An Alternative." *Aware,* 70 (May 1991) 12-13,

———. *The Origins of the Brethren, 1825-1850*. London: Pickering & Inglis, 1967.

———. *Who Are the Brethren and Does It Matter?* Exeter: Paternoster, 1986.

O'Brien, Peter T. and David G. Peterson, eds. *God Who is Rich in Mercy*. Homebush West, NSW, Australia: Lancer Books, 1986.

Ryrie, C. C. *Basic Theology*. Wheaton, Illinois: Victor Books, 1986.

Sanders, E. P. *Paul and Palestinian Judaism*. Philadelphia: Fortress, 1977.

Saucy, Robert L. *The Church in God's Program*. Chicago: Moody Press, 1972.

Schaff, Philip. *The Creeds of Christendom*. 3 vols. New York: Harper, 1877. Reprint ed. Grand Rapids: Baker Book House, 1983.

Schürer, Emil. *The History of the Jewish People in the Age of Jesus Christ*. 3 vols. Edited by Matthew Black, *et al*. Rev. ed. Edinburgh: T. & T. Clark, 1979-1987.

Schweizer, Edward. *Church Order in the New Testament*. Translated by Frank Clarke. London: SCM, 1961.

———. *Neotestamentica: German and English Essays 1951-1963*. Stuttgart: Zwingli Verlag, 1963.

Scofield, C. I. *The New Scofield Reference Bible, KJV.* Edited by E. Schuyler English. New York: Oxford Univ. Press, 1967.

Smalley, William A., ed. *Readings in Missionary Anthropology.* Tarrytown, NY: Practical Anthropology, 1967.

Smith, David L. *All God's People: A Theology of the Church.* Wheaton: Bridgepoint, 1996.

Snyder, Howard. *The Problem of Wineskins.* Downers Grove: InterVarsity Press, 1975.

Sohm, Rudolf. *Outlines of Church History.* Translated by May Sinclair. 8th German ed., 1893. London: Macmillan, 1913.

Solzhenitsyn, Aleksandr. "Why Study Church History?" *Christian History,* 25 (1990) 41.

Stenhouse, Andrew. *The Sin of Sectarianism.* Toronto: Christian Book Room, 1957.

Stott, John R. W. *Between Two Worlds: The Art of Preaching in the Twentieth Century.* Grand Rapids: Eerdmans, 1982.

―――. *Christ the Controversialist.* Downers Grove: InterVarsity Press, 1970.

―――. "Setting the Spirit Free." *Christianity Today* (June 12, 1981) 17-21.

―――. *The Spirit, the Church, and the World: The Message of Acts.* The Bible Speaks Today. Downers Grove: InterVarsity Press, 1990.

Strauch, Alexander. *Biblical Eldership.* 3rd ed. Littleton, CO: Lewis and Roth, 1995.

―――. *The New Testament Deacon.* Littleton, CO: Lewis and Roth, 1992.

Strauch, Alexander, and Richard Swartley. *The Mentor's Guide to Biblical Eldership.* Littleton, CO: Lewis and Roth, 1995).

―――. *Study Guide to Biblical Eldership.* Littleton, CO: Lewis and Roth, 1995.

Streeter, Burnett Hillman. *The Primitive Church Studied with Special Reference to the Origins of the Christian Ministry.* London: Macmillan, 1930.

Strong, A. H. *Systematic Theology* (Valley Forge, PA: Judson Press, 1907), 900.

Summerton, Neil. *A Noble Task.* 2nd ed. Carlisle, UK: Paternoster, 1993.

Swete, H. B., ed. *Essays on the Early History of the Church and the Ministry.* London: Macmillan, 1918.

Tenney, M. C., ed. *The Zondervan Pictorial Encyclopedia of the Bible.* 5 vols. Grand Rapids: Zondervan, 1976.

Thiessen, H. C. *Introductory Lectures in Systematic Theology.* Grand Rapids: Eerdmans, 1951.

Thomas, Geoffrey. "The 1994 Westminster Conference." *The Banner of Truth,* 382 (July 1995) 11.

Thomas, W. H. Griffith. "Is the New Testament Minister a Priest?" *Bibliotheca Sacra,* 136 (January 1979) 65-73.

―――. *Outline Studies in Acts.* Grand Rapids: Eerdmans, 1956.

―――. *The Principles of Theology: An Introduction to the Thirty Nine Articles.* Rev. ed. London: Church Book Room Press, 1956.

Tinker, Melvin, ed. *The Anglican Evangelical Crisis.* Fearn, Scotland: Christian Focus Publications, 1995.

Torrance, Thomas F. *The Doctrine of Grace in the Apostolic Fathers.* Grand Rapids: Eerdmans, 1959.

Trench, Richard Chenevix. *Commentary on the Epistles to the Seven Churches in Asia.* 6th ed. London: Kegan Paul, Trench, Trubner and Co., 1897.

Van Impe, Jack. *Heart Disease in Christ's Body.* Royal Oak, MI: Jack Van Impe Ministries, 1984.

Wagner, C. Peter. *Leading Your Church to Growth.* Ventura: Regal, 1984.

Ware, Timothy. *The Orthodox Church.* Rev. ed. New York: Penguin, 1983.

Watson, J. B. *The Church: A Symposium.* London: Pickering and Inglis, 1949.

Weeks, Noel. *The Sufficiency of Scripture.* Edinburgh: Banner of Truth, 1988.

White, John. *Flirting With the World.* Wheaton: Shaw, 1982.

Zahn, Theodor. *Introduction to the New Testament.* 3 vols. Translated by M. W. Jacobus, et al. Edinburgh: T. & T. Clark, 1909.

SCRIPTURE INDEX

Person & Title Index